THE ENEMY
OF THE PEOPLE

THE ENEMY
OF THE PEOPLE

A Dangerous Time to Tell
the Truth in America

JIM ACOSTA

HARPER

An Imprint of HarperCollinsPublishers

HarperCollins books may be purchased for educational, business, or sales promotional use. For information, please email the Special Markets Department at SPsales@harpercollins.com.

All photographs courtesy of the author unless credited otherwise.

FIRST EDITION

Library of Congress Cataloging-in-Publication Data has been applied for.

ISBN 978-0-06-291612-9

19 20 21 22 23 LSC 10 9 8 7 6 5 4 3 2 1

For H.O.P.

Contents

THE ENEMY
OF THE PEOPLE

Prologue

"This is CNN breaking news. . . ."

I was sitting on a plane just minutes after takeoff when the news alert flashed across the cabin's TV screens. It was the morning of October 25, 2018, and I was en route from Washington's Ronald Reagan National Airport to San Francisco, where I would be delivering a speech at San Jose State University on the state of the news business under President Donald J. Trump and accepting an award from the school's journalism program. I'd been planning on using the flight to work on my speech, but suddenly I was glued to the screen in front of me.

The New York City Police Department had units surrounding the Time Warner Center at Columbus Circle, across from Central Park. CNN's headquarters was being evacuated after a suspicious package had been discovered in the building's mailroom. A pipe bomb had been sent to CNN in New York, but its intended target was former CIA director John Brennan, a frequent Trump critic. The device was similar to bombs that had been mailed to Trump's leading Democratic Party adversaries, including former president Barack Obama and Trump's rival in the 2016 election, former secretary of state Hillary Clinton.

It has all been building up to some kind of act of violence, I thought.

I had feared the day would come when the president's rhetoric would lead one of his supporters to harm or even murder a journalist. And when it happened, the United States would undergo something of a sea change, joining the list of countries around the world where journalists were no longer safe reporting the truth. Perhaps we have already entered that era, a dangerous time to tell the truth in America.

Of course, there wasn't a damn thing I could do about it from where I was, strapped to my seat at the beginning of a five-hour flight to Northern California. All I could do was watch as the images of domestic terrorism played out on my tiny in-flight TV.

Yes, for a reporter, there are few things worse than missing a big story like this one. But "fear of missing out" was not the emotion I was feeling at that moment. I was pissed off. Really, really pissed off. This was a terrorist attack on my news organization and, without a doubt, on the American free press.

Since the days before the Iowa caucuses in 2016, I had covered both Trump's unimaginable rise to power and his tumultuous presidency. My photographers, producers, and I had covered the rallies where Trump demonized the press, where he called us "disgusting" and "dishonest," before moving on, at a news conference he held before being sworn into office, to dub my network and me "fake news." We had listened to the chants of "CNN sucks" from his crowds of supporters, seen them give us the middle finger, and heard them call us "traitors" and "scum." And of course, who could forget when the president of the United States said we were "the enemy of the people"?

On the way to California, I ripped up my original speech for the folks at San Jose State and started from scratch. The students, I had decided, would get the unvarnished truth about what I had been witnessing during my time covering Trump. I was afraid the president, I later told the crowd, was putting our lives in danger. But this was no time to back down. The truth, I argued, was bigger than a president who is acting like a bully. We were in a fight for the truth, and the stakes couldn't be higher.

Throughout Trump's race for the White House and during his first two years in office, I have been jotting down anecdotes, collecting quotes from sources, listening to stories from Trump aides and associates past and present, and stockpiling reflections on what is clearly the most important political story of my life. In many ways it is one I have been preparing to tell ever since I knew I wanted to be a journalist.

Growing up in the DC area, I have politics in my blood. The *Washington Post* was delivered to our house every morning. My parents were blue collar, but Mom read the *Post* from cover to cover each day. Dad worked at local grocery stores and came home with stories of meeting the likes of Dick Gephardt, the former Missouri congressman and Democratic presidential candidate. As for me, I went to high school with the daughter of U.S. senator Trent Lott. My best friend Robert's father, Eugene Dwyer, worked at the State Department.

Unlike a lot of young journalists these days, I took the traditional local news route to my jobs in network and cable news. Over the years, I worked everywhere, from DC to Knoxville to Dallas to Chicago, learning from some great journalists and covering everything under the sun. In local news, I was constantly on the go, running between city hall, the courthouse, and police headquarters. That's how I began to cultivate sources, generate scoops, and, above all, report things to the best of my ability in a fair and accurate fashion.

Eventually, CBS News gave me the opportunity of a lifetime: working under the likes of Dan Rather and Bob Schieffer. I covered the war in Iraq, Hurricane Katrina, and the presidential campaign of John Kerry. It was an amazing transition for me, one that opened up a huge world of possibilities, but it was CNN that gave me the job I had always wanted, as a political reporter. In 2008, I covered Barack Obama's epic battle with Hillary Clinton. In 2010, I carved out a niche for myself covering the rise of the Tea Party (an assignment that would prepare me well for surviving Trump's rallies many years down the line). And two years later, the network had me covering Mitt Romney's failed presidential bid.

After Romney's defeat, CNN moved me over to the White House to cover Obama's second term. "No drama Obama," as he was known, experienced plenty of drama during his final four years in office. The Benghazi attack, the ill-fated rollout of the Obamacare website, the rise of ISIS, and the scandal at the Department of Veterans Affairs were all serious challenges that plagued Obama, damaging his legacy as the president who stopped a second Great Depression and ordered the mission to take out Osama bin Laden. As it turns out, many of the stories that kept us busy during Obama's second term, such as ISIS and the president's inability to pass immigration reform, teed up some of the themes Trump would ride into the Oval Office.

Long before he became a presidential candidate, Trump was a political fixture on cable news partly because of his devotion to the "birther" movement, which was fueled by the false conspiracy theory that Obama had not been born in the United States. Trump was one of the biggest proponents of this bogus claim about the nation's first African American president. With his successful reality TV show, *The Apprentice*, Trump was already a star, but the "birther" conspiracy made him something of a household name in conservative circles, as he began popping up on "the shows" to talk about his strong suspicion that Obama wasn't really an American. It was shameful.

The Washington establishment, truth be told, did not consider Trump a credible figure. And President Obama brushed off the attacks coming from him as the rants of a "carnival barker." Still, I remember that we in the press gave that outlandish birther lie a ridiculous amount of coverage.

After Trump declared his run for president in June 2015, few folks inside Obama's West Wing gave him good odds on winning the White House. For them, he was considered more of a punch line than presidential material. Hillary Clinton, they were convinced, would be the next president.

It didn't take long for that view to change.

By the fall of 2015, as Trump was beginning to draw large crowds at his rallies, I remember attending an off-record reception at the office of National Security Advisor Susan Rice. (Think drinks with the staff.) A top official asked me if I thought Trump could actually win the Republican nomination. Sure, I said. Just look at the massive audiences showing up at his events.

The Obama people were beginning to pay attention, but they were still fully confident that Clinton would become the forty-fifth president. So was just about everybody else.

After Obama's State of the Union address in 2016, I exited the gates of the White House with a new assignment on the horizon. For the next ten months, I would cover the Trump campaign, from the Iowa caucuses to Election Night in Midtown Manhattan. I would then settle into my hotel across from Central Park for the transition period, until, mercifully, I was finally able to get back home to Washington.

I'll never forget what I saw on the campaign trail and what I have witnessed covering the Trump presidency. Even now, more than two years into his presidency, it's still shocking to remember Trump, as a presidential candidate, saying he could stand in the middle of Fifth Avenue and shoot somebody and get away with it. It's still shocking to remember him mocking the captivity of a war hero the way he mocked John McCain, poking fun at a disabled reporter, and describing Mexican undocumented immigrants as "rapists"—and still escaping the kind of accountability that would have knocked anyone else out of the race.

Beyond the slash-and-burn tactics employed by his campaign against his rivals, Trump has often twisted the truth, lied, and attacked those who would call out his falsehoods—most notably the national press corps. The *Washington Post* fact-checkers have catalogued nearly ten thousand false or misleading statements in the first two years of his presidency. He has thrived in this upside-down, through-the-looking-glass landscape because facts don't carry the same currency they once did. The late senator Daniel Patrick Moynihan once said, "Everyone is entitled to his own opinion, but not to his own facts." But that's hardly the case anymore. These days, everybody has his or her own set of facts. The result: facts are under attack, every minute of every day, in our fractured news spectrum—think Breitbart and Fox News—and of course on social media. Just try to ask a question the president doesn't want to answer, and you're sometimes labeled "fake news" or "the enemy of the people." Or worse than that: one administration official nicknamed me, I think affectionately, "public enemy number one."

The hardest part to understand is how too many of my fellow Americans have accepted and, in some cases, even adopted this degradation of our political culture. In short, America has changed right before my eyes. I see this phenomenon in the death threats and violent messages streaming into my social media accounts. Self-described Trump supporters have left countless messages saying I should be murdered in all sorts of medieval ways. The comments posted on my Instagram and Facebook pages recommend that I be castrated, decapitated, and set on fire. Out of curiosity, I will click on the accounts responsible for these horrific messages. Theirs was the same kind of hatred that had now driven someone to send pipe bombs to CNN.

Knowing that I still had hours until the plane touched down in San Francisco, I sat back in my seat and stared blankly at the TV screen, thinking about everything that had led up to this moment. In spite of the fear I felt for my colleagues and myself—the threat of physical violence now felt suddenly, horribly real—I knew this was no time to be intimidated. This was the time to ask the hard questions.

I remember sitting down for drinks one afternoon with a senior White House official who blurted out, "The president's insane." The official went on to confide that when he came into office, Trump did not understand the Constitution. What were the rules for appointing Cabinet officials? Trump wanted to know. How long can an acting secretary stay on? The official was frustrated with Trump's ignorance, his behavior. A lot of us are. But is Trump really to blame for what we see every day? Or should we look in the mirror for a change? Do we want this to be the state of our politics? Over the last couple of years, there has been plenty of conversation about whether we have allowed our political discourse to descend to a level that is beneath all of us. There is a growing chorus, not just among Democrats and liberals, but of Republicans and conservatives as well, who are exhausted with the disintegration of decency in our elections. In the decades to come, what in the world will we put in our history books to explain what has happened to America?

The answer: That depends on what we do right now. Because it's all riding on us.

I have seen my life turned upside down covering Trump. His attacks on me and my colleagues, dedicated and talented journalists, have real-life consequences. My family and friends worry about my safety. I hope at the end of the day the sacrifice will be worth it. No. I *know* it will be.

1

Empty Frames

As the inauguration of Donald J. Trump as the forty-fifth president of the United States approached, there were reminders everywhere of how dramatically the world was about to change. On January 19, 2017, I was reporting from the White House on the final day of Barack Obama's administration. But the story was no longer Obama; his time was up. The story was the arrival of Trump. And there was a sense of dread inside the Obama West Wing.

That day, the last before Trump would be sworn into office, I decided to roam the media-accessible hallway of the West Wing that leads to the area known as "Upper Press." This is where the office of the White House press secretary is located, and I was milling around, looking to say farewell to some of the people who had worked for Obama. The last press secretary of the Obama administration, Josh Earnest, had already cleared out his office. He was gone. So, too, was Eric Schultz, Obama's deputy press secretary. Schultz and I had developed a good working relationship during my time covering the Obama White House.

Anybody who knew Eric understood full well that he had his own misgivings about the press. He thought we chased Trump's bright, shiny objects too much, and he was right. Schultz also enjoyed

needling me over my question to Obama at a news conference at the
2015 G20 summit in Turkey. That was when I pressed Obama on his
administration's inability to control the spread of the terrorist group
ISIS as it stormed across Iraq and Syria, creating a caliphate that de-
stabilized the region and was responsible for murdering a number of
foreign journalists.

"Why can't we take out these bastards?" I asked Obama at that news
conference.

Obama offered a detailed and somewhat detached, almost clinical
response to the question. Obama, for all his strengths and intellect,
seemed to have misread the public's anxiety over ISIS, something
his own aides would later admit to me privately. People inside the
White House were incensed over the question at the time, and Schultz
never let me forget that the Obama team disliked the question. From
that day forward, Eric would email me news reports of various success
stories from the Obama White House battle against ISIS.

"We got one of the bastards," he would email me from time to time.
He meant it, in part, in good fun—or so I thought—but it was also a
way for him to let me know I had pissed them off.

In the days following Trump's victory, I'd caught up with Eric in
his office. Schultz had an unforgettable look of sleep-deprived agony
on his face. During the run-up to the 2016 campaign, he and I had
lengthy discussions about the wisdom of Hillary Clinton running
for president. Schultz, like many in the Obama White House, was de-
spondent that Clinton seemed to have botched what should have been
a thoroughly winnable campaign. They had all suffered a crushing
loss. They had all banked on the conventional wisdom that was mar-
row deep in Washington that Trump had no chance of winning. How
could the man who had laughably accused Obama of not having been
born in the United States succeed the first African American president
of the United States, they all wondered with dread. How could it all
end like this? they thought.

Now, standing in Upper Press on the night of January 19, I saw that Eric and the rest of the Obama gang had vanished from the press-accessible areas of the West Wing. All I could find, as I looked around, were empty walls, empty desks, and an eerie silence. It is a sight few Americans ever get to see. Obama's aides had packed up to leave. This was the transition of power under way. Out with the old and in with the new. This is how our democracy works.

No image crystallized this cold reality more than the picture frames hanging in the hallway outside Upper Press. During the Obama years, photographs of the forty-fourth president and his family hung there. But on the night of January 19, the frames were empty. The photos of Barack, Michelle, Malia, and Sasha Obama had been taken down. Over the next several weeks, pictures of Trump and his family would fill those frames. Until then, they were a blank canvas.

In a sense, every new administration is an empty frame, and we were all about to learn how Trump would fill his. For all the bluster on the campaign trail, no one knew for sure exactly how he would govern. Of course, some things were easy to envision. Trump's ability to pit one group of Americans against another, his bullying of immigrants, and yes, his demonizing of the press and assaults on the truth were also hallmarks of his rise to power. Trump was brash, but that's being too kind; he could also act like a bully. With this style of governance, the question was clear: would he change the office, or would the office change him?

So many pundits and respected presidential historians, perhaps out of a sense of national anxiety, predicted that the office he was about to assume would transform Trump. There was a feeling that the great weight of the presidency of the United States, with all its trappings and ceremony, would rest upon Trump's shoulders and humble him, turning the New York businessman into a leader all Americans could admire. But as Obama's longtime strategist David Axelrod has observed, presidential campaigns have a way of magnifying one's character—like an "MRI of the soul." Trump's soul was about to be magnified and projected onto the world stage. And the lessons learned from the moments leading up to January 20, 2017, suggested that the nation was about to undergo a remarkable and pivotal test.

On that night of January 19, I did find one last staffer from the Obama administration. A press aide, Brian Gabriel, greeted me and remarked on the incredible turn of political events that was about to unfold the following day. I joked to Brian that he basically was the White House. It was hard for him to crack a smile.

As I stood there with Brian, a question dawned on me that I thought I had better get out of the way while I had the chance. Trump's treatment of the press had worried me throughout the campaign, so I asked Brian if he wouldn't mind sharing a secret with me.

"Did you guys have the ability to listen in on our conversations in the press areas of the White House? Any listening devices in the booths?" I asked, referring to the small work areas set up for the TV networks and wire services in the press areas of the West Wing.

"No. Not that I'm aware of," Gabriel responded, a puzzled look on his face. I'll confess, at the time it seemed like a nutty question, but his answer did give me some relief. At least the Trump people would not have infrastructure already in place to spy on us, I thought.

———————

ON THE EVE OF TRUMP'S PRESIDENCY, I HAD GOOD REASON TO BE worried based on what I'd seen on the campaign trail. As a reporter who'd covered previous administrations as well as much of Trump's campaign, I suspected the office would not transform the man. Trump struck me as potentially unprepared for the White House. Neither Trump nor his top advisers thought he was going to win. Still, they had put on a good show.

Two nights before Election Day, I was in Pennsylvania and spotted a sign that the Trump wave was coming. Trump was doing a tarmac event near the Pittsburgh airport. The crowd was big and rowdy. Trump's supporters were so loyal that they booed as a Bruce Springsteen song played over the loudspeakers. They weren't yelling "Bruce"; they were booing, perhaps in response to Springsteen referring to Trump as a "moron" in the weeks before the election.

But that wasn't the memory that stayed with me. It was when Trump's Pennsylvania campaign manager, David Urban, came up to me and said, "Follow me." We made our way outside and then walked the length of the line of people waiting to get inside. It was easily a mile and a half long.

"Does this look like a losing campaign to you?" Urban asked.

"No, it doesn't," I replied. It was a sight to behold. A thought occurred to me: If Trump wins Pennsylvania, Clinton is in very big trouble.

The next night, we covered Trump's last event of the 2016 campaign, a rally in Grand Rapids before thousands of screaming Michiganders wearing red "Make America Great Again" hats. Trump had remarked that the large crowd hardly had the look of a second-place finish. How right he was! With crowds like the ones he was receiving in the final days of the campaign, Trump didn't need the press. And what happened after his final rally in Grand Rapids made that all too clear.

Although Trump's plane was parked on the tarmac right next to the press plane, the Republican candidate refused the time-honored tradition for a presidential candidate of posing in front of the plane for a photo with the journalists covering his or her campaign. One of Trump's traveling press aides, Stephanie Grisham, told us he was unavailable. (Yeah, right.) Disappointed, we schlepped onto the press plane for the final ride back to New York.

It was hardly surprising that Trump would stiff the press out of the planeside picture. He had spent the better part of the last year savaging the news media. We were, in his words, "disgusting," "dishonest," "scum," "thieves," "crooks," "liars," and so on. Trump simply could not stand us.

As a journeyman correspondent, I had already covered three presidential campaigns before "the Donald" came along. My first Election Eve picture with a candidate was in 2004, with John Kerry, who lost. I'll never forget that day. Unlike Trump, who rode on his own private plane (dubbed Trump Force One by the press), separate from the press plane, Kerry and the media all traveled on the same charter jet. (That's the campaign norm, one of many that Trump was happy to break.) And on Election Day 2004, Kerry walked to the press cabin and handed out red fleece jackets. Emblazoned on each were the words "Kerry Edwards Press Corps." (One small problem with the jackets: "Kerry Edwards" was written in a bright white stitching. The words "Press Corps" were barely visible in a dark blue—so dark that at a gas station on the way home after Kerry lost, a motorist looked at my new fleece and said, "Sorry, you lost." He couldn't make out from the jacket that I was with the press.)

No one thought a fleece jacket would be forthcoming from the Trump campaign. There had been no candidate bonding time with Trump as the 2016 campaign came to an end, so it wasn't exactly a surprise when Trump skipped the group photo and one last moment as a candidate to make peace with his imagined enemy. Leaving nothing to chance, his staff had arranged it so that the two planes didn't even land at the same airport, with the press plane landing in Newark, far away from Trump Force One's home at LaGuardia.

I felt bad for the younger campaign reporters, some barely into their twenties, who had spent the last eighteen months chronicling Trump's candidacy. I had wanted them to have that picture. So, as we got off the press plane in Newark at 3:30 a.m. on Election Day and started plodding toward the sad, dark buses awaiting us, I shouted at everybody to assemble in front of the plane. We were going to have our goddamned picture.

One of my colleagues had procured a cardboard cutout of Trump. We propped it up in the middle of us and all gathered together on the tarmac for the money shot. And with the flashlights on our mobile phones angled up at our faces to provide some much-needed lighting, we managed a pretty damn good middle-of-the-night photo in front of the plane. After all the taunting and all the abuse from a candidate who repeatedly lashed out at the news media, posing for that picture gave us all a good laugh.

———————

IT WAS 4:30 IN THE MORNING ON ELECTION DAY WHEN THE CAMPAIGN reporters following Donald J. Trump's unlikely, unconventional, un-believable bid for the presidency arrived, haggard, half-drunk, and bleary-eyed, at the Manhattan hotel preferred by the press corps, the JW Marriott Essex House.

We were standing in line, waiting patiently for our room keys, when in walks Reince Priebus, the chairman of the Republican National Committee. Priebus had become a trusted adviser to Trump, sticking by the real estate tycoon when times were tough. I had always liked Priebus. A Wisconsin nice guy, he was the GOP's smooth operator, easygoing with the party and the press. He seemed genuinely human to me, a rarity in the Washington viper pit.

The RNC chair had been with Trump through good times and bad. He had dutifully gone on the "shows" and fought the good fight, in-sisting against all evidence to the contrary that the former host of the reality TV show *The Apprentice* was going to win the presidency.

But privately, Priebus was less confident. In the lobby of the Essex House, he walked right up to me and said, "It's going to take a miracle for us to win." Priebus was a little tipsy that morning. Still, I couldn't believe my ears. He just walked up in a bit of a stupor and uttered those unbelievable words. So, I let him talk.

Priebus laid out what all the data were telling them: that the Trump campaign would lose but by a narrow margin. In Reince's mind, that was a small victory.

"Didn't you think we were dead after the *Access Hollywood* thing?" he asked.

"Yes," I said. "I said so on TV." I had, actually. On *The Situation Room with Wolf Blitzer*, the very day the *Access Hollywood* tape surfaced. On the tape, as most of the world knows by now, Trump was caught on a hot microphone saying he could grab a woman "by the pussy" and get away with it, among other outrageous remarks. At the time, I said that the tape probably meant the end of his campaign. "The bottom of the barrel" was how I described Trump's behavior on the recording. Oh, how wrong I was.

Priebus repeated himself: "Didn't you think that was the end?"

"Yes," I said, uncertain why he kept asking me the same question.

Then he started looking on the bright side, noting how the Trump campaign had managed to pull back from the abyss and make the final weeks of the election competitive. It was going to be close, not a blowout loss to Clinton. These were all good points, and all true. This is what the Republican Party chairman, at a desperate moment, no doubt, in his career and his life, was trying to get across. Again, I liked Reince, so I felt bad for him.

He went on to say how it appeared the Republicans would definitely not lose the House and might hang on to the Senate. Again, the slightly inebriated RNC chair was speaking the truth. That was my expectation as well.

And with that, he walked off. He had said his piece.

Needless to say, Priebus was wrong. We all were. Five days later, Trump announced that Priebus would be named the next White House chief of staff.

I was hardly the only person to serve as a sounding board for Reince's concerns about Trump. The incoming forty-fifth president had heard the dire predictions from him as well. Before the election, Reince had made it clear inside the Trump campaign that he thought the GOP nominee was in deep trouble after the *Access Hollywood* bombshell. After taking office, of course, Trump loved needling Priebus for his lack of faith in the final days of the campaign. Reince would laugh it off, but Trump never forgot. Sure, he needed Reince, to send a signal to establishment Republicans that he wasn't about to burn Washington to the ground. Trump, however, never forgives people for a lack of loyalty. Priebus entered the White House as damaged goods in Trump's eyes.

Election Night was a surreal experience. There we were in the Hilton Midtown ballroom, nearly all of us in the Trump press corps expecting a humiliating defeat for the GOP candidate. (Indeed, we were making plans for drinks later that night.) Even the Trump supporters on hand seemed to be preparing themselves for the end of the road. With the exception of a cake shaped in the likeness of Trump, it was hardly a celebratory atmosphere. For much of the night, the ballroom was half empty. Then the results started pouring in. States were falling into Trump's column faster than anticipated. Florida and North Carolina went to Trump early, surprising analysts and campaign insiders alike. A buzz was building inside the Hilton that perhaps Trump was going to do a lot better than nearly all the experts had predicted.

There is no need to recount, minute by minute, what happened next. We all remember. But it was a scene to behold. The ballroom eventually became packed with cheering Trump supporters. Some were heckling the press. I glanced over at my campaign colleague Katy Tur, of NBC News who shot back a look of astonishment. My fellow CNN Trump reporter Sara Murray emailed me that she had "told me so." Sara, to her credit, had predicted that Trump would win the election. I, wrongly, refused to believe you could boast about grabbing women by their genitals and get away with it. Mine seemed like the safer prediction.

The final results wouldn't come in until the wee hours of the morning of November 9. By that point, the place was wall-to-wall red MAGA hats. As I looked out onto the crowd, I remember thinking that a new, ultranationalist political movement had arrived in America, unlike anything I had seen in my lifetime. Then, out came Trump and his family, along with now vice president–elect Mike Pence and the rest of the campaign entourage. There was an odd absence of excitement in the room. It was almost as if those assembled were just as dumbfounded as the rest of us. When it was all over, I remember climbing off the press riser and walking right up to Pence, whom I had covered during his days as an Indiana congressman. He told me that they were ready to go to work. I didn't believe him. They had no idea what had hit them.

The true sense of how things were going inside the Trump campaign came from Jessica Ditto, a communications staffer, who was also on the ballroom floor at that early morning hour. I offered my congratulations to her and a couple of other Trump staffers who were milling around. Ditto replied acidly, "Well, maybe now we'll get better coverage from the media."

A thought ran through my mind: They are still wounded. They are still aggrieved. It dawned on me that the relationship between the press and the incoming administration would continue to be contentious.

It was nearly 4:30 a.m. when my head finally hit the pillow in my hotel room. I had not eaten any dinner. I downed a small can of Pringles, chugged a beer, and passed out. My phone rang about three hours later. Trump was going to be president, and the whole world was starting to freak out.

––––––––

IT FELT AS IF NOVEMBER 9 WOULD LAST FOREVER. AFTER MY THREE-hour nap in the morning, I went for a run. And then it was back to work. We did a piece for *The Situation Room with Wolf Blitzer* that evening. And before long, it was time to do a live shot for *Anderson Cooper 360*. It was back on the hamster wheel. The frenetic pace of the campaign did not end on November 8. If anything, it was accelerating.

As we were preparing to do our 8:00 p.m. live shot, something incredible was beginning to happen. Thousands of people were marching on the streets of Manhattan, descending on Trump Tower, chanting, "Not my president!" I was walking down West Fifty-Seventh Street, toward Fifth Avenue, and the demonstrators were everywhere. The election of Donald J. Trump had ended. The resistance to Trump was born.

But this new political force was an unstable source of energy, not completely directed at the incoming president. As I was getting set up for my 8:00 p.m. live shot, with my producer Kristen Holmes and a security official standing with me, the swarm of protesters was starting to gather around us. The demonstrators, understandably, were angry. Many of them were emotional and raging, and not all of them were friendly toward us. Then I started to hear the chant.

"CNN elected Trump . . . CNN elected Trump!" some of the demonstrators were shouting, a few of them directly at me. Theirs was a point shared by others. We seemed to give Trump too much coverage during the GOP primary season. The network brass has since admitted as much. We didn't elect him, but, as I like to remind a lot of Trump supporters, the press as a whole gave their candidate a boost during the primaries that no money could have bought.

The hostility we encountered that night felt unrestrained and possibly dangerous. As soon as our live shot was over, the show producers for *Anderson Cooper 360* told us to get the hell out of there. Our security guy escorted us through the crowd, and we were gone. After months of taking abuse from people at Trump rallies, now we were getting an earful from the other side. It was a sign of the new world we were all about to enter. Trump's election had not soothed tensions on either side; it had poured gasoline over them. The whole country, Trump supporters and opponents alike, was pissed off, in a state of near rage.

The Democrats of course had quite a bit of soul-searching to do.

As I saw all too clearly out on the campaign trail, there was extreme Clinton fatigue, something I believe Democrats never fully appreciated at the time. This was a major miscalculation, in my view, by the Democratic Party. I know from my interactions with Obama aides inside the White House that they overwhelmingly preferred Hillary Clinton to Joe Biden, despite the fact that Biden simply matched up better against Trump. The vice president, given his appeal to everyday Americans as "Uncle Joe," could easily have carved into Trump's working-class appeal and probably kept Pennsylvania, Michigan, and Wisconsin in the Democratic column. The "Blue Wall" might have withstood that late-October Trump surge. There would never have been James Comey's memo, raising questions of impropriety in Clinton's use of a private email server, to turn the tide eleven days before the election.

The vice president wasn't perfect, of course. He could be too candid, which the press loved. I remember being at a Christmas party at the vice president's official mansion, on the grounds of the U.S. Naval Observatory, in late 2015. The house was filled with reporters and operatives from Bidenworld. Unlike Obama, who rarely mixed and mingled with reporters, Biden relished working the room at his holiday parties. He held court with a couple dozen reporters for nearly an hour at the end the night, before they kicked us all out. Biden was handicapping the presidential field. He seemed to be masking his concerns about Hillary Clinton with some good ol' "Uncle Joe" humor.

"Marco Rubio is the most charismatic candidate in the field," Biden told us. "In both parties," he went on, in an apparent reference to Clinton.

"What about Ted Cruz?" somebody asked.

"That son of a bitch," Biden said. "I mean that son of a gun."

The reporters around him howled. But it was vintage Biden. He had the kind of humor that could go toe to toe with Trump.

But as Biden toyed with the idea of running for the presidency, he simply couldn't muster the energy to mount a campaign. He had just lost his son, Beau, to cancer in August 2015. A Democratic official had tipped me off to a call Biden held with Democratic National Committee members in the middle of the vice president's deliberations. At one point during the call, Biden told Democratic officials listening in that he wasn't sure he had the "emotional fuel" to run. It was Biden being Biden. He was candid. But he was exhausted. The same Biden who had lost a wife and daughter in a car accident at a young age had suffered another tragedy.

It was too much to ask Biden to run again. And the White House had made its choice clear. Obama's people wanted Hillary. It was "her turn," we were told. They loved Biden inside the West Wing, but there was little appetite for a Biden candidacy.

All that being said, defeating Trump in 2016 should have been a layup. It wasn't. The Democratic Party had written off, even laughed off, Trump's chances from the very moment he entered the race. And now, somehow, he was president.

During his transition to power over the next few months, Trump appeared to do little to bring the country together. Instead, he did what he knew best: he turned much of the transition into a reality TV show. As he assembled his Cabinet and White House team, he paraded candidates for various positions through Trump Tower. But the one episode of "Trump Transition Apprentice," as I thought of it, that crystallized this haphazard process most was the president-elect's treatment of Willard Mitt Romney.

It's probably too much to call me an authority on Mitt Romney. But I covered him during the 2012 presidential campaign. Romney ran a hard-fought, respectable race, but lost, handing Barack Obama a second term. It was the former Massachusetts governor's second attempt to win the presidency, and for a brief period in 2015, he was considering a third go at it. But as the 2016 campaign was heating up, Romney made it clear he did not want to be a three-time loser. That left him in an awkward place. He desperately wanted to be president. Members of his family were willing to support him had he decided to run in 2016. But Mitt, a thoroughly decent human being, tamed his ambitions and stayed on the sidelines.

And yet, Romney would not stay silent. Having courted Trump's support in 2012 (an event I covered in Las Vegas), he clearly felt the need to atone for that mistake. Romney, sources told me, regretted asking for Trump's support, an endorsement that came on a wild day—publicly because it featured two men who could not have been more different and personally because I believe it marked the first time Trump went off on me.

Trump appeared on *The Situation Room* via phone, as he so often did with CNN and other outlets, right after my live shot on his endorsement of Romney. My report had focused on Romney's decision to accept Trump's endorsement, despite the fact that the Manhattan businessman and avowed birther was something of an affront to the former Massachusetts governor's good manners.

After my report was over, Trump complained that my live shot sounded as if it had been written by the Democratic Party.

Later, an Obama operative emailed me: "[D]id Trump just go negative on you?"

"Yep," I replied. We were still years away from "fake news," but I had clearly gotten under his skin.

Flash forward to 2016, and it was as if Romney were trying to undo Trump's endorsement. At a critical moment in the early stages of the 2016 GOP primary cycle, the former Massachusetts governor raised a giant caution flag to the world. In an auditorium on the campus of the University of Utah, I watched, somewhat stunned, as Romney delivered a sustained, scathing takedown of the man whose support he had once gladly accepted.

"He's playing the members of the American public for suckers," Romney said. "He gets a free ride to the White House and all we get is a lousy hat."

The former governor's speech was a brutal, unmistakable fire

warning to the nation. Here was the Republican Party's 2012 nominee, as mild-mannered as they come, describing the GOP's eventual
nominee as little more than a reality show clown. Romney, a man
whose idea of letting loose was cracking open a can of Diet Cherry
Coke, was describing Trump as a unique threat to the world conning
his way into the White House.

I understood the earnestness of Romney's message all too well.
As a reporter on his campaign plane, I had come to see the Romney
the rest of America didn't really get to meet. Stiff and awkward on
the trail, he could be funny and disarming in his off-the-record
interactions with reporters. Most of us in the Romney press corps
viewed him as a rather admirable father figure—but golly (as Romney
would say), he was a disastrous presidential candidate. Despite all
his decency and his qualifications as a businessman and governor,
Romney was a gaffe machine. Those gaffes seem downright quaint
now. And there were many during the 2012 campaign:

"I like to be able to fire people."

"Corporations are people, too."

"Binders full of women."

And so on.

At Trump's rallies four years later, Trump ridiculed Romney over
his loss in the 2012 race. "He choked like a dog," he would howl.
Romney "walked like a penguin," he would joke. The Republicans in
Trump's crowds ate it up. They laughed at Romney's awkwardness
with a cruelty that took me by surprise. Trump's tirades were hardly
unintentional. They were often verbal spasms emanating from a candidate who delighted in inciting an audience. Trump didn't commit
gaffes. He trolled with taunts that he absolutely meant, and that were,
in many cases, simply hateful. He masterfully tapped into this sadism
time and again.

In the end, the GOP brushed off Romney's warning in Utah and was
somewhat vindicated for it. In the election's aftermath, even Romney

seemed to bow to the moment. During the transition to Trump's presidency, Romney let it be known he was interested in becoming Trump's secretary of state. Many in the Republican establishment felt he would be the perfect fit. He would normalize Trump, some thought. Calm things down. But that unlikely marriage would never come to pass. The president-elect instead chose to humiliate Romney, to rub it in that he, Trump, had accomplished something the former Massachusetts governor, a fellow billionaire (at least on paper), could not.

I was sitting in CNN's New York bureau one night during the transition when we received a tip that Trump and Romney were having dinner together in the city. One of CNN's campaign-embedded producers, Noah Gray, found out where: Jean-Georges, at the Trump International Hotel, across from the CNN studios in Manhattan. My producer Kristen and I made a reservation for 5:30 p.m. The two of us sat in the restaurant, running up the tab for two hours, before Trump and Romney finally came in. We were stalling until the moment they arrived. We could not have been luckier. They were shown to a table about fifteen feet away from us.

Not only could we see them talking. We were close enough to see what they were eating. The body language was revealing: Trump sitting there with his arms crossed like the alpha male as Romney tried to close the deal. RNC chairman and future White House chief of staff Reince Priebus was also at the table.

At one point, Trump turned around and said, "Hello, Jim Acosta."

We were busted. But we were customers, too, and they couldn't do anything about it. I went live on the air, over the phone, with Anderson Cooper to give CNN a full report. Was it a bit much to be doing a live report from a five-star restaurant on a dinner starring the president-elect and his one-time rival? Perhaps. But it was a striking moment of political theater, one that gave the public a glimpse into what could have been a moment of unification for the incoming Trump administration.

Had Trump selected Romney, he would have sent a powerful

THE ENEMY OF THE PEOPLE

message. To some extent, he would have been seen as a unifier, capable of healing the nation's political wounds. But, of course, Trump isn't a unifier. "Secretary Romney" was never going to happen; this meeting was just stagecraft. The press was brought in to snap photos, and the picture that made the rounds that night showed Romney with an expression on his face of a man having crow for dinner. It was not one of his best moments.

I got mixed signals from senior officials as to whether Trump and his people wanted to humiliate Romney by showing this thoroughly decent but defeated man bowing to the next president. A senior White House official insisted Trump actually considered the idea. As they left the restaurant, I asked Trump if Romney would be the next secretary of state. He responded, "We'll see." And they were gone.

About fifteen minutes later, I spotted Romney outside his hotel a couple of blocks away. He was standing in the rain, alone, umbrella in hand.

"I got nothing for you, Jim," he said to me.

"Of course," I responded. And we left it at that.

It struck me as a sad and poignant scene: a man who just four years ago was the Republican nominee for president standing in the pouring rain alone. No Secret Service agents around him. No entourage. Mitt Romney had tried to warn Republicans to stay away from Trump and he'd been kicked to the curb.

THE OPEN WOUNDS ON DISPLAY DURING THE TRANSITION ONLY made me more skeptical about what was to come with Trump's inauguration. Consider the morning of January 11, 2017. With a little more than a week before being sworn in, President-elect Donald J. Trump held his first and only news conference since winning the White House (actually, his first since late July 2016).

My guess was that he would not take a question from me, but I also thought he might. Trump seems addicted to conflict. And I had certainly had my moments with him for much of the 2016 campaign.

Regardless of whether Trump was going negative on me during the Romney campaign in 2012, his real piss-and-vinegar attitude toward me got its start at a news conference in Florida in 2016, shortly after he had won the South Carolina primary. This one was held, like most of his events, at a Trump property, his golf course in West Palm. The seating configuration for the news conference was the first sign of trouble. In a massive ballroom decorated with golden chandeliers and other over-the-top Trumpian touches—pictures of Trump were everywhere—the event's organizers had set up approximately twenty rows of chairs. The first fifteen or so were reserved for guests. Way in the back of the room were the seats for the press. It seemed we were expected to shout our questions *over* the guests assembled in the ballroom. This was clearly designed to limit our questions to those that would meet the guests' approval.

This press conference came after the infamous Republican debate where Marco Rubio made fun of the size of Trump's hands. Trump, as we all sadly recall, had defended his hand size at the debate by joking that he doesn't have to worry about any other corresponding inadequacies (i.e., the size of his penis). Yes, we were going *there*, in 2016. The news coverage went on for days, with discussions about Trump defending his manhood at a debate. Trump didn't seem to care that he was demeaning the office of the presidency by gleefully dragging the national political discourse into the gutter.

Which brings us to my question at this news conference. I asked Trump just that: Is it presidential to engage in talk about the size of one's manhood? Trump snapped at me.

"You should not have asked that question," he said, clearly irked.

One of the guests, a woman sitting in front of me, registered her disgust. "What an asshole," she said loudly.

But Trump then went on to defend the size of his hands, describing them as big and beautiful. He even turned to one of his friends in the front row to brag about his ability to drive a golf ball. It was odd to hear him go on in this fashion. To be clear, that's not what I was asking. Then he answered the question, vowing to be the most presidential president since Abraham Lincoln.

Still, the episode damaged my standing with the Trump campaign. Later on, in March 2016, he abruptly scrapped a press conference he had scheduled at Mar-a-Lago on the night of the Florida primary, a contest he had won decisively, driving Rubio out of the race. I called his spokeswoman, Hope Hicks, asking why Trump had canceled.

"Why? So you can ask him about the size of his hands again?" she asked sarcastically.

And then there was a run-in I had with Trump in May 2016, when he called me a "real beauty." Trump was holding a news conference at Trump Tower to answer questions about his charitable giving, or lack thereof, to veterans' groups. Much of this dated back to the real estate tycoon's decision a few months earlier to skip a debate in Iowa and instead hold an event to raise money for veterans' causes. In the months since, it was starting to become clear that Trump hadn't been as generous as he said he would be. By the time May rolled around, reporters were asking the hard questions. Where was the money he had promised to veterans? How much had Trump contributed? He hated the scrutiny but loved the coverage.

At a Trump Tower news conference in May, in responding to questions, Trump turned to his arsenal of biting one-liners. I asked him why he couldn't withstand the scrutiny that comes with running for president of the United States. The question went to the heart of one of his biggest liabilities, his temperament. Trump could have easily answered the question by saying, "I can handle the scrutiny. Nice try, Jim. Next question."

Instead, of course, he went on the attack: "I've seen you on television before. You're a real beauty," he growled.

Needless to say, by the time his Trump Tower pre-inauguration press conference in January 2017 rolled around, he had a pretty good idea what would happen when he called on me in a press conference.

Part of the reason I figured he would avoid my question was that my colleagues at CNN had just broken an important story that the president-elect had been told about concerns inside the U.S. intelligence community that the Russian government might have compromising information on him. Another news outlet, BuzzFeed, had reported some of the salacious but unsubstantiated allegations contained in the dossier, which came to be known as the Steele Dossier. CNN did not delve into those details, determining that they were unproven and, therefore, outside the bounds of fair reporting.

None of this was sitting well with Trump. For weeks, Democrats had charged that he was already an illegitimate president-elect, having lost the popular vote to Hillary Clinton and been linked to possible Russian interference in the election. There were questions at the time about his financial ties to the Russians, but there was no hard evidence of any possible collusion at that point. Trump's team saw the Russian story as yet another attempt to diminish the new president, softening him up for 2020. And Trump was already thinking about 2020—yes, even before he was sworn in. So, he decided he would return to one of his favorite lines of attack from his campaign playbook: an assault on the media, specifically CNN and BuzzFeed, for having reported the Steele Dossier story.

Trump's incoming press secretary, Sean Spicer, launched the first salvo, describing CNN and BuzzFeed's reporting as "a sad and pathetic attempt to get clicks." The accusation was particularly frustrating to my colleagues at CNN because we intentionally had not reported the details provided by BuzzFeed, as they were unsubstantiated at the time. CNN had decided, however, that the very fact that the intelligence community had presented Trump with the information about the Russians was, by itself, news, and it was. There was no denying that it was a major development.

But Spicer and the Trump team decided to lump CNN and BuzzFeed together in an attempt to chip away at the credibility of the news media at large. "For all the talk lately about fake news, this political witch hunt by some in the media is based on some of the most flimsy reporting and is frankly shameful and disgraceful," Spicer said.

Note the use of the term *fake news*. The "fake news" attack was a cynical ploy. The U.S. intelligence community had determined that Russian operatives had unleashed a blizzard of "fake news" stories on Hillary Clinton's campaign in an effort to boost Trump. The most sinister of these bogus reports had accused the Clinton campaign of running a child-sex ring out of a pizzeria in Washington, DC. It was a ridiculous and sickening lie, but a deranged man from North Carolina believed it was real enough and showed up at the restaurant with a gun, which he fired inside the eatery. Fake news was more than malicious. It was potentially deadly.

But Spicer wasn't alone when it came to making "fake news" the talking point of the day. The incoming vice president, Mike Pence, continued the scripted attack, referring to the Russia stories as "fake news," too.

"Today, we'll get back to real news, to real facts and the real progress our incoming president has already made in reviving the American economy and assembling a team that will make America great again," Pence added.

Then, at his press conference, the president-elect himself ratcheted up the rhetoric even further. He first tried to divide and conquer, pitting one news outlet against another. "I want to thank a lot of the news organizations for some of whom have not treated me very well over the years—a couple in particular—and they came out so strongly against that fake news and the fact that it was written about by primarily one group and one television station," he said.

Minutes later in the press conference, Trump used the line again. "I saw the information; I read the information outside of that meeting," he said, referring to the Steele Dossier. "It's all fake news. It's phony stuff. It didn't happen."

And again . . .

"Well, you know, President Putin and Russia put out a statement today that this [the dossier] fake news was indeed fake news. They said it totally never happened," Trump said, taking the word of the Russian leader over American journalists and, for that matter, the U.S. intelligence community.

Later on, Trump was asked by Major Garrett of CBS News if he defended a tweet he had posted that compared the U.S. intelligence community to Nazi Germany. The president-elect had accused leaders of the intelligence agencies of leaking the material to the news media to damage him.

The word *fake* was uttered once more.

Trump also tied CNN to BuzzFeed, which he called a "failing pile of garbage." BuzzFeed had also been a thorn in his side during the campaign, so much so that he'd even gone so far as to ban the news site's reporters from attending his events. To be fair to BuzzFeed, many of its reporters are excellent, and some of them went on to be hired by CNN.

The president-elect, along with his new press secretary and vice president–elect, had assailed CNN's credibility time and again in the run-up to the election. Now, at Trump's press conference, I was deep in thought about what was unfolding in front of all of us. Trump was not only attacking the credibility of one of the world's largest news organizations in CNN, but was also unleashing a profound assault on the truth. The fact that the U.S. intelligence community warned the president-elect about a potential Russian plot was not in dispute. This was something that had happened. This was an attempt to tell the public that up was down, that black was white, that real was fake. And it was all happening in front of our eyes.

Trump had told some whoppers during the campaign. The biggest whopper of them all may have been his vow to build a wall and make

Mexico pay for it, especially in light of Trump's repeated efforts to force U.S. taxpayers to foot the bill for the immense project. Still, there was much more to Trump's mountain of stump speech manure.

He falsely accused Ted Cruz's father of being a part of the conspiracy to assassinate John F. Kennedy.

Trump questioned the validity of the U.S. unemployment rate, arguing it was more than 40 percent when it was really in the neighborhood of 5 percent.

He said he witnessed Muslims celebrating the terrorist attack on the World Trade Center in 2001. That never happened.

Trump claimed he was against the Iraq War even as past interviews demonstrated that he had supported the Bush administration's military misadventure there.

He lied about how much Trump family money he received to start his own business, falsely stating his father gave him only $1 million, a fraction of the actual amount of that financial support.

It is no wonder Trump demonizes the press. As Lesley Stahl of CBS News once told Judy Woodruff of PBS, Trump confided to her that he calls the media "fake news" so people won't believe what the press is reporting.

There we were, sitting inside the lobby of Trump Tower, listening to the next president of the United States rip us to shreds. But Trump was simply doing what he had done throughout the campaign: attack the messenger. Same as at the rallies. Over the course of the 2016 campaign, he had called us:

Dishonest
Disgusting
Liars
Scum
Thieves
Sleaze
The worst

The "fake news" attack on CNN and BuzzFeed at the press conference felt like a coordinated strike. As Trump likes to put it, when he
gets hit, he hits back ten times harder. After listening to this withering
criticism of my employer, and after months of hearing Trump's crowds
chant "CNN sucks" on the campaign trail, I decided I was going to get
my question answered. One way or another, I had to ask Trump about
the Russians. Did they have the goods on him? And perhaps more important, had his associates had any contacts with the Russians during
the course of the campaign?

Finally, my opening arrived. For most of the press conference,
Trump had been waving me off. While I called out, "Mr. President-
elect," loudly but respectfully at least a dozen times, he selected other
reporters for questions. He would look at me and shake his head as
if to say, "No question." So, I had a decision to make: either I would
let the attacks stand and we'd walk out of that news conference
after taking his abuse one more time, or I would disrupt the news
conference and try a move he hadn't seen coming.

Here's what I was thinking: Trump had attacked CNN's credibility.
He had called us "fake news." It was only fair that we ask a question,
even if it meant causing a bit of a scene. So, that's what I did.

ACOSTA: Since you're attacking us, can you give us a question? Mr.
President-elect—
TRUMP: Go ahead [spoken to another reporter].
ACOSTA: Mr. President-elect, since you are attacking our news
organization—
TRUMP: Not you. Not you.
ACOSTA: Can you give us a chance?
TRUMP: Your organization is terrible.
ACOSTA: You are attacking our news organization, can you give us
a chance to ask a question, sir? Sir, can you—
TRUMP: Quiet.

ACOSTA: Mr. President-elect, can you say—
TRUMP: He's asking a question, don't be rude. Don't be rude.
ACOSTA: Can you give us a question since you're attacking us? Can you give us a question?
TRUMP: Don't be rude. No, I'm not going to give you a question. I'm not going to give you a question.
ACOSTA: Can you state—
TRUMP: You are fake news. Go ahead [again, to another reporter].
ACOSTA: Sir, can you state categorically that nobody—no, Mr. President-elect, that's not appropriate.

I shook my head. There was no need to go any further. My point had been made. In hindsight, I wish I had said something more than "that's not appropriate." But there it was; it had happened: a U.S. president had impugned the integrity of a news organization with a catchphrase that sounded a lot like "You're fired," from his days on *The Apprentice*.

As the PBS documentary program *Frontline* later revealed in an episode on the Russia investigation, broadcast in the fall of 2018, I did manage to spit out my question despite Trump's repeated interruptions:

"Did you or your aides or associates have any contacts with the Russians during the campaign?"

Not surprisingly, he didn't answer.

My disruption was not received well by the Trump transition team. Out of the corner of my eye, I saw the president-elect's incoming chief strategist, Steve Bannon, motion to Trump's private security team. Bannon wanted me tossed out.

Moments later, Sean Spicer moved in my direction. He looked at me and said if I did that again I would be removed from the news conference. To punctuate his point, he gestured in the same way a baseball umpire calls a batter out. If I tried that again, Spicer made clear, I would be out of the game.

After the news conference was over, Spicer walked up to me again and scolded me further, insisting that in disrupting the news conference I had crossed a line and that my behavior was inappropriate. I tried to shake his hand, but he refused. He had a job to do. He had to stand up for his boss. But I had had a job to do as well. My job, in that moment, had been to ask a question of the president-elect. It was obviously a question Trump did not want to address.

He did finally answer it, though. At the tail end of the news conference, a reporter from ABC News, Cecilia Vega, posed the same question I had tried to ask: whether any of the president's associates had had contact with the Russians during the campaign. But her query was only the first half of a two-part question. Trump answered the second half of the question from the podium but notably sidestepped the part about contact with the Russians.

He finally answered as he was walking to the elevator at the end of the news conference. "No," he said, before racing out of the lobby. There was no time for a follow-up. The elevator doors had closed.

As the world would learn much later, as many as fourteen individuals associated with him and his campaign had had some form of contact with Russians during the course of the campaign. And because the question had been asked, now Trump was on record with an answer. It just so happened that that answer wasn't true.

AFTER THE NEWS CONFERENCE, THE MAGNITUDE OF MY ACTIONS started to dawn on me. In the moment, I had merely acted to try to get Trump to take my question. Now, as I made my way across the lobby of Trump Tower, I realized I had done something that would be considered pretty controversial: I had made myself part of the story.

I was curious how the moment had come across to my colleagues. First, I turned to my producer for the Trump Tower press conference,

Elizabeth Landers. I won't forget the look on her face: her jaw had dropped. She was speechless. I then turned to my former producer and longtime friend Matt Hoye. He was there, producing for my colleague and correspondent Sara Murray. "What did you think?" I asked him.

"It was great!" he exclaimed.

Landers then turned to me and grabbed my attention. I was in a bit of a daze at that moment. CNN wanted me on the air immediately. Reporters from other news outlets tried to stop me as I made my way to the camera. The question was essentially: why'd you do that, Jim?

I then recounted live on CNN the events that had unfolded at the press conference. I explained that CNN had been under attack from the incoming president. We deserved a question, I argued. Unfortunately, Spicer had made things personal. In subsequent interviews on the Trump campaign's favorite network, Fox News, Sean would call me a liar and a "disgrace," demanding that I apologize to the president-elect for my behavior, which he called disrespectful. I tried to take the high road. As I later explained on CNN, I didn't take Spicer's attacks personally. In fact, I mentioned that I had known Sean for years, and added that I liked and respected him.

CNN released a very strong statement defending my attempts to ask a question at the news conference. "Being persistent and asking tough questions is his job, and he has our complete support," the statement read. That was a relief. It's good when the company backs you up, especially with something as big as this.

The CNN statement addressed some of Spicer's criticism and the incoming press secretary's own occasional challenges with telling the truth. "As we have learned many times, just because Sean Spicer says something doesn't make it true. Jim Acosta is a veteran reporter with the utmost integrity and extensive experience in covering both the White House and the President-elect," the statement read.

That moment at Trump Tower put Spicer and me on something of a collision course, one that would play out countless times during the daily White House briefings. As for Spicer's demand that I apologize—sorry, but that's not happening. I was just doing my job. Also, I don't recall Trump ever apologizing for his behavior.

At that news conference on January 11, 2017, all I did was try to ask a question. I am a reporter. That's what I do. And as the press was under assault throughout the 2016 campaign, here's what I told myself: My job is to ask questions of government officials and, as the old saying goes, speak truth to power. But after Trump's election, it had quickly become clear that the duty of the press was even bigger than that: We had to fight for the truth, because suddenly it was a battleground. For years we had done our jobs under the given that certain facts and truths are universal; with this administration, that was no longer the case. Everything had to be questioned. I wanted to make clear that they could attack us all they wanted, could call us all the names they wanted, but we were still going to search for the truth. And when we were confident we'd found it, we were going to report the news. Not fake news. Real news.

The Russia story was real news because there were so many legitimate questions at the time. We would have been derelict in our duty had we not asked them.

The American public seemed to agree. Ever since that moment at the press conference, people were walking up to me to thank me—at the airport, at the train station, at the grocery store. Ladies were applauding me at the hair salon. Strangers on the street were stopping me to ask for a selfie. A neighbor put a bottle of bourbon in my mailbox. That was not the last bottle sent to me, either. I suddenly had more than I could drink, in fact.

Here's what I felt then, and feel even more strongly today: I don't believe reporters are supposed to be the story. That's how I was trained.

But at that press conference, I had faced a choice: Do we just absorb Trump's attacks? Or do we push back and stand up for ourselves? It's a difficult decision, and one that members of the press confronted repeatedly during Trump's first two years in office. In my view, Trump represented a new kind of president, one that required a different kind of playbook for journalists.

But there was a more pressing emergency that day: Trump's disregard for the truth. The incoming president was questioning the validity of a perfectly legitimate news story. Trump knew we weren't going to buy it, but he also fully realized that millions of his supporters would accept his version of events. Hold on a damn minute, I thought that day. This man at the podium is about to be sworn in as president. He can't do this. This was no longer the brash businessman shattering conventional wisdom, as Trump's defenders had described him. This was a man about to take over the most powerful office in the world.

One thing I tried to make clear at that news conference is that the truth is worth defending. It's the force that maintains order in our world—in the end, it's all we really have. The incoming president was throwing that force off balance. Trump, who had been described by Jeb Bush as the "chaos candidate," excelled at creating disorder. As a very senior White House official would later tell me, this was all by design.

"He rules by instability. He wins by making everything around him unstable," the official told me. That way, the official said, Trump controls the chaos.

At that infamous news conference in Midtown Manhattan, Trump was destabilizing our collective sense of the real world. What was real had been deemed "fake." Trump had denied reality time and again during that crazy campaign. But what was the harm in a novice political candidate doing so over the course of an election? folks thought.

This was different. This was serious. With less than ten days to go before Inauguration Day, a terrible visual flashed in my mind: that we were all about to be pulled into the dumpster fire. On January 11, 2017, in my view, Donald J. Trump had declared war on more than just the press. He had declared war on the facts. Our fight for the truth had just begun.

2

The First Lie

Inauguration Day had finally come, and I had a job to do. My assignment was to cover the president, as in President Donald J. Trump, from the White House that day—well, to be more precise, I would be stationed out in the middle of the North Lawn of the White House. Yes, smack dab in the middle, where I would do my live reporting on what would become the first of many more surreal days of this administration.

Now, this was an odd place to be positioned. Normally, the press would go live from "Pebble Beach," the designated, tent-covered media stand-up area on the far western side of the North Lawn. But on this day, the White House and Secret Service were allowing us to report from the middle of the front yard of the Executive Mansion, where a long blue carpet was laid out linking the front door of the White House to the presidential reviewing stands for the Inaugural Parade. This enviable location would allow me to observe Trump's movements as he departed the parade route and made his way into the White House for the first time as president.

And a thought occurred to me: I was in a glorious position to shout a question to the new president.

But before Trump even arrived, we had a story on our hands. The reviewing stands along the pedestrian section of Pennsylvania Avenue in front of the White House were largely empty. Row after row was vacant. Sure, there were thousands of folks lined up along the parade route, but my experience in covering inaugurals for Barack Obama told me that these stands should not have been empty. Trump would notice this. (Anybody would have noticed it.) And Trump being Trump, he would not be happy.

The empty stands were either a sign that Trump's inauguration crowd was much smaller than that for Barack Obama's two Inauguration Days or an indictment of the presidential inaugural committee for not having made sure those stands were filled—or, perhaps, a bit of both. That unmistakable image of empty reviewing stands, and the pictures of the smaller crowd size overall, would become part of a critical story that was about to unfold.

Despite the dark tone of Trump's inaugural address, in which he spoke of an "American carnage" destroying the country, the new president was in good spirits. As he and First Lady Melania Trump crossed the North Lawn, I decided to ask—okay, shout—a fairly benign question. For once, I lobbed a softball.

"How was the day, Mr. President?" I asked.

"It was incredible," he said with a smile. Melania, who had always been a friendly face up until that point, appeared genuinely happy as well.

So many of my colleagues sent me emails congratulating me on receiving a response from Trump. That's so good for you, Jim, a few said. It was a sign, some thought, that there would be peace with the press or CNN or perhaps just me. But having covered him, I knew this was just Trump being Trump. He is capable of being charming, even to those he considers the opposition. Still, this was his day. This was his inauguration. There is no way, I thought, I can get away with shouting a confrontational question. Those days will come. And they did.

AS IT TURNED OUT, THOSE DAYS CAME MUCH SOONER THAN ANY OF us could have imagined. For many Americans who had voted against Trump, the first two weeks of the new administration were the worst-case scenario coming true, as the forty-fifth president took charge. Although I thought I had seen just about everything during the campaign, there were some appalling moments that surprised even me. Indeed, two main controversies during those weeks, the administration's war on the media and its harsh immigration policies, were deeply personal. And their arrival at such an early moment helped lay the foundation for much of my coverage in the years to come.

It started on Saturday, January 21, Trump's first full day as president. With one look outside the windows of the White House residence that morning, Trump could see and hear that he was leading a bitterly divided nation. A day of protests was under way across the country, including in Washington. The demonstration outside the White House was so loud that we could hear it inside the Briefing Room. So, Trump could hear it as well.

Trump would have the opportunity to view some of that democracy in action firsthand as he made his way out to Virginia for the highlight of his schedule that day, a trip to the Central Intelligence Agency in Langley. He was not happy with the CIA at that time. He had blamed the intelligence community for those leaks to the news media regarding compromising information the Russian government may have had on him, not to mention all the stories of Kremlin interference in the election on his behalf.

But the president was seething over something else that day. As he often does, Trump had watched the news that first morning in office, and he grew furious over reports that his inauguration crowd, while decent, had been fairly modest when compared to inaugural

crowds in recent memory, particularly those for his nemesis Barack
Obama.

Trump later made his bruised feelings clear in a fiery speech at
the CIA. Standing in front of a memorial dedicated to fallen Agency
officers, the president ripped into the news media, accusing the press
of intentionally lying about the size of his inauguration. Fake news,
he cried.

"It's a lie," the new president said at the CIA.

"I have a running war with the media," he continued, as if he were
at a Trump rally. "They are among the most dishonest human beings
on earth, right." To Trump, there was no difference between a hockey
arena in Western Pennsylvania and the nerve center of America's intelligence community.

"We had a massive field of people. You saw them. Packed. I get up
this morning, I turn on one of the networks, and they show an empty
field. I say, wait a minute, I made a speech. I looked out, the field
was—it looked like a million, million and a half people. They showed
a field where there were practically nobody [sic] standing there."

Not true but he went on and on.

"Honestly, it looked like a million and a half people. Whatever it
was, it was. But it went all the way back to the Washington Monument.
And I turn on—and by mistake, I get this network, and it showed an
empty field. And it said we drew two hundred fifty thousand people.
Now, that's not bad, but it's a lie. We had two hundred fifty thousand
people literally around—you know, in the little bowl that we constructed.
That was two hundred fifty thousand people. The rest of the twenty-block
area, all the way back to the Washington Monument, was packed."

I knew all too well from the campaign that Trump is obsessed with
crowd size figures. He would complain at rally after rally that the
photographers (as we in the industry refer to our camera operators) at
his events wouldn't turn their cameras away from the stage to show

the thousands of people on hand for his speeches. He would needle reporters if they dared report on any empty seats in their news stories. Crowd size reporting, to Trump, was as important as or more important than whatever a journalist said about the content of his speeches. Call him out on his rhetoric? No big deal. Call his crowed small? *Yuge* deal.

Resurrecting all this during the CIA visit was particularly troubling. With the public split over its new president, Trump was doubling down on his attacks on the news media at a sacred site—a spot where CIA officers are memorialized for their sacrifices to their country, for defending the same democracy that was supposed to protect a strong, free press in America. To the amazement of many in the room, and certainly to many around the world, there was some applause for Trump's latest broadside against journalists. Like so many episodes to come in this new administration, it was at once both stunning and disturbing.

Either way, a message had been sent: This was Trump's CIA now. He was in charge of a powerful agency that could, conceivably, be used with ill intent. It was a chilling reminder to the news media, I thought, that our liberties could potentially be in jeopardy. But Trump and his new team were far from finished in unleashing their anger on the press.

On that same day, Trump's first full day in office, reporters at the White House were summoned to the Briefing Room for some kind of statement from the incoming press secretary, Sean Spicer. Before he was tapped as White House press secretary, Spicer was widely regarded throughout Washington as a fairly reliable and even congenial spokesman for the Republican National Committee. Nearly every reporter in the nation's capital had Sean's contact information stored in his or her mobile phone. Sean could be friendly. He liked to drink with reporters. And most important, he was pretty responsive. If you texted him to confirm a story, unless you were on his bad side, you'd usually receive a reply. It's not revealing any kind of government secret that he had been a source of mine prior to the 2016 campaign.

So, it should come as no surprise that most folks in the Washington media breathed a collective sigh of relief when Spicer was selected as press secretary. Many reporters, including me, thought Trump had made a good pick. The press corps needed some kind of conduit to the president-elect, and Sean seemed like someone who understood the important role that office had to play in bridging the massive gap between Trumpworld and the press.

It was on this first day that we realized we'd all miscalculated.

Spicer's performance that day, needless to say, was a memorable one. It was clear that we were going to a bad place when photographs of the Trump inaugural crowd flashed on the large flat-screen monitors in the Briefing Room. Spicer, like the president, lashed out at the press, accusing reporters of misstating the facts about the number of people in attendance for the inaugural. Spicer stated emphatically that Trump's inauguration crowd was the biggest ever.

"This was the largest audience to ever witness an inauguration, period, both in person and around the globe," Spicer told reporters. He added the "around the globe" part in a blatantly dishonest way, as if the number of people watching the inauguration on TV or their devices somehow added to Trump's crowd size. Then came another threat, this time from the press secretary.

"There's been a lot of talk in the media about the responsibility to hold Donald Trump accountable. And I'm here to tell you that it goes two ways. We're going to hold the press accountable, as well," Spicer said.

After a few remarks on other topics, and without taking any questions, Spicer bolted from the room. The fact-checkers would later pan his performance. "Pants on fire!" roared PolitiFact. Spicer, it should be noted, later said his comments that day were a mistake.

I was seated in the CNN seat in the front row, right next to Reuters White House correspondent Jeff Mason. We looked at each other in stunned disbelief, wondering what in the world we had just witnessed. A few moments later, I reported live from the Briefing Room, as I had on so many occasions during the Obama administration. But this was a new experience. This was not how the Obama White House press briefings used to work. Not by a long shot. Yes, the Obama people could spin, BS, and equivocate, too. But this was different. Sean Spicer, the new White House press secretary, had just asked the media, and the rest of the world, not to believe their own eyes; incredibly, he was asking the world to believe Trump instead.

After regaining our senses, we went to work. My producer that day, Kevin Liptak, helped me dig up some key facts disproving Spicer's truth-challenged rant. Spicer had told reporters that white ground coverings used to protect the grass on the Mall had been installed for the first time for Trump's inaugural, creating the impression that fewer people were on hand for the festivities. Nope. That was false. As we discovered by looking into the CNN archives, white ground coverings were, in fact, also used at Obama's second inaugural. Spicer also said that magnetometers and fencing were deployed for the first time on the Mall, preventing hundreds of thousands of people from attending. This was also false. As we would later find with other claims the White House would go on to make, Spicer's inauguration nonsense could easily be fact-checked with, of all things, Google.

Spicer's performance was just the first wave of truth twisting. Kellyanne Conway, during an appearance on *Meet the Press* the following day, coined what will likely go down as the most Trumpian term of the era as she attempted to swat away questions from Chuck Todd about Spicer's performance.

"Don't be so overly dramatic about it, Chuck. You're saying it's a falsehood, and they're giving—Sean Spicer, our press secretary, gave alternative facts to that," Conway said.

But in an interview in her office, with her famous red, white, and blue inauguration outfit hanging on the wall near the table where we were sitting, Conway offered perhaps her most extensive comments to date about the controversy, explaining to me that she essentially misspoke that day.

"'Alternative facts' was a slip of the tongue. I rushed through 'alternative information and additional facts,' and it got mushed together. It was never meant to be Orwellian or to excuse lies. Everyone who still says it and uses it that way themselves are liars," Conway said, pointing out some of the factors that impacted the crowd size, an issue she confided she disliked.

"You could see me like I shook my head. And I meant to say what I was thinking—that Spicer was relying on alternative information and additional facts. And by that he meant that there were increasingly more ways to view the inauguration without incurring the cost of coming to DC and physically being in the crowd. We now use our phones and other personal devices. There was rain in the forecast. There were barriers put up and warnings about security and access," she continued, acknowledging it was basically a screwup.

"I know it sounds naïve," she said.

It reminded a lot of reporters of what Scottie Nell Hughes, a former Trump campaign surrogate and ex-CNN contributor, told National Public Radio's Diane Rehm a few weeks after the 2016 election: facts are no longer facts.

"One thing that's been interesting this campaign season to watch is that people that say facts are facts—they're not really facts," Hughes famously said. "There's no such thing, unfortunately anymore, of facts [sic]."

This attitude aligned with what I had heard numerous times from one of my sources inside the Trump campaign, who would go on to become a helpful provider of information from inside the White House. "The truth is a moving target," this source would sometimes say.

A disturbing theme was quickly emerging.

Looking back, this initial falsehood about crowd size barely registers in importance. Down the road, people's lives would be much more impacted by other deceptions, with far greater consequences. Ultimately, though, this first debate over crowd size mattered then and continues to matter today, mostly because it was the first lie of the administration. Of course, Trump had lied countless times throughout the campaign, but here, on his first day in office, when he was firmly in control of the bully pulpit, we understood that he was going to use the power of the presidency to continue to subvert the truth when it suited his purposes—even if it meant picking a fight over facts that could easily be disproven. After all, you could see from photographs later released to the public that Trump's 2017 inauguration crowd was smaller than Obama's at each of the latter's 2009 and 2013 celebrations. With this fiction, though, Trump was announcing that he would engineer his own reality regardless of what our eyes told us. As we learned days later, he even called the head of the National Park Service to complain about the agency's handling of the crowd size controversy. An Obama administration official working for the Interior Department had alerted me to the phone call, but I couldn't confirm it before the *Washington Post* broke the story. Given Trump's behavior, the official was afraid to speak out publicly. I couldn't blame him. The *Guardian* newspaper later revealed that a National Park Service photographer cropped out empty space in photos of Trump's inaugural crowd, in an attempt to satisfy White House officials, including Spicer. Trump's refusal to believe reality that day immediately set the tone for both his duplicity and the confrontations with the press that would follow.

For his part, Spicer would come to regret his handling of such a trivial issue. In his very first briefing, he had shattered his credibility. He had flat-out lied to the press, something reporters never forget. More important, Spicer fell into the Trump pattern of attacking the notion of objective truths. It was a devastating showing. Looking back on it now, Spicer's first performance in the Briefing Room signaled that he simply wasn't cut out for the job.

STANDING AT A LECTERN AND BRAZENLY LYING TO THE PRESS IS THE stuff of despots and dictators. Honestly, it sounded more like something that would have happened back in my dad's native country of Cuba. I can just picture a similar headline in the Cuban state newspaper: *Fidel Castro Had the Biggest Crowd Today. Que Grande!* The realization was an unsettling one.

My dad was born in Havana, Cuba, in 1950 and was raised in a small town outside the capital called Santa María del Rosario. In the fall of 1962, when he was just eleven, he left Cuba. My aunt Anabel, who had fled the island before my father and grandmother, was living in Miami. Reading the newspaper headlines about hostilities escalating between Fidel Castro and the United States, she and other family members believed it was time to bring my dad and grandmother to the States. So, on September 29, 1962, my father and grandmother fled Cuba. They landed in Miami with only the proverbial clothes on their backs. Three weeks later, the Cuban Missile Crisis would bring the world the closest it's ever been to nuclear war, forever altering relations between the United States and Cuba and making my dad's arrival a remarkable case of lucky timing.

This story of my father's arrival in America was a big influence on my childhood. As a boy, I was fascinated with Cuba—not just the Cuba he was raised in but the one he left behind as well. As a young journalist, I think I had a deeper appreciation for things such as freedom of speech and a free press. They remained in the background of much of my professional journey, shaping my sense of why it was so important to ask difficult, blunt questions. The hard questions have to be asked, not only because they challenge our leaders, but because we are lucky enough to live in a place that allows us to ask them.

Speaking truth to power like this came full circle for me when I traveled to Cuba with President Obama in 2016 as the United States reestablished diplomatic ties with the island nation. At a historic joint news conference featuring both Obama and Raúl Castro, I had the opportunity to question the Cuban leader about his country's practice of jailing political prisoners. Castro was so taken aback by the question that he removed the interpreter headphones from his ears and lashed out at me. The expression on Obama's face was priceless—like "Damn, Jim." One of my CNN colleagues jokingly asked how I was planning my escape from the island. But in my mind, there had been no alternative but to press Castro on human rights in Cuba. Ben Rhodes, Obama's deputy national security advisor, who had brokered the diplomatic breakthrough between the United States and Cuba, was seated a couple of rows in front of me. He passed me his Black-Berry with a message letting me know he was glad I had made the effort to push the Cubans to do better.

In part because I spent so much time thinking about Cuba growing up, I understood the importance of having an actual functioning democracy that values a free press. After all, I didn't have to look far back into the past to appreciate what the United States had done for me and my family. We have rights and freedoms in America that have been denied to the Cuban people for decades. That means we are free to question our leaders without fear of reprisal. Sure, I'm a proud Cuban American, but I don't want America to become more like Cuba.

I thought a lot about Cuba during those first weeks of the Trump administration, about what it meant to live under a dictatorship. It was hard to imagine our institutions being weakened to that extent, but in the wake of Spicer's press conference debacle, I was starting to worry.

After all, American democracy is only as strong as the people willing
to hold it accountable.

———————

IN ADDITION TO HIS BLOSSOMING WAR ON THE MEDIA, TRUMP FOCUSED
on another urgent concern during his first week in office: immigration, the issue that had catapulted him to the top tier of Republican
candidates during the 2016 campaign. As I like to put it, Trump's
enemies when he came into office can be boiled down to the "three
M's": Muslims, Mexicans, and the media.

Trump launched his campaign with what many critics say was the
most overt act of racism by a politician on the national stage in a generation. At his speech at Trump Tower on June 16, 2015, when he
rode down that escalator and began to turn the GOP political establishment upside down, the Manhattan real estate tycoon stereotyped
Mexican immigrants as rapists and criminals.

Most reporters can just about recite the "They're rapists" line from
memory, but Trump went further in that speech. He painted a similar caricature of Arabs and Muslims, saying that immigration from
the Middle East has "got to stop fast," a sneak preview of coming
attractions.

Later in his campaign, at a rally in Mount Pleasant, South Carolina,
Trump read from a press release issued by his campaign earlier in
the day: "Donald J. Trump is calling for a total and complete shutdown of Muslims entering the United States until our country's
representatives can figure out what the hell is going on," he said to
cheers from the crowd.

Trump knew exactly what he was doing. He was essentially going
where no decent American politician, Democrat or Republican, would
ever dare go. Here was a major Republican presidential candidate telling Americans that it was just fine to listen to their prejudices and
to their fears about Muslims. Tolerance would not keep them safe,

Trump insisted. He would. Trump, as he so often did, was sowing the seeds of division, and, yes, hatred. Nobody thought it would ever work long term, though. He was experiencing short-term political gains with his superheated rhetoric, sure, but the gains couldn't be sustainable. It was one of those areas where (looking back, of course) we could see we were all wrong.

On January 27, 2017, little more than two years after announcing his Muslim ban during the campaign, Trump turned his prejudice into policy, signing an executive order that barred people from seven predominantly Muslim countries from entering the United States. With the stroke of a presidential pen, all people hailing from Iran, Iraq, Libya, Somalia, Sudan, Syria, and Yemen—or approximately 218 million people—were blocked from setting foot on American soil. It was another mind-boggling moment for Americans. In a nation founded on a Constitution that opposed the establishment of an official religion and where religious intolerance had been strictly forbidden by its system of justice, Trump had initiated a policy that sought to discriminate against people who worshipped Islam.

"The United States cannot, and should not, admit those who do not support the Constitution, or those who would place violent ideologies over American law," he stated in his executive order.

Just as demonstrators poured out into the streets following his inauguration, protesters gathered at the nation's airports to decry Trump's travel ban. Poorly implemented as it was, the ban caused chaos at the airports, as scores of people, many of them American citizens, arrived at terminals to await relatives already en route to the United States from the banned countries in Trump's executive order. Grandmothers and grandchildren who had taken off with the understanding that they would be allowed into the country arrived in America in legal jeopardy. People were sobbing while waiting for loved ones who had been stopped, turned around, and sent back to their countries of origin.

"It was just chaotic and messy," a senior White House official told me, looking back at the rollout of the travel ban.

The official pointed the finger at the new chief strategist at the White House, Steve Bannon, for pushing the travel ban and other nationalist policies to the top of Trump's agenda in the early days of the administration. Before jumping aboard the Trump campaign, and prior to his arrival at the White House, Bannon was the conservative firebrand who led the Breitbart website, a haven for nationalist fear-mongering.

"We had way too many people not paying attention to what was being done, and some people doing two counterproductive things. One, fomenting fear and foisting their own agenda items. Two, pretending they had been elected to rule," the official said.

This chaos, of course, found its way back to the White House, where some officials, such as White House press secretary Sean Spicer, were also unprepared for the fallout. But there was another top aide to the president who appeared to be much more in control of the fast-moving events than the public really understood at the time.

That mysterious individual was none other than senior domestic policy adviser Stephen Miller, who would quickly become a household name in the Trump White House. Miller was well known in Washington. Before Trump, he had served as a little-known but loyal aide to Jeff Sessions when the Alabama Republican was in the Senate before becoming Trump's attorney general. While working for Sessions, Miller was the guy who would email reporters every day with the latest anti-immigration talking points coming from the senator's office. And when Sessions jumped on the Trump train, Miller hopped aboard, too, as a speechwriter. Trump loved Miller's bomb-throwing linguistic flourishes so much during the campaign that he had him serve as an occasional warm-up speaker at the rallies, allowing the once low-level staffer to make something of a name for himself out on the trail. It was a puzzling sight. There Miller was, at numerous Trump rallies, warming up the crowd mainly with his over-the-top immigration rhetoric. I remember thinking, How in the hell is this former Senate aide warming up campaign rallies for Trump? Other reporters who covered Washington and observed this had the exact same reaction. That's Stephen Miller? On the stage? For a presidential candidate? Behind the scenes, Stephen was the enforcer on the immigration issue. When another outlet reported that Trump was going wobbly on his promise to build a border wall, Miller vowed to me that an impenetrable barrier would be built across the U.S.-Mexico border. He was emphatic, as in I could take it to the bank.

Miller was one of the main architects of the travel ban, crafting the policy but also responsible for its haphazard rollout. A senior GOP congressional source told me that Miller was impossible to work with on immigration. He did much of his dirty work behind the scenes, on calls with congressional staffers and Trump surrogates who thought the former Senate staffer was essentially chasing an anti-immigration "pipe dream," as one White House adviser put it. Miller knew exactly what he was doing from a policy standpoint—indeed, in those early days, he may have been one of the few people in the Trump administration who did. It appeared he'd come to the White House to weaponize his biases, and the travel ban was his first order of business. If there was confusion in the White House about the severity of the travel ban and the motivations behind it, it was only because people weren't asking Stephen Miller about it. Miller wasn't drinking the immigration Kool-Aid. He was *making* it.

Miller would go on to be a key player inside the West Wing on nearly all the administration's plans on immigration, from the travel ban to a proposal to dramatically reduce the number of legal immigrants coming into the United States to the national emergency Trump declared in early 2019 in order to build his wall on the southern border with Mexico. If a policy had anything to do with immigration, Miller's fingerprints were on it, always with Trump's blessing.

As Miller operated in the shadows, Spicer seemed out of the loop, becoming the face of the administration's struggle to explain an inhumane policy. Sean was trying to sugarcoat what was clearly a draconian, hard-right turn for the nation's immigration system, one that immediately sent a message to the world that a new, less welcoming America had arrived on the scene. The press secretary, spiraling farther down his rabbit hole of deception, insisted that the new policy was nothing more than an enhanced vetting system for travelers and migrants coming into the United States.

"It's not a Muslim ban. It's not a travel ban," Spicer cried at a January 31 briefing, less than two weeks into the new administration. There was only one problem: Trump kept calling it a ban, over and over.

If the ban were announced with a one week notice, the "bad" would rush into our country during that week. A lot of bad "dudes" out there! Trump had tweeted the previous day, using the word *ban*.

"He's using the words that the media is using," Spicer maintained, to eye rolls in the Briefing Room.

But Trump would go on to undercut his press secretary, a constant source of frustration in the West Wing. Of course, Trump didn't care. Sean could try to dance around the truth or flat-out bullshit the public, but there was no hiding what Trump was trying to do. The issues that had animated his campaign would do the same for his administration. He was demonizing immigrants to keep "the base" happy. There is just no getting around that. Immigrants would become a scapegoat for Trump in ways we had not seen from an American president in decades.

As with Trump's attacks on the press, immigration was an issue that touched my sense of self as a journalist and an American. I'm a reporter, of course, but I'm an American first, and it was impossible to see these events unfolding without feeling tremendous sadness and concern. Watching the chaos at the airports and in the West Wing in real time, seeing the faces on some of the kids caught up in it, I found it hard not to think once more of my father and his experience coming from Cuba. He was only eleven at the time. Surely, he was scared, arriving with his mother (my grandmother), uncertain how they would assimilate in this new world. Taking in the scenes from the airports, I found it impossible not to think about his journey here.

My father's arrival was not met with hostile crowds or a president spewing hateful rhetoric. As my dad tells the story, he and my grandmother found warmth (both the wardrobe and human kind) at a Presbyterian church in Vienna, Virginia. Rather than settle in South Florida, as so many Cuban refugees during that time did, my dad and *abuela* migrated again after their arrival, from Miami to Northern Virginia, right outside Washington. The people at the church in Virginia gave them coats and sweaters to keep them warm during their first DC winter. Dad went to elementary school and started to understand life as an American, experiencing kindness and a welcoming spirit. One of his teachers would pull him aside to tutor him in English until he became proficient and then fluent.

Now, I don't want to paint a rosy picture of life for my dad and grandmother in the 1960s. Virginia, even Northern Virginia, was . . . well, Virginia in the early 1960s—probably not the best time or place to be a Cuban immigrant. I remember, as a child of the 1970s, seeing people act rudely to my grandmother—whom I called Waya, because I couldn't say *abuela* when I was younger—in reaction to her broken English. To this day, I still recall one woman at a supermarket flashing a look of hatred at my Waya. The look on my grandmother's face broke my heart. She was clearly embarrassed. So was I.

My dad graduated from high school and went on to work in grocery stores for the rest of his life. Remember that person working the checkout line in the supermarket? That was my dad. He did that (as well as other tasks, stocking groceries and so on) for forty years. Most

Americans struggled to say my dad's name, so he asked people to call him A.J., the initials for "Abilio Jesus." Anytime I visited him at the supermarket, the customers would tell me how much they loved A.J., and my dad loved serving them. The Safeway, in the affluent suburb of Great Falls, Virginia, gave him the opportunity to meet members of Congress, famous journalists, and star players for the Washington Redskins. My dad would tell me all their stories. He took photos with the Redskins players and shared them with me and my sister at home.

Listening to the rhetoric in the aftermath of Trump's travel ban, thinking about the scenes of hatred toward immigrants I'd seen on the campaign trail, I couldn't shake the sense that this was not a country I recognized. As the anti-immigration activists lied to people and implied that newcomers to the United States were lazy parasites, I simply pictured those millions of immigrants as being like my dad, working in that checkout line at Safeway until he literally could not stand anymore and retiring only when his legs were too weak to get him through an eight-hour shift. My dad paid his taxes. He paid into Social Security and Medicare. He earned his retirement. Fortunately, he also benefited from a union at Safeway that guaranteed him a pension along with the Social Security payment he receives every month. A.J. wasn't in the United States to game the system. My dad, like many of the young, undocumented so-called Dreamers, was brought to this country as a child. He played by the rules, worked hard, and, along with my mother, helped his two kids grow into successful adults, and is now enjoying his retirement—just what so many others deserve.

In the end, my dad flourished in part because, from the start, he had been welcomed much the way Americans had always welcomed immigrants. His success story, like those of millions of others, was made possible by the values America embodied and practiced—or at least it did up until Trump's executive order. Stories and experiences like those of my dad and the millions of others who've come to the United States seeking a better life were discounted in Trump's rush to institute his travel ban. If you came from a particular country, he and his top officials argued, you were automatically considered a danger to the public.

Trump's Muslim ban was troubling not only for how it played out but for what it foretold about things to come. On a personal level, the rollout of the ban and the tone of the Trump administration's position on immigration hit home. Prior to this, I'd always brought a passion for the truth to my job covering the White House, for finding the story, but it was difficult in those early weeks not to feel the weight of these attacks.

Like Trump's war on the media, his fraught immigration policies were still in their infancy, and it would take time to understand how far his administration was willing to go to dehumanize people seeking hope within America's borders. While I didn't alter my coverage on air or off, in the years ahead, I would often think about the initial chaos of the travel ban. Trump's attacks on this critical part of American life were personal for me long before he turned them into policy.

IN THIS INITIAL PUSH FOR THE MUSLIM BAN, THE ADMINISTRATION made it clear it had no problem erasing the boundaries between its immigration ideas and its fight with the media to suit its ends. This foreshadowed much of what was to come as the Trump team battled with the press, in large part, to clear the way for his policy designs for the nation.

During the first week of February, less than one month after moving into the White House, Trump, along with his counselor Kellyanne Conway, began to mischaracterize the media's coverage of terrorist attacks, pathetically insisting that somehow the press downplayed this threat out of some kind of political correctness run amok. Speaking to the U.S. Central Command on February 6, Trump made the absurd statement that news outlets didn't report on terrorist attacks. Anybody who has watched CNN's rolling coverage of such incidents is obviously fully aware that this is an outlandish lie, but Trump let loose that whopper anyway as he attempted to defend his travel ban to the public.

"It's gotten to a point where it's not even being reported," he told the Central Command. "And in many cases the very, very dishonest press doesn't want to report it."

This assault on the press followed an outright falsehood that came just a few days earlier, when Conway complained to MSNBC's Chris Matthews that the media had not covered something she referred to as the "Bowling Green massacre."

"I bet it's brand-new information to people that President Obama had a six-month ban on the Iraqi refugee program after two Iraqis came here to this country, were radicalized, and were the masterminds behind the Bowling Green massacre," Conway said.

It was "brand-new information" because there never was a Bowling Green massacre. Conway, who later said she made a misstatement, had her facts wrong in an astounding way. There was a case in Bowling Green, Kentucky, in which two Iraqi men were arrested for providing weapons to al Qaeda. But the men never carried out an attack of any sort in Bowling Green.

Despite that embarrassing episode for Conway, the White House continued to push the false narrative that members of the press were under-reporting terrorist attacks and that this served as justification for the travel ban. One day after Trump's comments to the Central Command, the White House released a list of seventy-eight terrorist attacks the West Wing claimed the media had not covered sufficiently. It was a laughable mess. Covering a time period stretching from September 2014 to December 2016, the White House list included, incredibly, the 2015 massacre in Paris and two mass shootings in San Bernardino, California, and Orlando, Florida. All three of these attacks were covered extensively by nearly every major news outlet in the United States for days on end. As I went through some of this on the air for CNN, I relayed the fact that the document was pure amateur hour, not to mention filled with misspellings. Just as Spicer had alleged from the lectern on the day after the inaugural, the White House was once again accusing the press of misreporting something when we hadn't.

"A head-scratcher" is how I described it on the air to CNN's Erin Burnett as we reported on the list that night. What an understatement!

Michael Short, an aide in the White House press shop, later emailed me to complain about my report, calling it "shoddy." But it was the administration's work that was shoddy. To include major terrorist attacks in such a list and claim they weren't being reported on was simply another example of the White House presenting "alternative facts" to the American people. And as in the case of the inauguration crowd size, the main thrust behind the terrorist attack list offered up by the White House was easily disproven with a simple Google search.

Shortly after that ridiculous White House list was released, on February 10, the Ninth Circuit Court of Appeals dealt a major blow to Trump's initial travel ban, ruling 3–0 against the executive order, stating that the public has "an interest in free flow of travel, in avoiding separation of families, and in freedom from discrimination."

Trump had lost, and he didn't take it well, tweeting in all caps, **SEE YOU IN COURT, THE SECURITY OF OUR NATION IS AT STAKE!**

The battle over Trump's travel ban would continue. The White House modified the ban twice more and ran into more roadblocks in the U.S. legal system, before ultimately receiving a favorable decision at the Supreme Court, which ruled that the third version of a ban could be rolled into action.

But all that was months ahead. In early February 2017, Trump was angry. He was being thwarted, not only by a news media that refused to roll over, but also by a U.S. justice system that was flexing its muscles as a coequal branch of the government. In the early days of the Trump administration, it was a sign of life from American democracy. The system, while under stress, was working.

Still, the cause for concern was everywhere you looked. For the moment, the issue of the Muslim ban had come to a halt, but in the aftermath, I began to understand, perhaps more clearly than ever before, just how difficult the coming months and years would be. What had been more academic in the weeks before Trump's inauguration had hardened into reality. As my colleagues and I were reporting on the latest twists and turns of the new administration, trying to keep up with a nonstop news cycle that had not relented since the days of the campaign, it felt as though we were stepping carefully across a minefield. One small screwup, and Trump would call us "fake news." We were constantly aware of that danger. But keep in mind that when he'd use the term *fake news*, he wasn't really talking about bogus reporting. Negative stories were what he cared about. He was just trying to bully the press into giving him more favorable coverage.

"He's trolling you guys," a Trump source of mine would tell me time and again. In other words, what was coming out of the White House was designed to drive us nuts and ratchet down what Trump perceived as negative coverage. He wanted us to pull our punches, use kid gloves, and soften the impact of our reporting. The heart of this strategy was, to put it crudely, shoot the messenger. Again and again, Trump was trying to shape the news by denouncing those covering it.

Now, every administration takes issue with its coverage by the press. Every administration complains about how stories are aired and characterized. Republicans in particular have been waging a war on the "liberal" media since the Nixon administration. Yet, this was something else entirely. Never had an administration been so combative with the media, or used open hostility as a way to push its policy agenda. Never had an administration been so willing to distort the truth publicly, or to rely on fabrications to justify its behavior. What had begun during the campaign as a way to get applause and cheers from raucous crowds at Trump rallies was now a bludgeon to elicit the positive coverage Trump craved. And this would become the new normal for the White House press corps.

What wasn't lost on me in all this was a simple reality of Washington power following Trump's election: Republicans controlled all three branches of the federal government. And though Trump would spend the next two years silencing one-off GOP dissenters, he was excellent at strong-arming Republicans on the issues that mattered to him. As it soon became clear, Republicans, despite their private frustrations with Trump, were not about to stop him, they were not going to use their powers in Congress to check his worst instincts.

In that vacuum was the press, one of the only major institutions of public life that Trump couldn't control. Those were the terms for our reporting from now on. And just because he couldn't control us, it didn't mean he would stop trying.

For his part, Stephen Miller seemed to revel in exacerbating these concerns about the Trump administration's undemocratic, autocratic instincts when he declared on the CBS Sunday morning news program *Face the Nation* that the president should not be challenged on such matters as the travel ban.

"Our opponents, the media and the whole world will soon see as we begin to take further actions, that the powers of the president to protect our country are very substantial and will not be questioned," Miller said.

This was the kind of declaration you'd expect from an authoritarian government. An administration that had started lying from the very beginning, about something as trivial as an inaugural crowd size, had taken its war on the truth to a disturbing new level, now claiming that it was beyond scrutiny. A couple of years from being an obscure staffer with no name recognition, suddenly Miller was on national television telling the American people that the Trump team wouldn't be questioned.

Watching the interview left me speechless, and I was wondering the same thing that a lot of people across Washington were wondering: who the hell does this guy think he is?

Trump had attacked the judiciary, Spicer had lied about the inauguration crowd size, Kellyanne Conway had pulled a nonexistent Bowling Green Massacre out of thin air, and Stephen Miller had said we couldn't question the president? It wasn't just this reporter, folks. Many of us in the press areas of the White House were looking at one another wide-eyed, jaws agape, dumbfounded. Sometimes it was just a knowing glance as we left the Briefing Room, but more often, we were all talking about it over drinks after work. (We certainly needed a few of those back in the early weeks of the Trump White House.) And we were all saying the same thing to one another, to our loved ones, to our family members, to our bosses, to anybody who would listen. It all boiled down to the same damn question: who the hell do these people think they are?

3

The Enemy

Reporting on those first few weeks of the Trump administration was like running through an ever-expanding hall of mirrors. One minute you're covering the travel ban. Then it's the Russia investigation. And all along the way, Trump is tweeting stuff that needs to be fact-checked in real time. Add in all the alleged falsehoods that challenged fact-checkers on a daily basis and you get a ridiculously exhausting exercise. Sources inside and outside the White House were all too eager at that time to dish the dirt about this official or that aide to the president inside the West Wing. In those days, two key rival factions inside the White House were constantly knifing one another. It was the people who had worked for the Trump campaign, such as Kellyanne Conway and Steve Bannon, versus the staffers who had come to the White House via the Republican National Committee, such as Sean Spicer, Raj Shah, and Reince Priebus. And, as you might expect, there was plenty of backbiting going on inside each faction. They'd talk about each other, sure, but getting them to talk about the important stuff, such as policy, was something else.

With this much backstabbing came a higher level of paranoia than I had ever seen before, which led to a major shift from my days reporting on the Obama White House. In the Obama years, officials would talk to you via email, text, or over the phone. Under Trump, who was lashing out at leaks among his staffers, top officials were fearful of getting caught speaking to the press. So, many of us in the news media had to move our conversations with sources over to encrypted apps, as a way to maximize privacy and secrecy. Some sources were adamant: they would talk on Signal or WhatsApp or they wouldn't talk at all.

Even with the encrypted apps, there was one subject that it was next to impossible to get anybody to talk about: the Russia investigation. Whether it was on the record, off the record, or on background (that is, anonymously), people were worried they would be ensnared in the investigation. One source in particular told me he would talk about anything as long as it wasn't Russia.

People inside Trumpworld fully understood why we in the press wanted to talk about Russia. By the time Trump got into office, the Russia story clearly had legs, as the FBI had already launched a high-stakes investigation into Moscow's interference with our 2016 presidential election. It didn't take long for the press corps to realize that this probe was into events not only that took place during the campaign, but also that were unfolding in real time. As such, it would be the first real test of how the new administration would respond to an actual scandal. Perhaps it shouldn't be surprising, then, that it failed spectacularly, raising more suspicions that seemed to keep the story going.

On the heels of Trump's rumble with the press over the travel ban in early February, another festering problem blew up in the president's face. On February 13, his national security advisor, Michael Flynn, was pushed out after admitting he had misled Vice President Mike Pence about his contacts with the Russian ambassador to the United States, Sergey Kislyak. Much of this did not come as a surprise to the White House. That's because the Justice Department had already warned the president's team in January—yes, right around when they came into office—that Flynn had been lying to federal agents (a crime in itself) about his contacts with the Russian ambassador regarding sanctions on Russia imposed during the presidential transition period by the Obama administration to punish Moscow for its meddling.

Before and after Flynn's removal, the White House displayed the lack of a coordinated response that had become something of a norm for the Trump team during the campaign. (They had been all over the place then, and that pattern continued as they came in to power.) Their original statement on Flynn's contact with Kislyak now looks laughably false. Here's how Spicer initially explained that contact to reporters on January 13, 2016, one week before Trump was sworn into office:

"On Christmas Day, General Flynn reached out to the ambassador, sent him a text, and it said, you know, I want to wish you Merry Christmas and a Happy New Year, I look forward to touching base with you and working with you. And I wish you all the best. The ambassador texted him back, wishing him a Merry Christmas as well, and then subsequently, on the twenty-eighth of December, texted him and said, I'd like to give you a call, may I? He then took that call on the twenty-eighth, and the call centered around the logistics of setting up a call with the president of Russia and the president-elect after he was sworn in. And they exchanged logistical information on how to initiate and to schedule that call. That was it. Plain and simple."

Plain and simple, it was not. It hasn't been ever since, and that raised more legitimate questions.

On February 9, 2017, the *Washington Post* first exposed Flynn's improper conversations with Kislyak, immediately setting off a scramble inside the West Wing to determine exactly what the new national security advisor had discussed with the ambassador. A well-placed senior White House official said that Vice President Mike Pence had summoned Chief of Staff Reince Priebus to discuss the matter immediately. Both Pence and Priebus obtained the Justice Department's transcripts of Flynn's conversations with Kislyak and reviewed them inside the White House Situation Room. Pence was alarmed over the *Post* story as Flynn had contradicted statements made by the vice president on the Sunday talk show circuit.

"They did not discuss anything having to do with the United States' decision to expel diplomats or impose censure against Russia," Pence said the previous month on CBS's *Face the Nation*.

Priebus then called Flynn to his office, where the chief of staff grilled the national security advisor in front of other West Wing aides, the senior White House official told me. Angered over Flynn's lies to the vice president and others on the Trump team about his conversations with Kislyak, Priebus wanted to make sure other staffers were in the room.

Flynn was immediately in trouble with the new president, the official told me. "The president was already tired of Flynn before the inauguration."

It's not like Trump wasn't warned about Flynn. Something extraordinary had occurred just after the election, when Trump met with Obama in the Oval Office: Obama warned him not to hire Flynn.

"Given the importance of the job, the president thought there were better people for it, and that Flynn wasn't up for the job," a former Obama administration official said.

But, as we reported for CNN a few months after Flynn was fired, one former Obama administration official in the national security realm told me that during the transition, there was one big reason that the outgoing White House team was worried about Flynn: Russia.

"Flynn's name kept popping up," said one senior Obama administration source about the Russia investigation.

Spicer later confirmed that Obama had raised concerns about Flynn to Trump during their meeting. "It's true President Obama made it known he wasn't exactly a fan of Gen. Flynn's," Spicer said.

The messaging around Flynn's departure was equally as muddled as the decision to hire him in the first place. Just hours before he was fired, Flynn was all of a sudden in a "gray area," a senior Trump administration official told me. That was just hours after White House counselor Kellyanne Conway said that Flynn had the "full confidence" of the president. Sean Spicer, in a bit of messaging disarray, told reporters that Conway was wrong and that Flynn's situation was being evaluated.

From the outside, the whole thing looked messy, and it was even messier on the inside. I remember standing for hours outside Spicer's office with other reporters as we all awaited Flynn's fate. About fifteen of us were crammed in the tiny hallway linking the "Lower Press" area of the West Wing, where the deputy spokespeople have their offices and the site of Spicer's lair. Officials were flying in and out of the press secretary's office, refusing to talk to reporters. It was a madhouse. I snapped a photo of all of us hanging out, waiting for Sean, to capture the moment.

By midnight, Flynn was gone. His departure was initially spun as a resignation, but he was shown the door. The next day, Spicer conceded that Trump had asked Flynn to resign over an "eroding level of trust" and pointed specifically to the former national security advisor's lies to the vice president about his contacts with Kislyak. Three weeks into the new administration, the president's first national security advisor was already forced out, and the reason could be summed up in one haunting word for Trump: *Russia*.

Naturally, just because Flynn was gone it didn't mean the problem had been solved. Far from it. If anything, Flynn's actions during the transition had actually bolstered the case for FBI director James Comey to expand the Bureau's investigation into Russia's meddling in 2016. It would have been law enforcement malpractice to shut down the probe at that point, despite Trump's cries of fake news. As for Trump's complaints about our reporting on Russia, how in the world could we have avoided the irony of Flynn's fall from grace? After all, it was Flynn who had been leading chants of "lock her up" at Trump campaign events, including at the Republican National Convention.

To me, Flynn's performances had been some of the most shocking sights during the 2016 campaign. I had attended rally after rally where Flynn, a retired general, had advocated the jailing of Hillary Clinton. People can blow this off as just harmless campaign rhetoric, but I disagree. It's unacceptable. We just don't do that in America. We don't lock up our political opponents. We settle our differences at the ballot box. The sight of Flynn, who had worn the uniform of a member of the U.S. Army, a retired lieutenant general no less, leading these cheers was nothing short of astounding, like something out of a banana republic.

In the end, neither Trump nor anyone else in the administration could effectively control the fallout from the Flynn debacle. General "Lock Her Up" Flynn faced the prospect of being locked up himself. In a sign of how future scandals would be mismanaged, no one from the administration was able to control or message the situation effectively, least of all the president.

That same week, on February 16, we all gathered in the East Room for Trump's first full news conference as president. We were told that he was holding the press conference to announce the nomination of Alexander Acosta (no relation) to be Labor Department secretary. But the Acosta nomination was just the setup. The real purpose of the news conference was for Trump to confront nagging questions from the Russia investigation and the departure of Flynn.

I was in a good mood that day, so I was having some fun with the Acosta news in my live shot before the president came out to the microphone. This, I suppose, is where some of the accusations against me for "showboating" come into play. I like to think of it as not being so damn stiff.

"I hope this is not fake news," I joked to Wolf Blitzer. " 'Secretary Acosta' sounds pretty good," I added. The reporters gathered in the room laughed. So did a few White House staffers. Other West Wing aides, who basically hated my guts, scowled, as they always do.

Trump was asked about Flynn right off the top. And the president launched right into what was becoming his go-to talking point, labeling the Russia investigation as "fake news." But there were real questions to ask. It was simply not in the cards to take his word for it.

The next question, posed by Jon Karl of ABC News, was (surprise!) the question I had tried to ask at the January 11 news conference.

KARL: I just want to get you to clarify this very important point. Can you say definitively that nobody on your campaign had any contacts with the Russians during the campaign? And on the leaks, is it fake news or are these real leaks?

TRUMP: Well, the leaks are real. You're the one that wrote about them and reported them, I mean the leaks are real. You know what they said, you saw it and the leaks are absolutely real. The news is fake because so much of the news is fake.

The leaks are real, but the news is fake. Did you get that? Let that wash over you for a second. It's a bit of a mind-bender. This was when, listening to Trump, I would feel my eyes glaze over. My thought at that moment was, What the hell is he talking about?

Trump shouldn't have been so hard on the press over leaks. I can speak for myself when I say that I held back on a number of stories based on leaks from the rival factions inside the West Wing. As I mentioned earlier, aides from the campaign days were constantly leaking damaging information about the staffers who had joined the Trump team from the Republican National Committee. Likewise, the RNC clan was willing to dish the dirt about the campaign veterans and about more visible Trump associates such as Kellyanne Conway, Boris Epshteyn, and Omarosa Manigault, one of the past contestants on *The Apprentice*.

Another staffer who made waves was Cliff Sims; he once bragged to me about how he had helped bring down a former Alabama governor who became embroiled in a sex scandal. Cliff cashed in and went public on the infighting with a tell-all book called *Team of Vipers* that, frankly, people inside the White House should have seen coming from a mile away. Several aides said Cliff went as far as to record Trump without his knowledge, a stunning breach of White House security. Sims has publicly denied the allegation.

When it came to Trump's complaints about real leaks and fake news, though, the stories weren't bogus. You couldn't believe the leaks, Trump was saying, because you can't trust the news. Then, a few moments later, he was back on the attack, of the press and CNN and . . . me.

TRUMP: I don't mind bad stories. I can handle a bad story better than anybody as long as it's true and, you know, over a course of time, I'll make mistakes and you'll write badly and I'm OK with that. But I'm not OK when it is fake. I mean, I watch CNN, it's so much anger and hatred and just the hatred.

There he goes again, I thought. We're not going to do this again, I told myself, and I put my hand up to interrupt him. Trump noticed me.

TRUMP: I don't watch it anymore because it's very good—he's saying no. It's OK, Jim (ph). It's OK, Jim (ph), you'll have your chance.

He's spoiling for a fight, I thought to myself. As I was preparing to ask the question, I noticed that there was great interest in what was about to unfold. For some reason, people kept handing me microphones. It was like the kids in the playground gathering around the two guys about to have a fight. By the time I started speaking, I was holding three different microphones. My exchange with Trump would last a good seven or eight minutes. But first, I tried to lighten the mood.

ACOSTA: Thank you very much, and just for the record, we don't hate you. I don't hate you.

TRUMP: OK.

ACOSTA: So, pass that along—

TRUMP: Ask—ask [CNN president] Jeff Zucker how he got his job. OK?

ACOSTA: If I may follow up on some of the questions that have taken place so far here, sir—

TRUMP: Well, that's—well, you know, we do have other people. You do have other people and your ratings aren't as good as some of the other people that are waiting.

ACOSTA: It's pretty good right now, actually.

TRUMP: OK, go ahead, John [*sic*].

ACOSTA: If I may ask, sir, you said earlier that WikiLeaks was revealing information about the Hillary Clinton campaign during the election cycle. You welcomed that. At one time—

TRUMP: I was OK with it.

ACOSTA: —you said—you said that you loved WikiLeaks. At another campaign press conference, you called on the Russians to find the missing thirty thousand emails. I'm wondering, sir, if you—

TRUMP: Well, she was actually missing thirty-three and then that got extended with a pile after that.

ACOSTA: Then your numbers were off, too.

TRUMP: No—no, but I did say thirty. But it was actually higher than that.

ACOSTA: If—if I may ask you, sir, it—it sounds as though you do not have much credibility here when it comes to leaking if that is something that you encouraged during the campaign—

TRUMP: OK, fair question.

After Trump defended his past praise of WikiLeaks, I tried to keep the conversation going. That's basically what we were having at that point, a conversation. It had ceased being a news conference. This was something akin to an interview. There were a million things to ask at that moment, but I had essentially one thing on my mind: Trump's repeated assaults on the press and our reporting represented to me a continuation of his attacks on truth itself. I felt compelled to explore this further. It wasn't easy. Trump was determined to turn our exchange into a vaudeville act.

> ACOSTA: Just because of the attack of fake news and attacking our network, I just want to ask you, sir—
> TRUMP: I'm changing it from fake news, though.
> ACOSTA: Doesn't that under—
> TRUMP: Very fake news.
> ACOSTA: —I know, but aren't you—

The room broke out into laughter. Trump has many flaws. Comic timing is not one of them. The jokes would continue. The president was all but under cross-examination, with question after question on the Russia probe. Yet, he seemed to be enjoying himself.

> TRUMP: Go ahead.
> ACOSTA: Real news, Mr. President, real news.
> TRUMP: And you're not related to our new [Trump refers to Alex Acosta]
> ACOSTA: I am not related, sir. No. I do like the sound of Secretary Acosta, I must say.
> TRUMP: I looked—you know, I looked at that name. I said, wait a minute, is there any relation there? Alex Acosta.
> ACOSTA: I'm sure you checked that out, sir.
> TRUMP: OK. Now I checked it—I said—they said, "No, sir." I said, "Do me a favor, go back and check the family tree."

I tried to steer us back on course.

ACOSTA: But aren't you—aren't you concerned, sir, that you are undermining the people's faith in the First Amendment, freedom of the press, the press in this country, when you call stories you don't like "fake news"? Why not just say it's a story I don't like?
TRUMP: I do that.
ACOSTA: When you call it "fake news," you're undermining confidence in our news media.
TRUMP: No, no. I do that. Here's the thing. OK. I understand what you're—and you're right about that, except this. See, I know when I should get good and when I should get bad. And sometimes I'll say, "Wow, that's going to be a great story." And I'll get killed. I know what's good and bad. I'd be a pretty good reporter, not as good as you. But I know what's good. I know what's bad.

Trump threw in a compliment about yours truly there, in case you missed it. But more important, he seemed, just for a moment, to concede the point about undermining the public's confidence in the press.

He went on for a few more minutes and then moved on. The entire news conference seemed to be, for Trump, nothing more than an opportunity to vent. He was hurt by the coverage, and he wanted me to know it. We had gone from a vaudeville act to the psychiatrist's couch.

Later in the afternoon, I received a phone call. It was a 202 area code followed by nothing else. I had seen this number before: it was the White House calling. I answered the phone. It was Trump's trusted aide Hope Hicks.

"Hi, Hope. What's up," I said, trying to be as friendly as possible.

"Hi, Jim. I just wanted to let you know that I spoke with the president and he wants you to know that he thought you were very professional today," Hicks said.

Okayyyyy.

"He said, 'Jim gets it,'" Hicks added. She was so chipper. Trump was complimenting my reporting, you say? After what went on in that room, I now "get it"?

What in the world is she talking about? I thought. He has called me "fake news" and "very fake news" to the entire world twice. I got *what*, exactly?

I thanked Hope but asked if it would be possible for the president to stop attacking the media. It was not helpful, I argued.

No dice. Hicks had a beef of her own. (She had something to say and she was going to get that out and move on.)

We just didn't understand the president, she complained. Trump truly does want to "make America great again," she told me.

This was going nowhere in a hurry. I thanked her, and we hung up.

"That was so weird," I exclaimed to my colleagues. But as I thought about it further, something dawned on me. Hicks was letting me in on Trump's thinking. She was doing me a big favor. When Trump told Hope, "Jim gets it," he was basically saying that I understood that his bluster was something of an act. When he called us "fake news," in his mind, it was an act. But here's the problem, and it is still a big one: not everybody was in on the act. This is where I have a problem with Trump's rhetoric. For starters, I didn't want to be a part of any kind of contrived reality TV presidency. This wasn't an episode of *The Apprentice*. And as I could plainly see in some of the disturbing and downright violent comments that were beginning to surface on my social media, countless Trump supporters didn't see me as a contestant on Trump's latest prime-time TV show, either. The press was increasingly being viewed as more than just "the opposition," as his chief strategist, Steve Bannon, had put it a few weeks earlier to the *New York Times*.

This trend toward demonizing the press would become all too clear the day after that news conference, when, shortly after Air Force One landed at Mar-a-Lago, in Florida, for a weekend of golf, the president posted a dark and dangerous tweet.

@realDonaldTrump
The FAKE NEWS media (failing @nytimes, @NBCNews, @ABC, @CBS, @CNN) is not my enemy, it is the enemy of the American People!

This was actually his second attempt at launching this extraordinary attack on the free press in America. Minutes before this, he had tweeted a similar message but left out the references to CBS and ABC. That first tweet was deleted and replaced with this one. Fox News, it should be noted, was not included in either tweet—as of this publication, the revised tweet still exists on Twitter, under the handle operated by the president of the United States.

Now, up until this point, a chorus of critics at a variety of news outlets had advised against my "taking the bait" from the president and responding to his "fake news" attacks. Trump, they argued, was luring the press into a trap. He wanted to troll and trigger outraged journalists, provoking them into a fight, one that he would always win, these critics complained. In my view, the Monday-morning quarterbacks were wrong.

Trump had crossed a clear, bright line. This was un-American. This should not go unchallenged.

Here's why. When he labeled the media the "enemy," the president, for all intents and purposes, was issuing a threat. Under the Soviet Union, Stalin had called the press "the enemy." So had Richard Nixon, during Watergate. Under Trump, who had whipped up his crowds to bash the press at his rallies, the danger was that the folks at home wouldn't know what he was doing. Was this an act? Was he serious? At that early point, it was an academic discussion. Too many of his supporters saw Trump's attacks on the press as a call to arms. My email inbox and social media accounts were routinely filled with threats of violence left by people who claimed to be a part of the MAGA movement. Once Trump called me "fake news," I changed the settings for the notifications on my Twitter account, as viewing all these posts would have been akin to peering into an open sewer or, more accurately, staring down an angry mob.

Memes featuring me began showing up all over Twitter. In one meme, my face had been superimposed over that of a 1940s gangster lying dead from gunfire. In another, a computer-animated scene portraying Nazis sending people into a gas chamber, my face was placed over that of the character hitting the Start button. It was ghastly, psychotic stuff. One person left a message on my Facebook account informing me that if he ever saw me out on the streets of DC, I would be dead. These were empty threats, I hoped. These people were merely venting their frustration at an easy target. I just wish they had been in on Trump's "act," as Hope Hicks had put it. If only they could see the man behind the curtain, in this dystopian Oz.

Even before he became White House chief strategist, Steve Bannon, a key figure during the presidential transition period, was talking about the press as the "opposition party," a catchphrase the former Breitbart boss used to describe what he thought was a torrent of negative stories about the incoming president. Press coverage was a subject Bannon and Trump continued to discuss in the early weeks of the administration. In an interview, Bannon explained to me that he and the new president had developed the "enemy of the people" label for the press during their conversations about media stories they didn't like. It was a bit of brainstorming or spitballing, Bannon said, that had occurred around that February news conference as a way to put Trump's frustrations into words. The term *enemy of the people* was a natural "corollary" that flowed from the terms *opposition party* and *fake news*.

"I think it's safe to say that we both came up with it in discussion," Bannon said of the "enemy of the people" label.

But he made sure that Trump got partial credit. "I think I threw out 'opposition media party' first, and then he threw out 'fake news is the enemy of the people,'" Bannon added.

The conservative firebrand was careful to explain that Trump didn't mean that all media were the enemy, though, Bannon said, it was obvious Trump felt that CNN and other outlets were "fake news." Therefore, CNN, in the president's mind, was the "enemy."

A senior White House official insisted Bannon was not taking full ownership of the expression. Bannon came up with "the enemy of the people," three aides to the president told me.

"'Enemy of the people' was first said in this White House by somebody who spent all of his time talking to the media," the senior official told me. "It's absolutely Bannon," the official added.

"It's meant to incite the media. Not the people," the official continued.

White House counselor Kellyanne Conway told me in an interview that she is not a fan of the expression.

"I don't use that phrase. Yet there is ample evidence that the media are often the enemy of the relevant," she said.

Then she acknowledged the risks of using that kind of language.

"It's fraught. It's danger—" Conway stopped midsentence, catching herself before saying "dangerous."

"I think calling the president a Russian asset is dangerous," she added.

Sounding almost professorial about Trump's attitude toward the press, Bannon insisted that the president was a creature straight out of the teachings of Marshall McLuhan, the Canadian philosopher who coined the phrase "the medium is the message," a theory taught in mass communications classes in college. (Disclosure: I have a degree in mass comm., and we studied this.) Trump understood, Bannon said, that a mastery of the news cycle was capable of fueling today's media-saturated presidential campaigns. Take control of the narrative, Bannon and McLuhan would argue, and you take control of the race.

This is Bannon's theory as to how Trump cut through sixteen GOP presidential candidates like a "scythe through grass," as he put it.

Bannon discounted the notion that Trump's rhetoric could lead to violence against journalists. But the former White House chief strategist said that attacking the media was a key element of Trump's strategy in the early days of his presidency. In the eyes of him and Trump, Bannon said, nobody cared about the Democratic Party at that point. Republicans controlled the White House and both houses of Congress. That made going after the press essential. Trump needed a punching bag, Bannon believed, to continue to drive the narrative and own the coverage. And that punching bag was the press.

As for Trump's Democratic critics, such as Connecticut senator Richard Blumenthal, a former senior White House official laughed. "Nobody knows who the fuck he is," the former official said, arguing that most people were more familiar with the anchors and correspondents from CNN and other networks who covered the Trump campaign and presidency.

A week later, on February 24, during a speech to the Conservative Political Action Conference (CPAC), Trump defended his new label for the press.

"A few days ago, I called the fake news 'the enemy of the people'— and they are. They are the enemy of the people. Because they have no sources, they just make them up when there are none. I saw one story recently where they said nine people have confirmed. There are no nine people. I don't believe there was one or two people. Nine people. And I said, give me a break. Because I know the people. I know who they talked to. There were no nine people. But they say, nine people, and somebody reads it and they think, oh, nine people. They have nine sources. They make up sources."

Ultimately, this "enemy of the people" designation mattered, not just because it was a threat to a free press but also because of the moment when Trump first uttered it. Coming in the wake of Michael

Flynn's firing and additional scrutiny from the Russia investigation, these words held new power to discredit our reporting and were an increasingly important tool for keeping his political allies close and his base closer. Why should Trump supporters trust stories about Russian collusion, after all, if those articles were written by "enemies" of the president? I'll tell you why. For starters, remember that Flynn had been fired by the president for lying about his contacts with Kislyak, a real (not fake) thing that happened. How could the press simply ignore something of that magnitude? The short answer is obviously we couldn't.

As menacing as Trump's public campaign to discredit us was for us in the press, it was in some of the quieter exchanges with the administration that the truly unsettling lies took place. Such was the case at the end of March, when I had my first run-in with Jared Kushner.

A White House official had summoned me to the office of Chief of Staff Reince Priebus, where I was joined by a couple of other reporters who had also heard about the looming departure of Deputy Chief of Staff Katie Walsh. Walsh, who came over to the White House from Reince's staff at the RNC, had become something of a scapegoat after the White House lost in its initial attempt to repeal and replace Obamacare. Stymied in its push for a travel ban, the White House had begun its attempted takedown of President Obama's signature legislative achievement, the Affordable Care Act. Trump was furious, blaming Democrats but also the Freedom Caucus, the gang of very-far-right House lawmakers who make it their business to torch legislation they don't see as sufficiently conservative. The White House was looking for someone to blame, and officials had landed on Walsh.

Following the departure of Michael Flynn, Walsh was viewed as the next high-profile departure from the Trump White House. I had gotten wind that she was about to be fired.

Yep, the Trump campaign people were eager to get that news out, as Katie was an RNC person, but I wasn't the only one to have received the tip. The White House had asked a small group of reporters, including me, to assemble in Reince's office. White House chief strategist Steve Bannon was also in the room. The two men walked us through what they wanted us to report, which was that Walsh was leaving to go to an outside group supporting Trump's agenda. We were also told that in no way was she being fired. All this was spin, of course, as Katie was being shown the door.

Then came the meeting's star attraction. Trump's son-in-law, Jared Kushner, popped in to join us. This was my first time meeting Jared. He seemed nice enough, polite and polished, though rail thin and a bit gaunt. The only reason I'm relaying the Katie Walsh story is because of what Jared said to me after the meeting was over: it was on Russia.

"Hey, you're the fake news guy," he said to me with a smile on his face. I got the sense he was trying to be friendly, but he had a point he wanted to make.

"We're real news," I told him. I then asked why he considered my news outlet to be fake news.

The Russia story, he responded. "There's nothing to it."

What did he mean? I asked. Flynn had just been fired for lying about Russia.

Nothing to it, he repeated, and walked away.

That was not true. Not by a long shot.

4

Russia, If You're Listening . . .

Contrary to what Jared Kushner wanted me to believe, there were indeed plenty of pressing questions about the Russia story. In fact, I'd had some of my own dating back to the campaign. One matter that was of particular interest to federal investigators during the 2016 campaign was that the Russians had succeeded in infiltrating Hillary Clinton's private email system on the very same day that Trump issued a plea to Moscow to hack into the Democratic contender's personal server.

The Trump campaign later said he was just kidding about that. It sure didn't seem that way from my vantage point sitting in the front row of that news conference at the Trump Doral Golf Course Clubhouse on July 27, 2016. Trump was asked about possible Russian interference—yes, even back then—as the Democratic National Committee had been hacked just days earlier.

Trump was peppered with questions about the DNC server breach. One particular line of questioning that seemed to get under his skin was whether he was too soft on Russian president Vladimir Putin. The Russian president, most foreign policy experts believed, was also meddling in other elections in Western states. Add it all up, and the growing consensus was that Putin was simply trying to reconstitute

Russia's standing in the world as a superpower, a long-stated goal of the ex-KGB agent who lamented the fall of the Soviet Union.

About twelve minutes into the news conference, Trump turned to me. "Why not get tough on Putin and tell him to stay out," I asked, in reference to the DNC hack.

"Why do I have to get involved with Putin for? I have nothing to do with Putin," Trump replied. "I don't know anything about him other than that he will respect me."

Then as he went on to do right into his presidency, Trump expressed doubts about the likelihood that Moscow was behind the hack. Keep in mind, even back during the campaign, the intelligence community was fairly certain Russia was responsible for the infiltration at the DNC. Trump was not having it.

"If it is Russia which it's probably not . . . nobody knows who it is," he went on to say. Then a few seconds later, continuing his response to my question, Trump said something that floored all of us in the room and, I suspect, federal investigators who were tuning in as well.

"Russia, if you're listening, I hope you're able to find the thirty thousand emails that are missing," Mr. Trump said during a news conference on July 27, 2016. "I think you will probably be rewarded mightily by our press. Let's see if that happens. That will be next."

"They probably have them. I'd like to have them released," he continued. "Now, if Russia or China or any other country has those emails, I mean, to be honest with you, I'd love to see them."

He then turned to another question. But that was that. All that the reporters in the room had to do was to glance down at their phones and see the notifications blowing up on their lock screens. Trump had, once again, broken the internet. Nearly every headline for the next twenty-four hours was Trump's invitation to the Russians to hack into Clinton's email server. The Clinton campaign went ballistic, accusing Trump of putting American national security at stake.

As would become increasingly clear over the first two years of the

Trump administration, the Russia story had legs, and plenty of plot twists (many of them quite real), and it was on us to cover them all in the face of increasing hostility from Trump and his team. What began with Michael Flynn quickly spread to other areas of the administration and stretched back to the campaign, as former aides and associates of the president were swept up in the probe.

It wasn't long before we would see Attorney General Jeff Sessions become the next piece of collateral damage in the probe. Sessions had come to the Trump administration by way of the Senate. In the early days of the campaign, then–Alabama senator Sessions surprised a lot of people in Washington when he endorsed Trump's candidacy in February 2016. This was way before the rest of the GOP had hopped aboard the Trump train.

Wearing a red MAGA hat, Sessions threw his support behind Trump at an August 2015 rally in Alabama. "I told Donald Trump this isn't a campaign, this is a movement," Sessions said.

Trump noted that he and Sessions were simpatico in their hard-right stance on immigration. "He's really the expert as far as I'm concerned on borders, on so many things," Trump said.

The Trump-Sessions marriage was a match made in heaven for supporters who vehemently opposed illegal immigration. Before the campaign, I had come across Sessions from time to time up on Capitol Hill. He almost always made himself available for an interview if the topic was immigration—that's how I first came to know Stephen Miller. During the campaign, Sessions led Trump's National Security Advisory Committee, and Miller became Trump's top speechwriter. Given what we saw during the campaign, it was hardly a surprise when Trump tapped Sessions to become attorney general.

Though Sessions was confirmed as Trump's attorney general with relative ease, by the end of February the ground beneath him had started shifting, largely because of statements he had made under oath during his confirmation hearing.

In the run-up to Sessions's confirmation hearing on January 10, reasonable questions had already been raised about possible links between the Trump campaign and Russia because of reporting from CNN, BuzzFeed, and many others. It was on this point that Minnesota Democratic senator Al Franken pressed Sessions:

FRANKEN: . . . If there is any evidence that anyone affiliated with the Trump campaign communicated with the Russian government in the course of this campaign, what will you do?
SESSIONS: Senator Franken, I'm not aware of any of those activities. I have been called a surrogate at a time or two in that campaign and I didn't have—did not have communications with the Russians, and I'm unable to comment on it.

Only, Sessions's response wasn't the whole truth. Reporting that unfolded in late February and early March (in the aftermath of Flynn's departure) would demonstrate that Sessions's words were not entirely accurate.

Sessions, as it turned out, had had interactions with the Russians himself, something he didn't disclose to Franken at the confirmation hearing. In April 2016, Trump gave a foreign policy speech at the Mayflower Hotel in Washington; I was there for that one. During the speech, Trump talked about his "America First" policy, took potshots at the Obama and Bush administrations for letting U.S. prestige run adrift, and vowed to crack down on illegal immigration along the border with Mexico. Consider where that prestige stands now. But more to the point, Trump's future attorney general and top GOP supporter in the Senate, Jeff Sessions, was there. And unbeknownst to just about everybody at the time, so was the Russian ambassador, Sergey Kislyak. Sessions, CNN and other news outlets later reported, met with Kislyak at a private reception prior to the foreign policy speech. The future attorney general, during his confirmation hearing before the Senate, did not fully disclose his contacts with Kislyak and neglected to mention this encounter at the Mayflower Hotel.

It still pains me to remember that I interviewed Sessions, live on CNN, following that Trump speech at the Mayflower, with absolutely no idea at the time that the Alabama senator had just met with the Russian ambassador at the event.

It was a brief interview, on Wolf Blitzer's 1:00 p.m. program on CNN. Sessions, of course, praised Trump's speech.

"He laid out a vision and, in many ways, [it] was electrifying," Sessions said, beaming.

In addition to that encounter at the Mayflower Hotel, Sessions had other brushes with Kislyak, meeting with the ambassador on the sidelines of the Republican National Convention in Cleveland, along with J. D. Gordon, a longtime GOP operative in Washington. Sessions also met with Kislyak in his Senate office in September 2016. But Sessions, his spokeswoman argued to reporters, had not lied to Congress because the senator had met with Kislyak as a legislator, not as an adviser to the Trump campaign.

Still, the damage had been done. Once it became clear that Sessions had not been forthright about this and other contacts with the Russians, he decided he could not legitimately oversee the Justice Department's probe into Kremlin interference. On March 2, 2017, nearly two months after that flawed testimony about events of one year earlier, Sessions recused himself from the Russia investigation, against the wishes of the new president.

"I never had meetings with Russian operatives or Russian intermediaries about the Trump campaign," Sessions told reporters at a news conference announcing his recusal. He would later say about his meetings with Kislyak, "In retrospect, I should have slowed down and said I did meet one Russian official a couple times, and that would be the ambassador."

But there was good reason to believe Sessions was meeting with

Kislyak as more than just a legislator. Roughly one month prior to the
Mayflower hotel speech, Trump's National Security Advisory Committee held a meeting to discuss a range of foreign policy subjects,
including Russia. The gathering on March 31, 2016, was captured in a
now-infamous photo that had been released by the Trump campaign
during the GOP primary season.

Seated around the table are individuals who now figure promi-
nently, and tangentially, in the Russia investigation. At one end of the
table is Trump. At the other is Jeff Sessions. To the left of Sessions are
two people who would later be questioned as part of the Russia probe,
J. D. Gordon and George Papadopoulos, a foreign policy adviser who
went on to plead guilty to lying to federal agents in the investigation,
prompting more valid questions about the Trump campaign's alleged
ties to Russia.

Gordon, who had also worked for the Herman Cain campaign,
in 2012, has gained some notoriety for his cameo appearance in the
Russia investigation. J.D. and I have known each other ever since he
worked for Cain. He's one of the few Republican officials in Washington who is bilingual in both English and Spanish, and he has often
appeared on CNN to speak with the network's sister outlet, CNN en
Español. He's one of those creatures in Washington you don't hear
enough about these days, a good guy who, as far I have ever been able
to tell, just wants to serve his country.

As for Papadopoulos, he may have been later written off as the
"coffee boy" by Trump's defenders, but according to J.D., George
played something of a pivotal role in that National Security Advisory
Committee meeting. Gordon says that it was Papadopoulos who raised
the idea of Trump meeting with Russian president Vladimir Putin
during the campaign. In a story with my CNN colleague Manu Raju,
we reported that Trump was intrigued by the idea. Trump "heard him
out," Gordon told us. Sessions, according to J.D., opposed the notion
of a Trump-Putin campaign summit.

Regardless of whether Sessions opposed the idea, this account raised doubts about what Sessions said during his confirmation hearing: that he was unaware of any communications between the Russians and the Trump campaign. The very idea of communicating with the Russian government was discussed at the meeting.

As an aside, Gordon told me that Papadopoulos wanted to be much more than the "coffee boy" for the campaign. He had pushed to be a surrogate on the Sunday talk show circuit, once noting that his last name rhymed with that of the host of ABC's *This Week*.

"Papadopoulos Stephanopoulos," George Papadopoulos told J.D. with a smile. Gordon thought Papadopoulos was out of his depth.

But that wasn't all that went down at that March 31, 2016, meeting. As I reported on CNN, Gordon said that Trump had told his advisers at the gathering that he "didn't want to go to World War III over Ukraine." Ponder that for a moment. Trump wasn't even the GOP nominee yet. He had zero foreign policy experience. And yet he was putting forward what was essentially a policy reversal for the United States. He was telling his budding foreign policy team that he wanted to dial back America's stance on Russian aggression. Nearly four months later, at the GOP convention in Cleveland, the Trump campaign argued against arming the Ukrainians in their conflict with the Russians, counter to what many foreign policy hawks back in Washington, such as Senator John McCain and others, were advocating. Gordon told me, and this is a critical point, that the party platform on Russia at the 2016 convention was a reflection of Trump's marching orders at that crucial March 2016 meeting.

Gordon later said he was irritated by some of the stories written about his comments to me about that meeting. J.D. insisted that he and his fellow campaign officials at the convention were not seeking to water down or soften the platform on the Ukraine question. They merely wanted to keep things from becoming more hawkish, he maintained. But Trump had other ideas. In an interview with ABC's

George Stephanopoulos, Trump said that the Russia platform had indeed been "softened." Either way, the signal had been sent from the GOP convention that Trump was seeking a new, closer relationship with Russia. And Trump would punctuate that message time and again from the campaign trail, where he repeatedly proposed better relations with the Kremlin. The hawks inside the Republican Party, including McCain, took note of this.

I trust J.D.'s recollection of events, but I also know that he is not happy with the way he was treated by the campaign. He told me he was never paid for his work for Trump. He also got a bad taste in his mouth working for Jared Kushner, once telling me a story about compiling reams of information on various foreign leaders whom Trump's son-in-law wished to meet, only to have Kushner disregard what he had prepared for him.

Like so many people who have given their lives to Trump over the years, J.D. got burned. Despite all his Washington experience in politics and government, not to mention his loyalty to Trump, Gordon ended up involuntarily giving away his expertise for free to a businessman with a reputation for stiffing his contractors. He was hardly the first Trump associate to feel cheated. CNN and other outlets have detailed the countless times Trump has refused to pay the contractors who helped the Manhattan tycoon build his hotels and casinos. J.D. and his fellow foreign policy advisers were simply the latest in a long line of victims.

To my amazement, Gordon would go on to appear on conservative news outlets to blast the Russia probe. In spite of how the Trump campaign had treated him, he had remained somewhat loyal to the president. That's hard for me to understand. But J.D. told me he was never convinced that there was any collusion between the Trump campaign and the Russians. He always saw what occurred as a kind of conspiracy of dunces, like something out of the Coen brothers' screwball comedy *Burn After Reading*, in which two numbskull gym employees discover a disk containing CIA information that they then try to peddle to Russian operatives. Trump aides repeatedly told me they were too dumb to run an organized campaign—how could they conspire with Russia? they joked.

But there was a very serious side of this for Gordon. As an eventual subject of the investigation into the Trump campaign and Russia, J.D. spent hours talking with the special counsel's investigators. They read back to him emails and texts he had sent to other people, communications the team of investigators had collected to spring on J.D. during his interrogations. He amassed legal fees in the five figures, he told me.

Nevertheless, that infamous National Security Advisory Committee meeting for Trump's campaign was a critical early sign of potential contacts between the GOP contender and the Kremlin.

THE FALLOUT FROM SESSIONS'S RECUSAL WAS SWIFT AND MESSY. Not to sound like Forrest Gump, repeatedly appearing at famous events, but I was with Trump the day Sessions recused himself, serving as the TV pool reporter for the networks. (Because it would be too much of a circus to have all the networks at every presidential photo op, one TV reporter and one cameraman, and typically a sound technician, are given the responsibility of covering these brief on-camera events on behalf of all the major TV networks. The same deal goes for the newspaper outlets and wire services. They, too, send in a few representatives from the print world to fill out the pool.) On March 2, 2017, I was in the pool, covering the president during a visit to Norfolk, Virginia, where he was touring an aircraft carrier. As we moved around the bowels of the ship, the other reporters in the pool and I peppered Trump with questions about Sessions, who, at that point, had not pulled the trigger on recusal.

"I don't think so," Trump said when I asked him whether Sessions should recuse himself. The president was also asked if he believed

Sessions had told the truth during his confirmation hearing. "I think he probably did," Trump replied.

Anybody who covered Trump extensively knew full well that he was back on his heels. His four- or five-word responses to questions about the Russia investigation were a pretty clear indicator that he was in no mood to talk. Sure, he would love to answer questions from reporters, just not on the Russia probe. Trump could certainly be abrupt when he didn't want to speak with reporters, but this was not one of those times. I had the sense that he wanted his trip to Norfolk to be a commander-in-chief moment. He was wearing an olive-green bomber-style jacket and a blue baseball cap, the stuff a president wears when touring an aircraft carrier. And we were ruining all that by annoying him with Sessions questions. Capturing it all to tweet it out to the millions of Trump's followers was the president's social media director, Dan Scavino. Later, before hopping aboard the Ospreys that flew the press back to Air Force One, I gave Dan a pat on the back. At that point, I still had pretty good relationships with some of the folks on Trump's team. Scavino was one of the "originals" from the campaign, the staffers I had befriended out on the trail, before Trump's war on the media.

When we landed back at Joint Base Andrews, just outside Washington, we waited on Air Force One, as was customary, for Trump to disembark and hop on Marine One for the chopper ride back to the White House. After close to an hour, and still on the plane waiting, we wondered what on earth was going on. It turns out, Trump had been sitting on the plane watching Sessions deliver his statement to the press, recusing himself from the Russia investigation. Though we were mere yards away from him, we had no idea the president was stewing over Sessions's recusal.

We all watched the coverage on our phones. Trump's aides had gone silent. It would become clear only in the days ahead that Trump was supremely pissed off at Sessions. Still, though he would later turn Sessions into a punching bag for nearly the duration of the former

Alabama senator's tenure as attorney general, at least that night, Trump stood by his man.

In a statement released that day, he said, "Jeff Sessions is an honest man. He did not say anything wrong [in his confirmation hearing]. He could have stated his response more accurately, but it was clearly not intentional," Trump added. "This whole narrative is a way of saving face for Democrats losing an election that everyone thought they were supposed to win. The Democrats are overplaying their hand. They lost the election and now, they have lost their grip on reality. The real story is all of the illegal leaks of classified and other information. It is a total witch hunt!"

Still, that statement contained the seeds of many hyperbolic Trump tweets to come—from "illegal leaks of classified and other information" to "witch hunt!" Even if Trump was being more gracious to Sessions for the moment, the offensive against the Russia probe was under way.

Not that Trump hadn't tried to stop Sessions from recusing himself. He had made his own overtures to the attorney general to prevent it from happening. Others in the White House had also chimed in. White House counsel Don McGahn had reached out to Sessions in an effort to discourage the attorney general from walling himself off from the investigation. So did the White House chief of staff, Reince Priebus, and press secretary Sean Spicer.

"I think it's fair to call it pressure," a senior administration official later told me about those phone calls to Sessions.

I reported this information on CNN on a Friday night—ah yes, the glamour of being a White House reporter—in early January 2018. Just before we went on the air with the story, I received a phone call from Spicer. At this point, Sean was no longer working for the White House; he had resigned the previous summer. Suffice it to say, we never really stayed in touch, but he called to deny that he had placed any pressure on Sessions to give up on the idea of recusing himself.

"For eight months the narrative was that I was out of the loop and now I'm part of it?" Spicer told me over the phone. "I don't think so." He added that he had called Sessions and his team only to talk about setting up a news conference.

But Spicer being Spicer, he couldn't resist becoming confrontational. He threatened that if I didn't kill the story, he would go after me on Twitter. Did I want to be called "fake news"? he asked. I politely told him that I wouldn't kill the story, and I said good-bye.

As for Priebus, who had also tried to stop Sessions's recusal, he declined to comment.

Despite the pressure on Sessions from the White House, he listened to the counsel of DOJ officials instead, who thought that, given the circumstances, he should recuse himself. The implications of his recusal were huge both for the Russia probe itself and for Sessions's tenure as attorney general. As Trump would make known repeatedly over the next year and half, he viewed Sessions's decision as a betrayal, perhaps the worst of his presidency. Demonstrating a fundamental misunderstanding of the job of leading the U.S. Department of Justice, Trump wanted the attorney general to behave as his own personal attorney. Sessions's recusal left Trump exposed, and now on his own, the president would use the bully pulpit of the office to shape public opinion and demonize those asking questions. His Twitter account would be the primary weapon in his arsenal.

BY LATE APRIL, ROD ROSENSTEIN HAD BEEN CONFIRMED AS THE deputy attorney general, becoming the DOJ official who would oversee the Russia investigation with Sessions on the sidelines. It did not take long for his independence to be tested.

Without Sessions to protect him, Trump would go on to rip into the Russia investigation at every twist and turn in the probe. For months the investigation had been an obsession for him, but the coming weeks would show him operating with a singular focus on it. Unable to keep Sessions from recusing himself, Trump found what he thought was another way to control the investigation: through the head of the FBI, James Comey.

Less than four months after taking office, Trump fired Comey. The president, in one of his more outward expressions of dishonesty, hung his decision to do so on Comey's handling of the Hillary Clinton email investigation—yes, the same probe that had arguably handed him the keys to the Oval Office. Trump pointed to a report completed by the new deputy attorney general, Rod Rosenstein, that sharply criticized Comey's performance in the Clinton email saga. Then, in a letter to Comey, Trump inserted what he believed to be something of an exculpatory side note, claiming out of nowhere that the FBI director had assured him he had nothing to worry about in the Russia probe.

"While I greatly appreciate you informing me, on three separate occasions, that I am not under investigation, I nevertheless concur with the judgment of the Department of Justice that you are not able to effectively lead the bureau," Trump wrote in the letter to the ousted FBI director.

In something of a coup for CNN, one of our White House producers, Noah Gray, received a tip that Trump's personal security aide, Keith Schiller, was about to hand-deliver the letter to FBI headquarters, just down the street from the White House. It was mind-boggling to watch. There was one of Trump's main security officials, whom we had all come to know during the campaign and who had gone on to assume the government equivalent of that position inside the White House, basically showing up at the FBI to fire James Comey on behalf of Trump. Typically, the firing of an FBI director would not go down like this. Usually, the director would be summoned to the White House to hear the bad news in person. But Trump didn't want to do the dirty work directly, so he sent Schiller. Who does that?

Serious legal commentators raised questions whether the Comey firing amounted to obstruction of justice, a possible impeachable offense. Trump fueled that speculation by revealing his true motivations in an interview with NBC's Lester Holt.

Trump told Holt that the Russia probe had, in fact, been part of his rationale for firing Comey. It was a stunning admission. As dishonest as Trump can be sometimes, he can also be remarkably candid. This was definitely one of those occasions.

"And in fact, when I decided to just do it," Trump told Holt, "I said to myself, I said, 'You know, this Russia thing with Trump and Russia is a made-up story, it's an excuse by the Democrats for having lost an election that they should have won.'"

Bannon warned Trump and other top White House officials that the president was making a serious mistake. Bannon was "pretty adamant about it," a former senior White House official told me, explaining that Comey's Russia investigation, at the time, was not driving the news coverage.

The day after Trump fired Comey, in another "you can't make this shit up" episode at the White House, the president invited the Russians over for a visit. Not just Kislyak, but Sergey Lavrov, the Russian foreign minister, was also welcomed into the Oval Office for a meeting.

In a bit of diplomatic trolling, the Russians posted photos of the encounter on one of the state media outlets. The new White House, filled with inexperienced staffers who simply lacked any kind of understanding of how calculating their Kremlin counterparts could be, had no idea the Russians would release the pictures.

"They tricked us," an angry White House official said to me. "That's the problem with the Russians—they lie," the official added. My story made a pretty big splash that morning, as it was dripping with the irony that officials inside the Trump administration could be so naïve about the intentions of the Kremlin.

A further case for independent oversight in the Russia probe came via Comey himself, in the form of both his testimony before Congress and reports of contemporaneous notes he had taken following meetings and phone calls with Trump. Comey memorialized their interactions in a now-infamous memo that detailed some of Trump's aggressive behavior aimed at terminating the Russia investigation.

In his prepared testimony to Congress about his conversations with the president, the former FBI director stated that on January 27, just one week into the administration, Trump asked him for a pledge of loyalty over dinner.

"I need loyalty, I expect loyalty," Comey recounted the president saying.

According to Comey, Trump tried to intervene in the Flynn case in a February 14 meeting in the Oval Office. This was one day after Flynn was fired over his false statements about his conversations with Kislyak.

"I hope you can see your way clear to letting this go, to letting Flynn go. He is a good guy. I hope you can let this go," Comey recalled Trump as saying.

On March 30, Trump asked Comey to lift the "cloud" of the Russia investigation, again according to the former FBI director's sworn testimony. Trump tried once more on April 11, asking Comey to "get out" that the president was not a target of the investigation.

The night that Comey's prepared testimony was published, I got a tip that the attorney Trump had initially hired to handle the Russia investigation, Marc Kasowitz, was seen celebrating at the Trump Hotel in Washington, a popular hangout for administration insiders and friends of the president. Kasowitz was handing out cigars and loudly bragging that Comey hadn't laid a finger on Trump in his testimony.

"We won. It's clear Trump didn't do anything wrong," Kasowitz was overheard saying, according to sources who heard the comments.

Kasowitz, who had just been hired by Trump in late May, didn't last long in that position. He left the president's outside legal team in July, after it was revealed by ProPublica that he had sent threatening emails to a man who suggested that he resign.

The trials and tribulations on Trump's legal team alone were enough to keep us busy in those early days of the Russia investigation. In the days that followed Comey's testimony, Trump tapped two high-profile DC attorneys to come to the rescue, John Dowd and Ty Cobb. Dowd wasn't particularly difficult to find. He had me in stitches from the moment he picked up the phone.

"Oh, I'm not supposed to talk to you. You're a bad guy," he said, laughing.

In the aftermath of Comey's revelations to Congress, with public pressure rising to dramatic levels, Deputy Attorney General Rod Rosenstein made some changes of his own, deciding to appoint a special prosecutor, a man with seemingly unimpeachable credentials: former head of the FBI Robert Mueller, a registered Republican.

For me and much of the DC press corps, the appointment of Mueller was the culmination of an astonishing eight-day stretch that had begun with the firing of Comey. While the events of that week in May 2017 would shape much of the news and its coverage for the rest of Trump's presidency, they also changed the larger calculus for Trump's media strategy on the Russia investigation. With the investigation in Mueller's hands and one more layer removed from Trump's oversight, his options for interference were even more limited. Seemingly backed into a corner, he would begin to do what he does best: go on the offensive against Mueller, the investigation, and the reporting around them, despite valid questions that needed answering. This would come in the form of not just tweets criticizing Robert Mueller but also broadside attacks on news outlets, leaks, and all manner of reporting on the Russia probe.

Spicer was getting more desperate at the podium, with reports coming in that Trump was considering pulling the plug on him and even the press briefings altogether. Just as Mueller was opening up shop in the special counsel's probe, Trump was attempting to clamp down on the press. On May 30, 2017, Spicer told reporters in the Briefing Room that Trump was frustrated with "fake news."

It was one of those moments when I felt it was important to poke the bear. What fake news? I asked Spicer.

> SPICER: I think that he is frustrated, like I am and like so many others, to see stories come out that are patently false, to see narratives that are wrong, to see "fake news." When you see stories get perpetrated that are absolutely false, that are not based in fact, that is troubling. And he's rightly concerned.
>
> ACOSTA: Can you give an example of fake news, Sean? Could you give us an example?

Spicer went on to complain about a mistake a BBC reporter had made about Trump's behavior at a G-7 summit, which had been retweeted by a reporter in the U.S. press corps. In answering my question, Sean had the chance to go off on some aspect of the Russia investigation, but he didn't. All he was able to come up with was a tweet he didn't like.

When he was asked to come up with other examples of "fake news," he couldn't.

"What I'm telling you is, is that the reason that the president is frustrated is because there's a perpetuation of false narratives, a use of unnamed sources over and over again about things that are happening that don't ultimately happen, and I think that is troubling. Thank you, guys, very much," he said as he abruptly left the Briefing Room.

Until this point in the Trump presidency, Trump's war on the media had felt more like an extension of his campaign: largely rhetorical, designed to elicit the most favorable coverage possible or at least to give pause to some reporters' negative coverage. As we would learn in the months ahead, all these things would continue to hold true, but there were new stakes, new battle lines that had hardened in the wake of Robert Mueller's appointment. From then on, all the reporting around the Russia probe and the White House took on larger significance to both the White House and the country at large. The same held true for Trump's attacks on the media. No longer just applause lines, they grew more sinister, and seemed designed to undermine the credibility of our reporting on this specific story.

A former senior White House official said that Trump remained glued to the news coverage of the unfolding Russia investigation, a viewing habit made clear by his tweets slamming the probe. "Trump watches you guys nonstop," the official said of the president's secret preference for watching CNN. "He watches Fox to make himself feel better," he added.

Publicly, the president would never admit that, as he made painfully clear in July 2017, when he tweeted out a video showing an image of him body-slamming a man with a CNN logo superimposed over his face, a depiction of violence that included the hashtag #FraudNewsCNN.

A former high-ranking FBI official reminded me that, unlike Comey's decision to inform the public that he was reexamining Clinton's email practices eleven days before the election, the bureau's director kept the investigation into possible Trump campaign ties to Russia under wraps.

If that had been revealed the last two weeks of the campaign, it "would have been game over for Trump," the ex-official said.

5

Spicy Time

It was against the backdrop of the Russia investigation that we also had our day jobs to do—the grind of attending the daily press briefings, deciphering myriad leaks from the White House, trying to get stories confirmed or commented on. All these typical operations of reporters covering the White House made it impossible for us to ignore the sheer scale of the dysfunction there. Through the first six months of the administration, the White House communications shop had shown a startling array of weaknesses. For all their bluster and confrontation with reporters, they were a disorganized mess.

Even after his disastrous performance on that Saturday following the inauguration, when he spoke in defense of the Trump inauguration crowd size, Sean Spicer would continue to fail in spectacular fashion. Not only did he mislead the American people from the podium in the White House Briefing Room, but he also berated reporters in an almost uncontrollable manner. To make matters worse, he routinely garbled his explanations of administration policy, occasionally turning the focus of the news cycle on himself with inexplicable word salads and tone-deaf language. The most infamous of these was when he referred to concentration camps as "Holocaust centers." On top of that, he attempted, unsuccessfully, to clamp down on press freedom with his ill-fated decision to turn off the cameras during the White House briefings, a move that only ended up calling more attention to the chaos of his news conferences. Each new day, it seemed, brought another setback for Spicer. And slowly but surely, the press corps' confidence in the White House press secretary dropped to levels I had never witnessed in my days covering Obama's second term. In the press areas of the White House, reporters whispered to one another, wondering how much worse it could get.

We weren't the only ones asking this question. In Trump's eyes, performance on television is a defining qualification. Either you can perform on TV—as he did for many years hiring and firing contestants and celebrities on *The Apprentice*—or you can't. Trump was coming to the conclusion that Spicer was not ready for prime time. How bad was the criticism? Right down to Spicer's wardrobe: Trump didn't like the ill-fitting suits Sean was wearing on TV.

The real problem for Sean, though, was that he was not cut out for the job of press secretary. As I had come to find out all too well, he sometimes had a quick temper and a nasty vindictive streak. I had never experienced this in my pre-Trump interactions with him. Back then, if I had questions about what was going on inside the RNC, he would call me back. He might take a good-natured jab, but he would still be helpful. Yet, as folks around Washington were starting to express in the early days of the Trump White House, Sean Spicer was changing.

"I don't know this Sean Spicer" was a common refrain around Washington in early 2017.

Journalists, GOP operatives, staffers on the Hill—we all wondered what the hell had happened to him. The change in him dawned on me prior to the inauguration-crowd-size fiasco, particularly at that January 11 news conference. But "Spicy," as we had started calling him, a reference to Melissa McCarthy's impersonation of him on *Saturday Night Live*, was getting worse.

On January 31, eleven days after the inauguration, Spicer and I had another run-in, this time at an event hosted by George Washington University. Frank Sesno, a former CNN White House correspondent and current GWU professor, had invited Sean and me to appear on a panel to discuss news coverage of the Trump presidency. Spicer again brought up the Trump Tower press conference of January 11, when I had my heated exchange with Trump. In Sean's version of events, I had told viewers that he had threatened to remove me from the news conference if I asked another "tough" question. I'd done nothing of the sort.

Spicer did warn me that I would be tossed out if I interrupted the president again, a remark I had passed along to viewers. But he had kept repeating his false version of the story, and did so again that night at George Washington.

"He misled viewers tremendously," Spicer told Sesno.

I was in the audience, listening in and, to be honest, trying to keep myself from laughing at this nonsense. So, I did what you would expect me to do. I interrupted him and the program to yell out, "That's not true."

Spicer also defended the inauguration-crowd-size claim he made at that first White House briefing on January 21. Though he would later refer to his comments at that briefing as a mistake, initially, at this event at GWU, he had only one self-critique. "We created a strategy on how to deal with the current media cycle going on, and I implemented it," he said in defense of his crowd-size remarks, and then conceded, "I probably should have taken questions."

Then it was my turn to get up onstage. Sean had left—he either didn't want to appear onstage with me or had had to leave.

"I think we heard some alternative facts there," I told Sesno. Later on, I made it clear where I stood (and stand now, as you are reading this): "They can throw us out of the White House, they can kick us down the street. We'll set up our trucks on Pennsylvania Avenue, we'll do the exact same stories every day," I told the crowd. "It does not matter what they do because we're here to do our job."

Getting back to Spicer, he did note, accurately, during the GWU event that I was still getting a chance to ask questions at the daily White House briefings. That was true at the time. And Sean and I had some good battles in the Briefing Room. Yes, they got messy, and yes, they got personal—although, I should point out that it was Spicer who initially made things personal.

No White House official, Democrat or Republican, really wants to hear a reporter questioning what he or she is doing. Press secretaries from both parties have a job to do. They want to get the president's message out, largely unchallenged. But what has been lost on some of Trump's defenders, both inside and outside the White House, is that the press has an essential task as well. When we interrupt or try to poke at certain vulnerabilities in a press secretary's argument, it's for the purpose of ferreting out information that may well be vital to the American people. When journalists dig and talk to sources, who in some cases will disclose what they know only anonymously, it's not for the purpose of behaving as political activists, as so many critics have alleged. It's to find the truth. So, call me a showboater or a grandstander or "fake news." I will go to my grave convinced deep down in my bones that journalists are performing a public service for the good of the country. The country is better off with reporters in the White House Briefing Room asking the hard questions, even if we sometimes sound a little over the top. That noise is the sound that a healthy, functioning democracy makes.

Part of the problem we have run up against as reporters in the age of Trump is that we have to serve as fact-checkers in real time. Because Trump sometimes begins the day with untrue or unfounded claims on Twitter, journalists must spend much of their time setting the record straight. That process is necessary, as tedious and as frustrating as our pushback might be to ardent Trump supporters. Picture a world where the American president gets to say whatever he wants and isn't fact-checked. I'm here to tell you that other societies have tried out that way of government, typically in the form of dictatorships where the rights of the free press are crushed and where citizens must accept what they're told or else. It may sound quaint, but when it comes to the federal government, if the taxpayers are footing the bill, they deserve to know they are getting their money's worth. With that mind-set, we in the news media have no alternative but to ask the tough questions when covering the White House, especially when the president displays a total disregard for the essential role of a strong, free press.

Given his years of experience in Washington, Spicer should have known all this. But if he understood it, he certainly didn't show it. At the briefings, he demonstrated a clear bias for conservative media. Rather than call on the Associated Press or another wire service first, as so many of his predecessors over the years had done, he would turn to Fox News to open the sessions, before moving around the room, ping-ponging from members of the conservative media to journalists representing more traditional news outlets. A senior administration official told me that the press shop had a strategy for calling on reporters in the Briefing Room. "Stick to the middle" was the mantra. If you look at the Briefing Room seating chart, you will find more folks from conservative media sitting in the middle seats, while more aggressive reporters, from CNN and NBC, are on either side. Spicer had plenty of GOP-friendly outlets to call on. For all the talk of the "liberal media," consider the sheer number of conservative news sites that regularly sent reporters to the briefings: Fox News, Fox Business, the Daily Caller, Breitbart, One America News Network, Newsmax, and the Christian Broadcasting Network are just some examples.

Trump, too, showed a clear preference for calling on conservative news outlets, for example, at his joint news conferences with foreign leaders at the White House. This had a major influence on the information coming out of these events. Typically, these joint news conferences feature two questions from U.S. reporters and two questions from members of the press corps attached to that visiting leader ("2+2s" we call them). If Trump could count on receiving softball questions, particularly those that steered clear of the Russia investigation, he could control the message.

My guess is that, today, Spicer realizes he had made some mistakes, and to be fair, he was dealt a terrible hand. He had been forced to defend so many of Trump's falsehoods—hell, let's just call them what they are: lies—that he was rarely on offense in the Briefing Room. At each briefing, invariably one of the first questions to come up would be about one of the president's ridiculous statements.

Consider Trump's claim, made shortly after he won the election, that millions of undocumented people had voted illegally. This was his excuse for having lost the popular vote to Hillary Clinton, a nagging sore point for Trump, who can't stand the fact that he finished the race with three million fewer votes than those cast for the Democratic Party's nominee. Trump repeated this claim once again in a meeting with lawmakers at the White House, on the Monday after he was sworn into office. It was clearly still on his mind. The next day, January 24, at the White House briefing, to support Trump's voter fraud claim, Spicer trotted out a study that didn't exist.

"There's one that came out of Pew in 2008 that showed 14 percent of people who voted were noncitizens. There's other studies that have been presented to him. It's a belief he maintains," Spicer told us.

But the 2008 Pew study was about out-of-date registration records, not election fraud involving the undocumented. Sean was apparently conflating that Pew study with a separate study that purported to find evidence of election fraud—a study that had already been widely discredited.

Still, Trump wasn't about to let facts get in his way. He went on to create an election fraud commission, the Presidential Commission on Election Integrity, which, as you may recall and have probably guessed, found zero evidence of widespread voter fraud, certainly not at the scale that would have delivered an additional three million votes to Hillary Clinton. Trump and Spicer were manufacturing their own "alternative facts," as they so often did, right out of the White House.

A senior White House official tried to blame some of Trump's tendency to spread false information on his wide network of friends who stay in contact with the president, either by phone or occasional visits to the Oval Office.

"Most of the misinformation the president receives comes from outside this building," the official said. "He's got a large circle of friends. He's got people always trying to impress him, always trying to stay in touch with him," the official continued.

But that's not the only source of information that leads Trump astray from the truth, the official said.

"I think he just reads stuff and he says, 'Did you know. Did you know. Did you know.'"

There were, of course, other lowlights for Spicer. At a press briefing on March 20, 2017, he tried to minimize former Trump campaign chairman Paul Manafort's role in Trump's election victory, as the Russia investigation unearthed questions regarding Manafort's ties to corruption in Ukraine and Russia.

"Obviously there's been discussion of Paul Manafort, who played a very limited role for a very limited amount of time," Spicer said.

This was silly, and continued to be a ridiculous talking point for the White House. Trump later parroted the lie about Manafort's "limited" role in the campaign. But truth be told, Manafort was hired by Trump in March 2016 essentially to close the deal for him during the upcoming GOP convention. Manafort, who had worked for other top-tier Republican politicians, was supposed to send a signal to the Washington establishment that Trump's candidacy was not going to take the party over a cliff. In May, two months later,

Manafort was promoted to campaign chairman, a post he maintained until later that August, when he resigned. As a top official at the Republican National Committee and a fixture of the Washington establishment himself, Spicer knew full well that Manafort had a prominent role with the campaign. But he wasn't being straight about that.

This brings us to Trump's infamous accusation that Barack Obama had wiretapped the Manhattan businessman at Trump Tower during the 2016 campaign. To me, it is one of the defining lies of the Trump era. Trump provided no evidence for this claim. As usual, he just tweeted it. And, as is often the case, much of Washington freaked out, shaking up the news cycle. You'll have to remember that, at that time, folks weren't yet accustomed to seeing the president blast out conspiracy theories to the masses.

Sadly—and this is the reason that this particular lie is so important— members of Trump's White House team immediately doubled down on the lie, in a rather comical but also frightening way.

For days, news outlets were consumed by discussions of the president's unproven claim that his predecessor had essentially spied on him. Obama's office released a brief statement, denying the claim, but the story had already been injected into the Trump-era news cycle, which means it was everywhere on social media, not to mention dominating much of the coverage in both mainstream and conservative news.

First, Spicer tried to shut the story down, releasing a statement insisting that the White House would have no further comment on the tweets. "Neither the White House nor the president will comment any further," Spicer said.

But even Spicer's own press shop lacked message discipline. His then-deputy, Sarah Huckabee Sanders, in an attempt to give the story legitimacy, made up a ridiculous claim that the wiretapping story had already been reported in the press. That may have been the first of Sarah's many lies to come.

"Everybody acts like President Trump is the one that came up with this idea and just threw it out there," she said on ABC's *This Week with George Stephanopoulos*. "There are multiple news outlets that have reported this," she added, a statement that PolitiFact rated as "False."

Then, adding to the absurdity of this episode, came Kellyanne Conway, who told a New Jersey newspaper that perhaps Trump had been the victim of a different kind of eavesdropping. Maybe it wasn't wiretapping, as the president had initially claimed. "What I can say is there are many ways to surveil each other," Conway told the Bergen County *Record*. She went on to suggest that Trump could have been secretly recorded using household appliances, such as a "microwave" oven. I don't know about you guys. I have a defrost setting on my microwave but no button for "Surveil." I'm pretty sure you can't "wiretap" a baked potato. But I digress.

All these fact-challenged defenses from Spicer and the larger communications team at the White House demonstrated why these confrontations kept occurring during the press briefings. We just weren't getting any answers, and that forum was our one chance every day to try to elicit some. We could not merely accept as fact Trump's assertion that Obama had bugged him. Sorry, but we weren't born yesterday.

Fortunately for everybody, the Trump team backed down, sort of. On March 16, twelve days after the original, unfounded tweet from Trump, Spicer came as close as he could to issuing a clarification of the president's erroneous statement. In an exchange from the briefing over the wiretapping accusation, Spicer noticeably shifted the explanation coming out of the White House. All of a sudden, Trump's claim of wiretapping, we were told, should not be taken literally. The president had put "wiretapping" in quotes, Sean explained, as if that made the falsehood ring true. Usually, you put things in quotes to make things more certain, not to speak about them more generally.

Surveillance, Sean claimed, is what Trump was really talking about. Though it should be pointed out, there remains zero evidence to this day that Obama ordered surveillance of Trump at his place of residence and business, as the new president alleged. Republicans and Democrats on the Senate and House Intelligence Committees have said as much.

There was a lot of interrupting, as we went back and forth over this, nearly two weeks after Trump posted the wiretapping tweets. But here's how it played out during the briefing:

ACOSTA: You have a Senate and House Intelligence Committee both leaders from both parties on both of those panels saying that they don't see any evidence of any wiretapping. So how can the president go on and continue to—

SPICER: Because that's not—because you're mischaracterizing what Chairman Nunes said. He said, quote, "I think it's possible. He's following up." So to suggest that is actually and you're stating unequivocally that you somehow—

ACOSTA: —literally, you said if you—

SPICER: Right, and I think that we've already cleared that up. And he said exactly that. But the President has already said clearly when he referred to wiretapping he was referring to surveillance.

ACOSTA: Right, but it sounds like, Sean, that you and the President are saying now, well, we don't mean wiretapping anymore because that's not true anymore, so now we're going to expand that to other forms of surveillance. What's it going to be next?

SPICER: No, no, Jim, I think that's cute, but at the end of the day—we've talked about this for three or four days. The President had "wiretapping" in quotes; he was referring to broad surveillance. And now you're basically going back. We talked about this several days ago.

There you have it. When the president had "wiretapping" in quotes, he meant surveillance. The white flag, mercifully, had been raised. Trump, let the record reflect, also walked back his original accusation. In an interview with Fox News, he tried to put the matter to rest by arguing that "wiretapping" could mean lots of things. It was all but an admission that Trump was just making stuff up.

"Don't forget, when I say 'wiretapping,' those words were in quotes," Trump told Fox. "That really covers, because wiretapping is pretty old-fashioned stuff. But that really covers surveillance and many other things. And nobody ever talks about the fact that it was in quotes, but that's a very important thing," he added, suggesting that if you put spoken falsehoods in "air quotes," you can basically say anything you want. Sorry, that's not how this works.

As my confrontations with Spicer went viral, it was becoming clear that our contentious exchanges were damaging any real opportunity for us to have some kind of professional relationship, on or off camera. Once you were on Spicer's bad side, you never really recovered. For me, I suppose, that day came back when I had dared to challenge Trump at the news conference during the transition and Spicer threatened to throw me out. Still, to give Sean some credit, there were times when he did his job as press secretary. He would occasionally call me on the phone, offer information, and try to clarify things, as he should have. But then, the next day, he would snap and go ballistic, leaving us wondering whether he could handle such a high-pressure position.

Part of the problem for Sean was he was trying to do two jobs at once. Spicer had come into the administration serving as both press secretary and communications director. He took on both these positions (a mistake he should have never made) after former Trump campaign spokesman Jason Miller surprisingly withdrew his own name from consideration for the position of White House communications director during the presidential transition period. Miller walked away from that coveted administration job after it was revealed that he had fathered a child out of wedlock. Jason and I had butted heads during the campaign—he insulted my reporting live on CNN—but I am not about to run him into the ground here. He made a mistake in his personal life and left Trumpworld to go be with his family.

But Jason's sudden absence placed Spicer in an unwinnable situation. Any White House veteran would have warned Sean that he was taking on two huge responsibilities. Being the White House press secretary requires enormous preparation. You have to be steeped in policy expertise on a range of subjects, from terrorism and North Korea to health care reform and budget issues. Sean, as we now know, was already unprepared for that kind of job. As head of communications for the RNC, he had mainly fielded questions on political strategy and fund-raising, not the intricacies of the Iran nuclear deal. Sounding poorly read on that kind of material can move markets, in the wrong direction.

Add to all that the gargantuan task of serving as communications director for a White House that was just getting off the ground, and you have a recipe for a public relations disaster. A good "comms" director is constantly thinking about the president's message, as in how to sell it and how it's being reported. The communications director isn't typically speaking from the podium. He or she is organizing messaging events with Cabinet members or the president himself. Under Trump, this job is even more impossible when you consider the fact that the forty-fifth president is undisciplined, to put it charitably, and prefers to do his own messaging, no matter how unreliable the information sometimes is. In short, there was no way Sean could do both those jobs—you can't prepare adequately for the daily briefing if you are planning messaging events, and vice versa—and this two-headed monster led to his eventual demise.

Around the middle of February, I received a tip that Michael Dubke, a little-known GOP operative based in Northern Virginia, was about to be tapped as the new White House communications director. After confirming the news with a White House official, we broke the story late at night. One sign that we had it correct? Sean wasn't knocking it down. But make no mistake, they were pissed off that it had leaked, and looking back, I see that it was probably leaked to annoy Sean.

The next morning, just before eight o'clock, my phone rang and the name "Sean Spicer" flashed on the screen. I answered. Spicer was, to put it mildly, losing his mind. Visualize veins popping out of his neck. It was that kind of call. He was screaming into the phone, taking issue with part of the story. I calmly tried to explain my reporting to him, but his feelings would not be soothed.

Spicer was obviously angry because somebody from inside Trumpworld had leaked the news. Think about how that looked. The man in the White House in control of rolling out stories hadn't been able to manage the news about the position in charge of rolling out stories.

There I was, standing next to my young son, who had come into the room, listening to Sean screaming at the top of his lungs, "You're a fucking weasel!"

When I hung up, I looked down at my son.

With a look of astonishment on his face, he asked, "Who was that?"

"Son," I said, "that was the White House."

NOT ALL SUCH EXCHANGES WITH SPICER HAPPENED IN PRIVATE. IT should not be forgotten how Spicer treated some of my colleagues in the Briefing Room. His appalling treatment of April Ryan, perhaps the most visible African American reporter at the White House, was awful. During one briefing, on March 28, he chastised her simply for shaking her head, which only made him look chauvinistic and petty. April, as tough a reporter as she is, had asked a pretty benign question that day, pressing Spicer on whether he had become concerned about the image of the White House. Sean tried to dodge the question, leading April to shake her head in disbelief. As reporters, we often shoot glances of disbelief at the press secretary, especially when that press secretary is named Sean Spicer. If you can't handle reporters shaking their heads at you, you shouldn't be at that podium. It's that simple.

As we filed out of the Briefing Room, I remember April, who is a friend of mine, asking me, "Can you believe that?"

"Unbelievable," I replied, an exchange April and I had on too many occasions heading back to our workspace in the White House basement.

One thing that April and I had in common was that Sean was making things personal with both of us. To April, I became her "brother from another mother"; April was my "sister from another mister." She and I had something else in common: we were both beginning to receive death threats, and at levels we had not experienced before. April would later confide that she had the FBI on "speed dial."

Ryan, like so many other veterans of the press corps, has covered the White House going back decades. She deserves more respect than that. Spicer's treatment of her pretty much summed up the White House attitude toward reporters in general. Certainly, it wasn't the way he used to treat us, but once you are drawn into Trump's orbit, it seemed, the press was the "opposition party" and, sadly, the "enemy."

Occasionally, I thought Spicer and I would turn a corner, but then, almost like clockwork, he would dash those hopes. One day, I was sitting in a booth in the press area of the West Wing when an aide stopped by to ask me to come up to Sean's office. No problem. Was Spicer calling me into his office to yell at me? To make peace? Perhaps we would finally bury the hatchet. I dropped everything and made my way to his office.

As it turned out, Sean had sent for me to complain about a chyron (a graphic summarizing the news of the day at the bottom of the screen) that was on air at that moment during a segment of Erin Burnett's *Out Front*. I can't remember what the chyron said. Whatever it was, I don't recall it being that bad. These things can always be toned down, I guess. But it had set Spicer off.

As I walked into his office, he was screaming obscenities into the phone. On the other end of the line was CNN's Washington bureau chief, Sam Feist.

"Hold on," Spicer says, as he stopped yelling at Feist and turned to me and barked, "What the fuck is wrong with you people?" Look at the chyron, he demanded, pointing at the TV in his office.

This was classic Spicer. He was so upset about the chyron CNN was running that, in a perverse circle of life, he was screaming at my bureau chief over the phone and at me in person at the same time. As ridiculous as this scene was, and after all the drama Sean and I had been through together, I still tried to help. I emailed the show about the chyron to see if they could tweak it, but it was too late. The segment was over. By that point, Spicer had finished his ranting, so I left.

There were moments of relative peace between Spicer and me. I'm happy to report that we did get along at the 2017 Easter Egg Roll. You know the event. Thousands of children and their families gather on the South Lawn to take part in one of the oldest White House traditions. The Easter Bunny is there. There are tables where children color Easter eggs. The First Lady sits and reads stories to the kids. And, as you may have seen, adorable little boys and girls, dressed in their Sunday best, gather to roll an Easter egg with a wooden spoon across the South Lawn grass. I reached out to Spicer to see if he wanted to do an interview. He must have been in a good mood that day, because he agreed. In the days leading up to that Easter Egg Roll, Spicer had been the target of ridicule over his past service as the White House Easter Bunny. There were photos of him in a bunny costume circulating on the internet, attached to some rather vicious, mocking stories.

This was one of those moments when I really felt sorry for Sean. Yes, he could be difficult and even downright nasty. At times, it seemed he had it coming. But making fun of a guy for playing the Easter Bunny? It just felt ugly to me, the kind of bullying that has begun to fill our public discourse, especially when figures like Sean are on the ropes. If it's wrong to bully people on social media, isn't it also wrong to ridicule the press secretary, even if it's Sean?

When I interviewed Sean that day, I didn't bring up the Easter Bunny gig. That would have been, in my view, just petty. I did ask him about North Korea and tried to cover other policy areas. But at the end of the interview, I decided to ask him about Melissa McCarthy, the comedian who had helped make Spicer a household name. Yes, her portrayal of Sean on *SNL* was brutal, but Spicer hadn't been the first political figure to be lampooned on *Saturday Night Live*. So, I thought, his insights on McCarthy's version of "Spicy" might be illuminating. Would he laugh it off? Would he throw a jab at McCarthy? Would he rage at me for asking the question? His answer might tell us a bit about how he was handling it all.

Instead, Sean gave a rather bland answer on the topic. "I'm usually fast asleep by the time that comes on," he said with a smile, but dryly. "I'm in bed, get up, go to church the next day, and look ahead," he added.

"I get made fun of, too," I said, trying to keep the conversation going.

"Well, maybe more deserved," he responded, with a grin.

This was about as boring as Sean could have been on the topic. And maybe that's how he wanted it. If he had gotten animated on the subject, it would have made news. The moment was perhaps the last genuinely civil exchange I've had with Sean.

It was not, however, the last time I felt sorry for him. In May 2017, after the firing of James Comey, Trump was ready to get out of Dodge. As previously scheduled, we all embarked on the president's first foreign trip, traveling to Saudi Arabia, Israel, Italy, and Brussels. In Saudi Arabia, Trump famously visited a Saudi facility purported to be a center for combating terrorism without a hint of awareness that most of the 9/11 hijackers had been from Saudi Arabia.

The president finished off the stop by placing his hands on some kind of strange glowing orb. Ever the showman, he was eating it all up. But the images sent out to the rest of the world were jaw-dropping. It was nothing less than a coup for Riyadh to have the president of the United States turn to the Saudis for their expertise in the fight against terrorism, this in a country that had been the source of so much violent extremism around the world. The administration appeared to be dodging any kind of on-camera accountability along the way. Top officials, including Jared Kushner and Ivanka Trump, spoke with reporters, but did so anonymously, on background, so they wouldn't have their names attached to whatever quotes they served up to the media. Secretary of State Rex Tillerson held a news conference, but for foreign press outlets only.

Still, the biggest absurdity of this first leg of the foreign trip was undoubtedly when Trump and his commerce secretary, Wilbur Ross, joined the Saudis in a ceremonial sword dance. I remember being in the press filing center seeing the video feed of Trump, Ross, and the Saudis all doing the cha-cha and wielding *Lawrence of Arabia*–type swords. The other reporters and I burst into laughter. Perhaps we were delirious from the jet lag, but we all scrambled up to the monitors to snap a photo of the images being fed in by the White House pool. Looking back, though, I see that the scene wasn't really funny. It was another example that, on the world stage, Trump seemed to prefer to have autocrats and dictators as his dancing partners. As we would all come to learn later on in the administration, with the murder of Saudi journalist Jamal Khashoggi and its aftermath, U.S. coziness with the kingdom in Riyadh has real-world consequences. In hindsight, I wish we hadn't laughed at the sword dancing. Yes, it was long before Khashoggi's violent death, but it makes me sick just thinking about it.

In addition to the critical foreign policy issues we were following on that trip, we were keeping tabs on a different sideshow: the fate of the press secretary. We were on Spicy-watch. There had long been questions looming over Sean, many of them fueled by Spicer's enemies in Trumpworld—he had many—who wanted to see him fired. Was Trump going to fire him? If the president fired Spicer, would Priebus go, too? Priebus and Spicer were always seen as a package deal. "The RNC crowd" is how Trump campaign veterans described them, both inside and outside the White House. Spicer, in their eyes, would never be seen as an "original" from the campaign. After disparaging Trump privately to anybody who would listen during the primaries, Sean had glommed on at the end of the election cycle and snatched up one of the top jobs in all of American politics. That generated a mountain of animosity inside Trumpworld and made him a lot of enemies. Mostly, though, he was despised because he had beaten them to the job.

For his part, Priebus is almost too nice a guy to be part of any story about Trump. He and I would frequently chat it up at the various media dinners around Washington. Still, he had his detractors. In many ways, his approachable, affable nature probably made him ill-suited to be Trump's chief of staff. Reince very much had an open-door policy during his tenure. Just about any Trump associate or friend could call the president on Reince's personal phone or make an appointment to visit the Oval Office. This was part of Reince's undoing.

Priebus seemed to compensate for his weak standing in the White House by resorting to the same sycophancy that Trump craved from his top aides. Case in point was the infamous Cabinet meeting in June 2017, when Vice President Pence, the Trump Cabinet, and other top aides went around the table praising the president.

"We thank you for the opportunity and the blessing to serve your agenda," Priebus gushed.

"I wasn't saying he was a blessing. I was saying the job was a blessing," Priebus later told me.

But nobody could top Pence: "The greatest privilege of my life is to serve as vice president to the president who's keeping his word to the American people." We were all waiting for him to describe Trump as their "Dear Leader," like something out of North Korea. This wasn't *The Apprentice*. It was *The Twilight Zone*.

Undermining Priebus perhaps more than anyone was Trump's former campaign manager, Corey Lewandowski, who had been fired by the candidate after more than a year on the job. He was constantly hanging around the White House during the first year of the administration, bending Trump's ear and using his access to promote his "consulting" work. Lewandowski wasn't alone. Jason Miller and Bryan Lanza, former campaign spokesmen, were other frequent visitors among the Trumpworld figures seen milling around the White House grounds. The Corey sightings inside the West Wing routinely led to speculation that he was about to replace Priebus at any moment. One outside Trump adviser told me that Corey never really wanted to work at the White House, but that the "campaign" people got a kick out of leaking Lewandowski's White House visits to the press primarily because those visits annoyed the "RNC" people inside the White House, such as Reince and Sean. To this point, Lewandowski would occasionally walk past the cameras on the North Lawn to draw maximum attention, guaranteeing that Politico or Axios would publish another "Corey story," as I called them. It was "catnip for the media . . . a bright shiny object," the adviser said of the Lewandowski-Priebus stories. "Something we enjoy doing." This is how Trumpworld played its games, making life miserable for people they didn't like inside the White House by leaking palace intrigue stories to the press.

"The knives were out!" was how sources inside Trumpworld were constantly describing Spicer's future. Sean was always portrayed as being on thin ice. "The boss is not happy [with Sean]," that same Trump adviser told me on a regular basis. CNN reported this kind of stuff infrequently because, after a while, we could see that people were just screwing with Reince and Sean.

Still, there were instances when it was abundantly clear that Trump's dissatisfaction with Spicer was indeed growing. There was ample of evidence of Sean's rapid descent during that first foreign trip. When we arrived in Rome, the news was breaking that Trump was hiring an outside counsel to represent him in the Russia investigation. Still, as massive as the Russia investigation was at that time, the development that grabbed the attention of nearly every reporter on that trip came the following day.

Trump was to meet with none other than His Holiness Pope Francis. There was plenty to dissect about the visit. The pope had not hidden the fact that he didn't really care for Trump. His statements coming out of the Vatican, not to mention his 2015 visit with Obama on the South Lawn of the White House, where he spoke about the threat posed by climate change, made it pretty clear that he was, for the most part, a progressive pontiff. But that's not the storyline that emerged from Trump's stop at the Vatican.

The president brought a small entourage with him for his brief encounter with the Holy Father. To the amazement of the entire press corps and much of Washington, Spicer was left out of that entourage. Now, I had been assured by a couple of White House officials that this had nothing to do with Sean; and other reporters were talking to the same officials and hearing the same thing. But we never believed any of it for a second. Spicer was a devout Irish Catholic. He was so filled with Irish pride, in fact, that he wore shamrock pants on St. Patrick's Day. He really did! Leaving Sean out of the mix for a meeting with the pope, of all the people on earth, sent a clear and vicious message. As I learned from other sources who advise Trump on a regular basis, the president was ready for Spicer to leave, but he didn't want to fire him. My sources told me Trump wanted Spicer to leave on his own.

"It was a slap in the face," a senior White House official described the snub to me.

When Spicer's absence from the Trump entourage became known, calls and texts poured in from sources, especially those who didn't like Sean. One particular enemy of Spicer's called rather upset, confiding to me that even she had to feel sorry for him at that moment. Here was Spicer, at the top of his political career as the White House press secretary, being humiliated on the world stage. He was probably the most visible Catholic on the Trump team, and yet he was being denied a meeting with the pope. When would he ever have such an opportunity again, to see the leader of his Church as part of the president's team? It's very likely he wouldn't.

"The president didn't do that. Other people did that." A senior White House official claimed Trump wasn't behind the snub. "That was petty," the official said. "Those people no longer work in the administration."

This sums up the nastiness of Trumpworld. The president often didn't pull his employee into a boardroom, as he had on reality television, and thunder, "You're fired." Instead, he or his people played games with Sean's head and, in this case, his faith. It was another reminder that Trump demands loyalty from his subjects but gives almost none in return.

I remember hopping on the phone with Sean later on during that trip. He sounded as if he had a few drinks in him. He sounded sad. Why wouldn't he? He had been all but excommunicated from Trumpworld, and at the Vatican no less.

———————

AS BAD AS I FELT FOR SPICER IN THAT MOMENT, THIS WAS NO TIME to let him off the hook. He was still the press secretary, and he was beginning to crack down on CNN even more. As spring turned to summer, he was starting to play games with the daily White House briefings. Breaking with years of tradition, he was freezing out certain networks and news outlets simply by refusing to call on some reporters, including me. CNN was feeling this more than any other network. For several weeks in a row between April and June, Spicer slowly but surely turned off our access. This, of course, was retaliation for our coverage of the administration.

There were two ways for us to respond to this. We could absorb this nonsense, as we had all the other abuse, or we could push back. My sense was that we had to push back. Trump had called us "the enemy of the people" and "fake news." As he would say to his base at his campaign rallies, what the hell did we have to lose? So, I decided to start interrupting Spicer during the briefings. If he wasn't going to call on CNN, I thought, CNN was going to call him out.

A case in point came in that tumultuous month of May 2017, after the Comey firing, when Trump suggested that he had the former FBI director over a barrel because there may have been recordings of their encounters, tapes that would prove that the president was right about everything, or so he imagined. This suggestion, which later turned out to be another one of Trump's lies, came per usual in the form of a tweet that, per usual, was designed to disrupt the news cycle. All this, once again, tossed Sean back into the ungodly madness of explaining away Trump's falsehoods in front of reporters.

Three days after Trump's tweet, at the May 15 briefing, Spicer repeatedly dodged questions about whether such records existed.

"The president has made it clear what his position is," Spicer told reporters. "I was clear the president would have nothing further on that last week," he added.

Spicer refused to call on me during that briefing. So, as he exited the room, I shouted out my question to him.

"Where are the tapes?" I asked him. He didn't respond, but the cameras were still rolling, and the briefing was still being carried live on CNN. The viewer had heard it.

To make sure Sean got the message that I didn't appreciate CNN being iced out of the briefings, I vented my frustrations on Twitter. Hey, if *they* can do it, my thought was, why can't *we*? For a few weeks, anytime I posted a tweet about Comey, I finished it off with the hashtag #wherearethetapes. I suppose there are some folks out there who would call this #grandstanding, but social media sites were now a part of the terrain for reporters covering the presidency. And I considered #wherearethetapes a catchy way to keep the story alive that Trump had blatantly lied to the public about the existence of Comey tapes, and the White House had zero chance of making the whole thing go away.

Trump and his team, it should be pointed out, held out for nearly a month before backing down and admitting that there had never been any Comey tapes. But until then, our confrontations would continue. During one news conference, on June 9, 2017, the White House press shop retaliated against us for our news coverage by moving our seat to the back of the Rose Garden, instead of putting us in the front row with the rest of the TV networks. This was clearly designed to punish us. There was no way we would be able to ask a question. To register my disgust with their pettiness, I decided to fire off a tweet.

@Acosta
CNN was placed away from the other TV networks in the equivalent of Siberia (no pun intended) at today's news conference.
3:26 PM-Jun 9, 2017

This went on for several more days. Spicer kept up his side of the battle by continuing to ignore us during the briefings. So, I escalated things on my end. My sense of it was the press secretary should not be able to get away with shutting out an entire news network for an extended time. I continued to take aim at Spicer's belligerence with some of my own.

@Acosta
As he often does, @PressSec avoided taking questions from CNN
today. #courage
1:20 PM—Jun 12, 2017

Admittedly, this confrontational approach created even more tension in the Briefing Room. A few reporters were starting to adopt
the same practice of shouting out questions and turning to Twitter
to take the press secretary to task. Of course, colleagues from other
outlets, I'm fully aware, were rolling their eyes, annoyed by some of
these tactics.

There were plenty of reporters out there who felt we needed to
continue to play by the old rules, even as this administration took
extraordinary steps to destroy the rule book. Trumpworld had shown
time and time again that, when it came to dealing with the press corps,
it would not respect the norms and boundaries, implicit or otherwise.
And as reporters, we found ourselves confronting hostility unlike any
we'd ever faced. Some journalists argued that the best way to move
forward was to focus on the news and stay in our lane. To me, it all
boiled down to a question faced by each and every journalist covering
the Trump White House: what would you do?

What often got lost in all the chaos and the scrutiny of my reporting
was the fact that journalists like me—people who both had followed
the campaign and were now covering Trump in the White House—
had been exposed to the worst elements of Trump's rise to power.
The campaign reporters had covered rallies where thousands of people screamed, "CNN sucks" and "Fuck the media," and hurled other
insults at us. Other reporters in the White House press corps had not.
They had stayed in DC. So, we were all coming into this new administration with a different set of experiences.

Perhaps nothing embodied these differences quite like the response
from the White House Correspondents' Association (WHCA). The

WHCA had only very rarely registered complaints with the Trump team over its behavior up until the election. I suppose part of the reason for this reluctance to criticize the then–GOP nominee was the attitude that Trump was going to be Trump. He was going to demonize the press because it energized his base. Truth be told, I still don't understand why there weren't more complaints coming out of the WHCA or other press organizations about Trump's treatment of the media. As a reporter at the rallies, it truly felt like it was every journalist for himself.

This cutthroat atmosphere from the campaign shaped much of my approach once Trump was in office. As a result, my view became that the abuse would not stop unless we stood up for ourselves. A different kind of president required a different playbook for reporters. A former member of the WHCA board once said to me, "We can't always take the bait," and I kept arguing back to her and my other colleagues that we couldn't just take it on the chin, either. This is not to say that I had many disagreements with my colleagues on the WHCA board. I really didn't. Indeed, former WHCA president and Reuters reporter Jeff Mason, who delivered an impassioned speech at the White House Correspondents' Association Dinner in 2017, an event Trump skipped to thumb his nose at the press, wisely retooled the event into a night to celebrate the First Amendment.

As for Spicer, he was certainly growing impatient with the occasional rebellions in the Briefing Room. Weary of the sparring, he was racking up episode after episode of embarrassing moments, all happening with Trump (quite often, we are told), watching from behind the scenes.

Then Spicer upped the ante. In June 2017, in the middle of the Comey tapes controversy, Spicer decided to suspend the practice of allowing television coverage of the briefings. Instead, the news conferences would be audio only, and could not be aired live. Keep in mind that the Briefing Room would still be wired for TV, with cameras, microphones, and lighting equipment everywhere. But the people who operated that equipment, Spicer mandated, would not be able to hit the On switch. Unfortunately—and this gets to the pack mentality of news organizations—the networks and other news outlets made the decision to go along with Sean's new crackdown on our coverage, as they felt it was still important to have access to the press secretary for information, even though Spicer could hardly be deemed a reliable source of information. In another concession to Trump team tactics, we all abided by the restrictions.

Personally, I thought this was a mistake. Given Trump's toxic attitude toward the press, there was the strong possibility that this would become permanent and that the daily White House briefing, something news outlets across the world relied on every day, would go dark for good. I reported as much on the air at the time. Cue the accusations of grandstanding, but, as I've said repeatedly, call me all the names you want. This was important. This was about standing up for our ability to cover the White House. There is no more important place to have access.

Now, Spicer had already dabbled in tactics aimed at punishing individual reporters. Back in February 2017, rather than hold an on-camera briefing, he opted for an off-camera gaggle (a short, less formal briefing) with a group of invited reporters. To send a message, he notably excluded Politico, the *New York Times*, the *Los Angeles Times*, and CNN. Among those getting an invite were such Trump-friendly outlets as Breitbart, the *Washington Times*, and the One America News Network. My CNN colleague Sara Murray, who was supposed to represent our outlet during that gaggle, instead went on the air to report on how the White House had once again retaliated against the press.

"When we went to enter, I was blocked by a White House staffer, who said we were not on the list for this gaggle today," Murray reported on CNN. There was no fallout for Spicer after this blatant attempt to intimidate our news outlet. This was all about sending a message: if we messed with the White House, we would be left out in the cold. Let's face it, this was pure divide-and-conquer stuff. Sean and the White House folks knew how journalists work. Reporters aren't typically going to turn down a briefing just because other reporters haven't been invited. That's not how it works in Washington. For some reporters, access is more important than solidarity. In the media jungle of Trumpworld, those reporters who stand with the White House instead of with their fellow members of the press are often rewarded with scoops. Sad but true.

Getting back to Spicer's draconian decision to ban cameras, this was not targeted retaliation, aimed at one particular news outlet. This was a blanket restriction on the entire White House press corps. As it turned out, it was a foolish move for Spicer and company. For starters, technology is not on the side of restricting access, as reporters all have mobile phones that can stream the briefings live anyway. But let's put that aside: it's the principle of the matter that's far more critical here.

Sean wasn't the first press secretary to become frustrated with televised interactions with reporters. The briefings, for the most part, had been open to cameras since the Clinton administration, and press secretaries, from time to time, had questioned whether they were worth all the hassle. In fact, one of Clinton's former press secretaries, Mike McCurry, would go on to argue that these events had descended into showboating exercises for network correspondents long before I got my White House press pass. One of McCurry's successors, George W. Bush's press secretary Ari Fleischer, arrived at the same conclusion. Were McCurry and Fleischer correct? Granted, you had press secretaries from both parties who said the briefings had gotten out of hand. Some of their frustration, I believe, could be chalked up to PBSD, post-briefing stress disorder. If you spent years taking questions from a bunch of demanding reporters, you'd probably hate this stuff, too. In the end, some of it comes down to press secretary strategy, and Spicer's strategy was to keep upping the ante.

So, on June 19, at one of those off-camera briefings, I decided once again to register my frustration on social media. Now, we'd been told we weren't allowed to turn on our cameras and put Sean's friendly face on TV. But there were no rules, as far as I knew, that said we couldn't take pictures in the room. So, to note the absurdity of what was about to unfold, I turned my phone toward the Briefing Room floor and snapped a picture. As the off-camera briefing was about to begin, I tweeted this:

@Acosta
The Spicer off-camera/no audio gaggle has begun. I can't show you a pic of Sean. So here is a look at some new socks I bought over the wknd

It was a bit irreverent, I admit. And, truth be told, not everybody at CNN was on board with the sock tweet. But one lesson I learned from Trump is that posts on social media—in particular, pointed tweets—do grab people's attention. The sock tweet went viral. (I mean, they were cool socks.) After the briefing was over, I walked out to the live-shot position on the North Lawn of the White House and let Sean have it.

"The White House press secretary is getting to a point where he's just kind of useless," I told CNN's Brooke Baldwin. "It just feels like we're sort of slowly but surely being dragged into what is a new normal in this country, where the president of the United States is allowed to insulate himself from answering hard questions."

I'll admit it. Calling Sean "useless" was probably too harsh. But keep in mind that the off-camera aspect of the briefing had been only part of the madness we dealt with that day. Spicer stonewalled in another sense, by refusing to answer some critical questions during the briefing, dodging questions on whether Trump believed human activity contributed to climate change. Sean was routinely telling reporters he didn't know because he hadn't talked to the president. It was a ridiculous response. How could the press secretary not know the answer to that question? Sean was stonewalling us, of course; he did know the answer. Trump was (and still is) a full-blown climate change denier; he had repeatedly described global warming as a "hoax." The problem for Spicer was that admitting the truth about Trump's actual feelings on the climate change issue was just too embarrassing.

So, yes, if the briefings were going to be both off-camera and substance free, then Sean, as press secretary, was, basically, "useless." That didn't mean we shouldn't cover his briefings. Indeed, covering these briefings, especially if they were going to be presented in this fashion, would only help reveal the absurdity of what these government officials were doing with our tax dollars.

Don't forget that. These are taxpayer-funded officials in the press office. Their job is to help inform the public, not misinform.

CNN, I should note, showed tremendous support for the stance I was taking in the Briefing Room. Our bureau chief in Washington, Sam Feist, understood the nuttiness of the off-camera spectacle. On June 23, during yet another off-camera gaggle, Sam sent a sketch artist over to draw pictures of Spicer answering questions from the podium. If Sean wouldn't let us turn on the cameras, we thought, we had to show the viewers something. Why not a sketch, like something out of a courtroom during a high-profile trial? Sam later gave a copy of the sketch to Sean, who seemed amused by it. It was one of many peace offerings from CNN to the White House that, as you might expect, led to only more abuse from the administration. Oh, we tried to turn down the temperature.

On June 26, I turned up the heat as Spicer scheduled another off-camera briefing. Once again, he was not calling on CNN. So, I interrupted him.

"There's no camera on, Jim," Spicer said.

"Maybe we should turn the cameras on, Sean. Why don't we turn the cameras on? Why not turn the cameras on? They're in the room, the lights are on," I responded.

After the briefing was over, I again vented my frustrations with CNN's Brooke Baldwin. Who the hell wants to hear my frustrations? Fair point. But it was important, I thought, to clearly explain the situation to the public in real time.

"I think that we just need to recognize what's happening here," I said on the air. "What we are typically accustomed to in this town, in terms of covering the White House, covering the United States government, that is being eroded away right in front of our eyes."

Three days later, Spicer's deputy, Sarah Huckabee Sanders, held the first on-camera briefing in a couple of weeks. The whispers coming out of Trumpworld were that Trump wanted to give Sarah a shot at doing the briefings. But her arrival on the scene only added to the Spicy-watch melodrama: when would Sean finally leave the administration?

Either way, Spicer seemed to take much of the public response to his policies personally. Case in point, a piece for the *Washington Post*, written by Paul Farhi, questioned whether I had crossed a line as a reporter with all my efforts to hold the White House accountable. In it, Spicer took the opportunity to unload on me.

"If Jim Acosta reported on Jim Acosta the way he reports on us, he'd say he hasn't been very honest," Spicer told the *Post*. "I think he's gone well beyond the role of reporter and steered into the role of advocate. He's the prime example of a [reporter in a] competitive, YouTube, click-driven industry," he added. "He's recognized that if you make a spectacle on the air then you'll get more airtime and more clicks. . . . If I were a mainstream, veteran reporter, I'd be advocating for him to knock it off. It's hurting the profession."

Farhi asked me for a response to Spicer's lengthy rant. I gave him my reaction: "I will let my reporting speak for itself just as I will let

Sean's performance as press secretary speak for him." Farhi, perhaps hoping I would return fire, didn't include the quote in his story.

One other takeaway from the *Post* story was that Sean lied about my reporting. At one point during my conversations with Farhi, he asked why I hadn't ever visited Spicer's office. Sean was lying and said that I hadn't. In fact, I had posted a photo on Instagram—ah, the value of social media—of me standing outside Sean's office with a dozen other reporters. And the night he was screaming at me about the chyron on CNN? I was standing inside Sean's office.

Sean also claimed to Farhi that I had skipped briefings that included the veterans' affairs secretary. This, too, was a lie. CNN furnished to the *Post* pictures of me sitting in the Briefing Room listening to the VA secretary taking questions from reporters. Fortunately, Farhi did not put those accusations from Sean in his story, but they were an early signal of just how far the White House would go to disparage my reporting. If they were willing to lie to a media journalist for one of the most important newspapers in the world, what else were they willing to do? We would later find out.

By then, it didn't really matter. Rumors were swirling that Spicer was on his way out. Also, stories were surfacing that Trump was searching for a new communications director to replace Mike Dubke, who had already quit. On July 21, 2017, the West Wing exploded in chaos. Trump selected a new communications director from his days on the campaign trail, a sharp-tongued hedge fund manager named Anthony Scaramucci, who had served as one of the GOP contender's surrogates during the 2016 cycle. Spicer had opposed Scaramucci's hiring, as had Reince Priebus. Both Priebus and Spicer saw Scaramucci, who was aligned with the RNC haters in the campaign, as a threat to their influence in the West Wing. And he was. My sources told me that they had tried to keep him out of the White House for as long as possible.

But the dam broke: Scaramucci was hired, Spicer quit in protest, and Sarah Sanders became press secretary. Priebus left the following week, replaced by retired general and homeland security secretary John Kelly. Kelly then fired Scaramucci after just ten days—Scaramucci disputes this and says eleven—prompted in part by a damaging story in *The New Yorker*, written by Ryan Lizza, who reported on a profanity-laced conversation he had had with the man known as "the Mooch."

I'm kind of glad I was on vacation when Spicer stepped down as press secretary. After all our battles, I didn't want to be seen as piling on. CNN asked me to call in with my take. Spicer, in my view, had so damaged his credibility in his first appearance in the Briefing Room, after Inauguration Day, that he was never going to recover. Why would we believe Sean's comments on Syria, climate change, or voter fraud when he had lied so blatantly on January 21 and said that the president had had the biggest inauguration crowd in the history of the United States? After that, we all knew that he was speaking, or in some cases misleading, on the president's behalf, and in the end, Spicer, like so many of the president's aides, was useful until disposable. That, I must say to this day, has made him something of a sympathetic character for me.

There is an even more charitable view of Sean's actions. Some in Washington believe that Spicer, along with former White House chief of staff Reince Priebus, felt somewhat compelled to work with Trump to normalize him and, perhaps, even to pull him into the mainstream. This is part of the "they tried to save America" defense you hear from time to time in Washington, about establishment officials who go to work for Trump. For a brief period, Spicer and Priebus gave Trump a bit of that establishment sheen.

Still, it can't be forgotten that Sean was making a choice. Even though every time he came out to the podium in the White House Briefing Room he looked like he was in a hostage video—reading from a script, mindful that the boss was watching—every day, he was making a decision to be there. Still, while he often received mysterious notes from press aides in the middle of briefings, prompting him to quickly wrap up things up, he wasn't a captive. He wasn't chained to his desk in the press secretary's offices, one of the most coveted corners of the nation's capital. Yes, Sean certainly had a choice, and his choice was to enable Trump as he divided the country in ways we had never seen before.

If Spicer thought the task of defending Trump had become impossible for him, he should have done himself and all Americans the favor of stepping down much sooner. Imagine the amount of good Sean could have done for the country had he taken a different route, such as resigning in protest and warning us of what was going on behind closed doors in the West Wing.

Perhaps the ultimate legacy of Sean Spicer, the one that would leave the longest and most indelible mark on the administration, on the press corps, and on the public, was that he was the first face of the administration for us beyond Trump. He set the tone from the beginning about what it meant to be the spokesperson for the Trump administration. He had told the first big lie of the administration about the inauguration. The transparent stonewalling, the twisting of facts, the demonization of the press—all these dangerous tactics had found oxygen in Spicer's approach in front of the cameras and behind the scenes. Years from now, he might be remembered more as a punch line than anything else. However, through his refusal to correct the lies and his allegiance to the man in the higher office over the higher good, he came to embody the character traits we'd see time and time again from those in this White House.

Most concerning of all, though, was how Spicer's tenure showed the need for absolute vigilance from the press corps. Repeatedly, our will to push back, to challenge the destruction of long-held norms, was being tested. While the debates over restricted camera coverage and freezing out networks might sound petty, they were early skirmishes in a larger conflict. There were stories brewing that would demand answers to hard questions, and it was increasingly unclear if the American people were going to get those answers.

The passage of time might soften my feelings here, but it's not fair to let Sean off the hook, is it? When it came to what sometimes felt like Trump's bonfire of the insanities, Sean was always there to light the match, toss on another log, and pour on the gasoline. Our battles in the Briefing Room left me with one simple lesson that should be taught in our schools and colleges to rising journalists and public servants: as a spokesman for the president of the United States, you serve the people of the United States, not the president. Sean lost sight of that crucial responsibility; he was derelict in his duty. He and the rest of Trumpworld stamped all of us in the press as traitors simply for trying to call out the administration on its brutal, unrelenting dishonesty. But in Trump's war against "the enemy of the people," Sean's departure didn't signal an end to the hostility to the facts. Spicer's replacement was more than willing to enter the battlefield. For Sarah Huckabee Sanders, her moment of untruth had arrived.

6
The Worst Wing

You'd think that after the reign of Sean Spicer—which introduced the American people to embarrassing claims (inauguration crowd size) and amateurish handling of sober topics ("Holocaust centers")—that Trump would have been ready to hire a professional for the job of press secretary. But we didn't end up with something out of the hit NBC show *The West Wing*. Trump had decided to elevate Spicer's deputy, Sarah Huckabee Sanders, who had impressed senior White House staffers, most notably the president himself. By and large, Sanders simply picked up where Spicer had left off. There was no honeymoon with the press.

Sanders, who, we were told, preferred to be called "Sarah Sanders," continued the Trump administration tradition of walking into the Briefing Room and often misleading the press. She has been caught on multiple occasions telling whoppers, often explaining this away as trying to "give the best information that I have." She, too, retaliated against CNN by refusing to call on us during the briefings. Instead of trying to repair the broken relationship with the press, she seemed to delight in it. She also continued the West Wing's practice of showing preference to conservative news outlets. Rather than holding briefings with reporters, Sarah turned to Fox News on a regular basis for less confrontational interviews. Returning from the Fox News live position on the North Lawn, she would be gracious enough to take a few questions from the rest of the White House press corps, which gathered to peck for any crumbs she'd leave on her way back to her office.

Oddly enough, Sarah was also once one of those veteran campaign operatives who generally got along with the press. We had all been out for drinks with her. She could throw back her Maker's and Coke with the best of them. Sarah was well known to reporters from her days working for her father, former Arkansas governor Mike Huckabee, who had mounted his own underdog presidential bid but lost in 2008 to John McCain. Huckabee once again flirted with a presidential run in 2012, but held back to make money over at Fox News. Perhaps the preference for Fox News, which for all intents and purposes, had become a state TV outlet for the White House, was in the blood.

Another veteran from the Huckabee presidential campaign days, South Carolina GOP operative Hogan Gidley, later went to work in the West Wing as Sarah's deputy. Hogan was also someone you could have a drink with. We got along pretty well when he worked for Rick Santorum's campaign in 2012. The Santorum people, including the candidate himself, thanked CNN for devoting much more coverage to their campaign than they were receiving from the other networks, which had assigned all their top correspondents to covering Mitt Romney. I had advocated for this approach behind the scenes, and my bosses agreed. You'd think that some of this would have accumulated some goodwill with Sarah and Hogan down the road. Unfortunately, that didn't happen.

Still, as Sarah came on board as Spicer's deputy, she was the press official who often came across as the less volatile voice of reason behind the scenes. Spicer would explode at us, and Sarah would tell folks how Sean was under a lot of pressure to smooth things over. She could also be candid in less formal settings. En route to Saudi Arabia during that first foreign trip, she told a bunch of reporters that she was hurt by *Saturday Night Live*'s depiction of her by an overweight comedian on the show. *SNL*'s first sketch about her described her as being the daughter of a "Southern hamburger."

"I don't even know what that means," Sarah complained, before downing a couple more drinks and sleeping for the rest of the flight. I remember feeling bad for her at the time.

Publicly, though, she was sending all the right signals to Trump that she was capable of misleading the press. A key case in point: On July 11, 2017, not long before Spicer resigned, publication of some of Donald Trump Jr.'s emails revealed that in June 2016, he, along with his brother-in-law Jared Kushner and Trump campaign chairman Paul Manafort, had met at Trump Tower with Natalia Veselnitskaya, a Russian attorney with ties to the Kremlin who was offering negative information about Hillary Clinton. But Trump and his team had engaged in a deception about that meeting, telling the *New York Times* in a statement that the meeting was actually about Russian adoptions, not the Clinton campaign. As we would later discover, Trump had dictated that misleading statement. This was another episode in the Russia investigation story that raised serious questions. Was a cover-up orchestrated to conceal the campaign's connections to a foreign adversary? It seems only natural to ask the question. If we hadn't pressed for answers, my goodness, we would be failing the American people.

But that's not what the public was initially told. After the emails became public, we were all pushing hard for the White House to provide some answers. In August 2017, Sarah insisted to the press that Trump had not dictated the statement when, in fact, he had. "He certainly didn't dictate [the statement], but he—like I said, he weighed in, offered suggestion [sic] like any father would do," she falsely claimed.

No matter what Special Counsel Robert Mueller would later conclude in his investigation, this was a clear example of the White House misleading the public, a part of a pattern of behavior that only fueled more interest in the Russia story. Getting caught in these misstatements, whether the falsehoods were intentional or not, just made things more complicated for the Trump team.

A memorable case in point for me came in December 2017, when she told me if I tried to ask a question of the president during a press availability (or "pool spray," as we call it), I might not be allowed into another such event. Now, keep in mind, a pool spray is not the same as a briefing or news conference. It involves fairly standard stuff: when the president signs a bill or executive order or meets with a foreign leader, at the conclusion of his remarks, members of the press have a chance to ask a question. The thinking behind pool sprays, which have been going on for decades during Republican and Democratic administrations, is that the president gets to spread his message at that particular moment and the press has an opportunity to ask off-the-cuff questions about the news of the day.

However, like so much in the Trump era, even these seemingly innocuous events had taken on far greater meaning. Much of this came from Trump himself, who often sets such a negative news agenda for himself that invariably the news of the day was, in part, spent dealing with his messaging from his early morning tweets. His tweets, usually composed and posted while he watched *Fox and Friends*, were often incendiary, offensive, and many times false. On this particular day, Trump had insulted New York Democratic senator Kirsten Gillibrand, a potential 2020 rival.

Here is Trump's tweet from the day Sarah threatened me, December 12, 2017:

@realDonaldTrump
Lightweight Senator Kirsten Gillibrand, a total flunky for Chuck Schumer and someone who would come to my office "begging" for campaign contributions not so long ago (and would do anything for them), is now in the ring fighting against Trump. Very disloyal to Bill & Crooked-USED!
8:03 AM-12 Dec 2017

As soon as he posted the tweet, the news cycle, as it often does, went bananas. Clearly, by saying Gillibrand would "do anything" for a campaign contribution, Trump was suggesting that the New York senator was somehow prostituting herself as a politician. Short of the most ardent Trump supporter, anyone could see that the president was obviously leveling a disgusting, sexist charge.

Later in the day, Trump was scheduled to sign a defense spending bill. And lo and behold, it was CNN's day to be in the White House TV pool.

Now, I would not have been doing my job as a member of the White House press corps, nor would I have been doing my job for the press pool, if I had not asked a question about his offensive tweet. Sanders knew exactly what I was about to do.

She walked right up to me. "Hey, can we talk?" she said.

"Sure," I responded.

Sarah explained that Trump was not in the mood to take questions. He was already pissed off that I had tried to ask questions at a previous pool spray.

Too bad, I countered. That's what we do.

Sarah then warned me that if I tried to ask a question, I might not be allowed into another photo opportunity. It was clearly a threat.

A few moments later, Trump entered the room. I emailed CNN president Jeff Zucker to let him know what had happened. His reply: don't be bullied. (In case you're wondering, Jeff, to his credit, has never tried to control what I do as a reporter. I can't say this about a lot of TV executives. That day, Jeff was simply trying to let me know that he had my back. Standing up to these guys, as he knows, isn't easy.)

So, I asked the question: "Mr. President, what did you mean when you said that Kirsten Gillibrand would do anything for a campaign contribution?"

Trump didn't respond, and that's okay; that's his prerogative. I could see he was furious. But the question had to be asked. The president's defenders can attack the press for shouting questions or being "rude," as Trump likes to say. But he doesn't get to fire off an inflammatory tweet or make an outrageous statement without some expectation of intense press coverage. Trump's tweet had continued to dominate the news cycle, and my question to him, in my view, indicated that there was still some semblance of accountability left in Washington.

If a penalty flag needs to be thrown in that pool spray, it should be for Sarah, not me. For starters, she shouldn't have threatened me. More importantly, it's not up to Sanders to decide which journalists represent the press pool at the "sprays." That's up to the news outlets that cover these events. Clearly, I thought, she was testing those boundaries.

Like Spicer, she wanted to let it be known that she believed her job was to protect the president. What she has never understood, though, is that the job of the press secretary is more than that. The job also includes working with the media. Yes, you have to make sure the president's message is delivered to the American people, but at its essence, the position requires a healthy respect for the mission of a free press. Reporters are a noisy, dysfunctional bunch of people. They are demanding and pretty distrustful of government. Yes, we respect the office of the presidency. Of course! That's why we believe it warrants so much scrutiny. At the end of the day, reporters simply want to write or broadcast a story that tells the American people what's going on in the White House, the United States, and the wider world. That's pretty much it. As soon as a press secretary understands that, the job should go much more smoothly. In my observation, it's a pretty straightforward position. Journalists have questions. Answer them. Reporters have deadlines. Help them meet them. Don't threaten us. And above all else, and as much as humanly possible, tell us the truth.

Like Spicer, Sanders never really understood any of this, so perhaps it's not surprising that my relationship with her continued to deteriorate. She once asked me via email if I had been "day drinking again." My response to her was "No, have you?"

———————

SANDERS DID TRY TO RETURN TO THE REGULAR ORDER OF THINGS during the on-camera briefings, which had been restored by Scaramucci, the single greatest accomplishment of his abbreviated tenure.

One of the other changes that came about after Sarah took over from Sean was that she would occasionally invite guests, senior officials from the administration, to chat with reporters about initiatives under way in the Trump White House. This quickly became one of the ways the White House tried to control the message at the briefings. These "mystery guests," as we called them, were often unannounced and gave the White House the ability to spend more time talking about a specific issue and less time taking our questions. Now, it's true that we had these sorts of briefings under Obama; and Sean brought in guests, too. But Sarah, as she was just getting started, did it more frequently.

The reporters would be gathered in the Briefing Room, anticipating that the press secretary would come out alone to take our questions. Then, instead, surprise! Out would come a Cabinet member or some other senior administration official to talk about a particular subject. Perhaps it would be the treasury secretary to talk about new sanctions on North Korea. On one notable occasion, it was the head of the Environmental Protection Agency, Scott Pruitt, to talk about the president's push to deregulate the very industries that polluted the environment.

Pruitt, who would later resign under an ethical cloud—he lived at a lobbyist's condo and once declared his desire to buy a mattress from the Trump Hotel in DC—and not for his hard-right environmental positions, clashed with reporters (including yours truly) over climate change during a briefing back in June 2017. I asked whether his head was "in the sand" on the issue.

"You know, people have called me a climate skeptic or a climate denier. I don't even know what it means to deny the climate. I would say that there are climate exaggerators," the EPA head told reporters at the briefing—

incredibly, given that he's widely recognized as a climate change denier. This was the kind of language used by energy industry lobbyists, not Cabinet secretaries working for a guy who had promised to "drain the swamp." Does gaslighting contribute to global warming? I digress.

A few weeks later, on June 28, 2017, we heard from the head of the border patrol, Thomas Homan, who fumbled to find an answer when I pressed him on whether undocumented immigrants committed more crimes than native-born Americans. Studies have shown that they don't. Homan tried to bolster his argument by noting that the undocumented commit crimes by crossing the border illegally. That's a misleading talking point.

"Aren't you concerned, though, about exacerbating fears about undocumented immigrants?" I asked. "You're making it sound as if undocumented immigrants commit more crimes than people who are just native-born Americans. . . . What is your sense of the numbers on this? Are undocumented people more likely or less likely to commit crimes?" I continued.

"Did I say aliens commit more crimes than U.S. citizens? I didn't say that," he replied. Homan, a holdover from the Obama administration, had clearly found himself right at home working for Trump. A senior administration official once described Homan to me as a "true believer" when it came to the hard-right positions of the anti-immigration think tanks in DC.

But it was Sanders who provided us with perhaps the most alarming of all the administration guests to waltz into the Briefing Room. Yes, I'm talking about Stephen Miller, the president's domestic policy and speechwriting guru, who had arrived to talk to us about his signature issue, immigration. Needless to say, anytime he spoke on the issue, I found myself recoiling from his words.

Miller came into the Briefing Room on August 2 to announce the new administration policy for cutting legal immigration by half. That's right. This was not a proposal to stop illegal immigration. Miller laid out how Trump wanted to sharply reduce the number of *legal* immigrants coming into the country. The administration, Miller told us, was proposing a merit or point system for those immigrants.

Speak fluent English? You receive more points than those applicants who aren't fluent. Other points are awarded if you have an advanced degree or even if you've won an Olympic medal.

As Stephen was going around the room and taking questions, it occurred to me that Trump, as he had in so many areas, was attempting to do more than just alter U.S. immigration policy. He was trying to change the very nature of America. For generations, the United States has welcomed people from all walks of life, all education levels, all races, colors, creeds, and religious backgrounds. That's what makes America . . . America.

Other countries have done what Stephen was proposing. That's fine. But those countries aren't the United States.

Now, at the time of this briefing, Trump's immigration policies weren't in the news every day, but I'd never stopped being bothered by them. Like Trump's proposal to build a wall on the border with Mexico (that Mexico had declared it would never pay for), his legal immigration reform plan seemed driven primarily by a prejudice particularly against newcomers to the United States who were not white. Listening to Stephen take questions, I wanted to challenge him not on the bullet points of the plan, but on the motivations behind it. My thought was that Trump's RAISE (Reforming American Immigration for Strong Employment) Act was uniquely un-American.

I didn't intend to confront Miller in any dramatic way, I simply wanted to ask him my question. As the briefing dragged on, I wondered if he would even call on me, but finally he did, on the final question. Stephen, who fancies himself something of a scholar on far-right immigration policy, engaged with the glee of a debate team captain.

All of a sudden the Briefing Room became a debate room. I held up what I felt was Exhibit A in the defense of America as a welcoming nation to immigrants: the Statue of Liberty.

> ACOSTA: What you're proposing here, what the president's proposing here does not sound like it's in keeping with American tradition when it comes to immigration. The Statue of Liberty says, "Give me your tired, your poor, your huddled masses yearning to breathe free." It doesn't say anything about speaking English or being able to be a computer programmer. Aren't you trying to change what it means to be an immigrant coming into this country if you're telling them, you have to speak English? Can't people learn how to speak English when they get here?
>
> MILLER: Well, first of all, right now, it's a requirement that to be naturalized you have to speak English. So the notion that speaking English wouldn't be a part of immigration systems would be actually very ahistorical. Secondly, I don't want to get off into a whole thing about history here, but the Statue of Liberty is a symbol of liberty and light in the world. It's a symbol of American liberty lighting the world. The poem that you're referring [to] that was added later is not actually a part of the original Statue of Liberty. But more fundamentally, the history . . .

I told Stephen I thought he was engaging in some "National Park revisionism."

Now, there are times of course when, for a reporter, it's better not to engage. Perhaps this was one of those times, but I felt I had to try to strip away Miller's rhetoric, as he seemed intent on painting a negative picture of undocumented immigrants and sometimes even immigration at every turn. I hadn't wanted to debate the policy in front of the whole press corps; I'd just wanted an answer to my question. Instead, Miller had opted for a debate.

Over the next several minutes, Stephen and I ended up going on at some length about what the Statue of Liberty represented in terms of numbers of legal immigrants, language requirements, and, more broadly, what was behind the larger policy of the Trump administration. My point to Stephen that day was that from the campaign trail to the Oval Office, the administration had repeatedly, consistently come across as hostile to immigrants. After years of racially loaded rhetoric around immigrants, its motivations around immigration policy would always be suspect.

If you look at the criteria Stephen was laying out—and feel free to look this up—there appeared to be an intention to put a premium on immigrants coming to the United States from more Anglocentric countries. As Miller laid out in the Briefing Room that day, immigrants coming from parts of the developing world would be at a serious disadvantage in the new Trump/Miller legal immigration system. The Irish, Italians, Germans, and Russians who sailed under the Statue of Liberty and up to Ellis Island were hardly fluent in English when they arrived on America's shores. So, what are we saying when we establish such criteria after those immigrants have been assimilated into the United States? I'll tell you what we're saying—or, at least, I'll tell you what the Stephen Millers of the world are saying: they are rolling up the welcome mat and telling the rest of the planet that people of color need not apply. Stephen, you could argue, was simply putting it in plain English.

One interesting moment in our exchange came when Miller, after being challenged on these points, lobbed what appeared to be a fresh line of attack. According to him, I was revealing my "cosmopolitan bias." What in the world is a "cosmopolitan bias," you ask? It is as bizarre to me now as it was then, but it is not an unfamiliar term. As it turns out, the term *cosmopolitan* was used by Joseph Stalin to purge anti-Soviet critics in the USSR. Former CNN anchor Jeff Greenfield wrote a piece about this slur in Politico, in which he unearthed this quote from Stalin: "the positive Soviet hero is derided and inferior before all things foreign and cosmopolitanism that we all fought against from the time of Lenin, characteristic of the political leftovers, is many times applauded."

"Enemy of the people?" "Cosmopolitan bias?" Anybody else see a pattern here?

The "cosmopolitans," Greenfield writes, were academics, writers, scientists, and often Jewish. Miller is from a Jewish family, so I hardly think he is espousing anti-Semitic views. Still, white supremacists, nationalists, and neo-Nazis who make up the "alt-right" have all adopted the term *cosmopolitan* when speaking of the opposing side. ThinkProgress uncovered passages from former Ku Klux Klan grand wizard David Duke railing against "cosmopolitan" views that Israel be a "Jewish-only state." The term was also employed by the anti-immigration forces at VDARE, a white nationalist group that describes the battle over immigration as "an ideological split between cosmopolitan elites who see immigration as a common good based in universal rights and voters who see it as a gift conferred on certain outsiders deemed worthy of joining the community." As noted in Volker Ullrich's book *Hitler: Ascent, 1889–1939, cosmopolitan* was an anti-Semitic term "used against the Jews by Nazis and Bolsheviks alike" who were "considered not only cosmopolitan, but also rootless, and in the late 1940s the term became a code word for Jews who insisted on their Jewish identity."

Time and again, before Miller used the insult, references to the term *cosmopolitan bias* appear in far-right literature as an attack on proponents of multiculturalism, tolerance of minorities, and diversity. Perhaps it's just a coincidence that Miller hurled that epithet at me during the White House briefing, but I think not. Miller is exceedingly fluent in the language of anti-immigration zealots. He has been advocating their ideas, their proposals, and their worldview for years.

Even without being accused of having a cosmopolitan bias, I found the conversation around the Statue of Liberty particularly troubling. Lady Liberty is such a powerful image for all Americans, one that lies at the heart of how we view ourselves and how, for generations, the world has viewed us. My father didn't travel to America by ship, sailing below the Statue of Liberty, as so many immigrants did decades ago, and he wasn't processed through Ellis Island, but he was welcomed into this new country. Were there people who were rude to him and my grandmother (who spoke little English) when they first arrived and at times during the years that followed? Sure, of course. All immigrants endure that. Still, my father was certainly not painted with a broad brush by the president of the United States as part of a community of "rapists" and criminals flooding into the country.

Moreover, Miller's alternative facts on Lady Liberty were insulting to a disturbing degree. Just go to the National Park Service website for the Statue of Liberty. There's a page dedicated to Lady Liberty entitled "The Immigrant's Statue." There you can find photo after photo of boats teeming with immigrants coming into New York Harbor, beaming with hope for their future in a new country. Italian, Irish, and other European immigrants are seen holding the hands of their children as they arrive on America's shores. Towering above them is, of course, Lady Liberty.

The poem "The New Colossus," by Emma Lazarus, still resonates today:

Not like the brazen giant of Greek fame,
With conquering limbs astride from land to land;
Here at our sea-washed, sunset gates shall stand
A mighty woman with a torch, whose flame
Is the imprisoned lightning, and her name
Mother of Exiles. From her beacon-hand

Glows world-wide welcome; her mild eyes command
The air-bridged harbor that twin cities frame.
"Keep, ancient lands, your storied pomp!" cries she
With silent lips. "Give me your tired, your poor,
Your huddled masses yearning to breathe free,
The wretched refuse of your teeming shore.
Send these, the homeless, tempest-tost to me,
I lift my lamp beside the golden door!"

Miller is right that the poem was mounted not on the statue itself, but inside the pedestal's lower level, but let's get the history right here. Lazarus, herself the child of Portuguese Jewish immigrants, wrote the sonnet in 1883 to raise money for the construction of a pedestal for the statue. According to the National Park Service website, the chairman of the statue project commissioned Lazarus's work. In 1903 the poem was added to Lady Liberty, immediately transforming the statue into a symbol for immigrants coming to America. Regardless of when the poem was added, the larger meaning of its inclusion on the statue remains the same.

It was astonishing to sit in that Briefing Room as Stephen Miller pretended his administration was not motivated by racially prejudiced attitudes toward immigrants. Of course it is. A senior administration official who worked in both national security and on the issue of immigration once told me that Miller's zeal to roll back the flow of migrants into the United States was indeed colored by his own personal beliefs. Stephen "didn't hide his hatred," the senior Homeland Security official told me privately. "It bled into all of the White House policies." Stephen did not respond to my requests to discuss this.

Similar to my exchanges with Spicer, confronting Stephen required a shift in strategy. Unorthodox tactics, such as reading a poem from the Statue of Liberty, sometimes do a better job of getting to the heart of the matter than asking the boilerplate policy-based questions. Go ahead and try to ask the question directly: Stephen, isn't this a racist policy? He's not going to bite at that apple. But poke the stick in places he's not expecting, and you might throw him off his game and perhaps prompt a candid remark that reveals everything.

A couple of weeks later, Sarah Sanders was briefing reporters on Air Force One when she noted that it was Stephen Miller's birthday. She joked that he was hoping for a text from Jim Acosta. To show, once again, that there were no hard feelings, I sent him a text and wished him a happy birthday. He immediately wrote back, "Thanks!"

For the record, I would debate Miller anytime anywhere on the subject of immigration—not because I have a passion for flooding America with immigrants from south of the border, as the xenophobes would have you believe. (Miller accused me at that briefing of being in favor of "open borders," a tactic used by anti-immigration zealots. Nothing could be further from the truth.) I would do it because the president of the United States of America and the people who work at the White House should always be champions for our nation's immigrants. That's the American way, even if it's not Trump's way, or Stephen's.

Like my confrontations with Trump, my exchange with Stephen Miller struck a nerve with the public. Yes, the death threats once again rolled in, but so did gestures of gratitude. One CNN viewer sent me a T-shirt depicting the Statue of Liberty and featuring Emma Lazarus's poem. Another viewer sent me a children's book about Lady Liberty's true meaning. Despite an official attempt from the White House to change the significance of this enduring symbol of American freedom, the people at home weren't fooled. So many Americans, I was reminded, were on the side of truth and tolerance. In the days that followed, I met Indian Americans, Arab Americans, Latinos, and Asian Americans, all of whom thanked me for standing up for the immigrant story that had come to define

America. My encounters with them have stayed with me. Sounds corny, I know, but they believe in the America I grew up learning about. They believe in the America I believe in, an America for all of us. We are and should always remain a beacon of hope, the brightest light in the universe.

7

Charlottesville

For the first six months of Trump's presidency, life for the White House press corps was a bit like the movie *Groundhog Day*—no matter what happened the day before, you would wake up and realize that Trump was still president, the world was still a mess, and we were covering it all, over and over again. Patterns began to emerge. The Trump tweets, hyperbolic, misspelled, and factually challenged, would come in the morning, throwing off the news cycle. Then there was usually some kind of media session with Trump during which he would attack an adversary, real or imagined, and the narrative of the day would change again, leaving Spicer, Sanders, and the mystery guest at the Briefing Room podium to parrot falsehoods or worse to the American public. Looking back on some of this now, I see that it was all rather predictable, an odd thing to say given Trump's frequent ability to shock the free world.

It was because of this strange rhythm, which normalized Trump's extreme and unpredictable behavior, that everyone immediately saw the profound and disturbing implications of what unfolded during August 2017. Words, of course, do matter, a lot—a lesson this country would learn over and over again that August.

It began on August 11. Trump had spent the first part of the day drumming up another confrontation with North Korea, which, troubling as it was, seemed largely on a par with what he'd been saying recently. Later that night, roughly twelve hours after he'd sent a tweet informing North Korea that America was "locked and loaded" (after first warning Kim Jong-un that he would be subjected to "fire and fury"), darkness fell on the tiny city of Charlottesville, Virginia, save for the dozens of torch-wielding white supremacists, neo-Nazis, KKK members, and other extremists from the nascent "alt-right" movement in America who were marching across the campus of the University of Virginia. These American fascists, who seemed to have come out of nowhere, had gathered for what they called a "Unite the Right" rally, which had been organized to protest the removal of a statue dedicated to the confederate war hero Robert E. Lee. The marchers carried Tiki torches and chanted such neo-Nazi slogans as "Jews will not replace us," "Blood and soil," and "White lives matter," before encircling the statue of Thomas Jefferson on the UVA campus.

At the statue, they brawled with counterprotesters, some with the antifascist movement known as Antifa. The cops came in and broke up the violence, at least for the night. There was no mistaking the images beaming out of Charlottesville and going viral around the world in a matter of seconds. A new face of hatred and evil had emerged in America.

The next day, on August 12, the Unite the Right demonstrators, many armed with weapons thanks to Virginia's loose firearms laws, returned to Lee's statue ready to do battle again, this time with deadly consequences. Carrying Confederate flags, and in some cases wearing red MAGA hats, the neo-Nazis and white nationalists fought again with counterprotesters on the streets of Charlottesville.

Then, in one horrific moment captured on video, a car driven by a white supremacist plowed into a group of people demonstrating against the extremists, killing a thirty-two-year-old woman named

Heather Heyer. She had gone to the rally to speak out against the fascists. Nearly twenty other counterdemonstrators were injured. The driver, a twenty-year-old self-described Nazi sympathizer named James Alex Fields Jr., was charged with Heyer's murder. The day would claim two other lives in the area when two Virginia State Police officers were killed as their helicopter crashed after being deployed to bring order to Charlottesville.

Having grown up in Virginia, I couldn't believe what had happened in my home state. Yes, the state was once the heart of the Confederacy, but the Virginia of my childhood and college days had evolved into a multiracial and much more moderate place. Indeed, it was a point of pride for me that it was home to the nation's first elected African American governor, Douglas Wilder. My high school in the DC suburb of Annandale, Virginia, had actually been very diverse. Situated outside the nation's capital but just inside the Beltway, Annandale High School boasted a student body of just about every race, creed, and color. My classmates all got along pretty well.

Yet I can still remember debating the root causes of the Civil War as a student at James Madison University, a college named after one of America's founding fathers, who was also a slave owner. I can remember some of my classmates arguing that the War Between the States was the result of "Northern aggression," while I took the view that the conflict was due in large part to the South's unwillingness to give up its dependence on slave labor.

Later, as a young reporter, I witnessed events that demonstrated pretty clearly that America had not sufficiently dealt with the issue of race. I once covered a neo-Nazi march while working at Chicago's CBS station, WBBM-TV. The neo-Nazis were nothing more than a bunch of racist thugs looking for a fight and brawling with the police. At the time, I thought, these guys hardly warranted the coverage. It was a dying ideology, in my view, destined to fade away with time.

But during the Obama administration, it was clear that the ghosts of the twentieth century hadn't fully been laid to rest. The election of the first African American president gave rise to the Tea Party, the fiscally conservative political movement within the Republican Party. Its members claimed to be devoted solely to the elimination of the national debt and opposed to bailouts handed out during the 2008 financial crisis. How did that work out? Well, as soon as they controlled the White House and Congress, the Republican Party went right back to deficit spending, handing out lavish tax cuts to the rich, just as they had done during the George W. Bush administration. What I witnessed time and again covering Tea Party rallies and marches was an outburst of racist imagery on signs and T-shirts; one sign at a Tea Party march depicted Obama and Pelosi in bed with each other.

One of the ringleaders in the long opposition to Obama's presidency, of course, was a New York businessman and TV star named Donald J. Trump, who had led the struggle to cast doubt on Obama's American citizenship, known as the birther movement. Trump, who pushed the envelope on the issue of race in the late 1980s when he called for the death penalty for five minority teenagers in the Central Park Five case (they were convicted and later exonerated), eventually soared to political stardom as he demanded to see Obama's birth certificate, once claiming he had sent private investigators to Hawaii to find out if the forty-fourth president was born in Honolulu. Trump's investigation never produced any proof that Obama was from Kenya, Indonesia, or wherever. It was all a sham. One of the key under-reported stories of the 2016 campaign was Trump's refusal to talk about his past birtherism. A former Trump campaign official told me that Trump knew the birther story was bogus but didn't want to admit it, something he finally did in September 2016.

But Trump remained a beloved figure among the fringe, race-baiting segment of the far right. So, it was no surprise when neo-Nazis, white supremacists, and other members of the alt-right gathered in

Washington less than two weeks after Trump's election to declare that their movement of hatred had been reborn.

"Hail Trump, hail our people, hail victory," exclaimed movement leader Richard Spencer, one of the organizers of the Unite the Right march in Charlottesville. Was Trump responsible for this disgusting spectacle? No, not directly, but whether he liked it or not, his rise to power had emboldened these dark forces, according to experts who study extremist groups. Trump's birther chickens had come home to roost.

Trump, who was on vacation in New Jersey during the unrest in Charlottesville, delivered a brief statement on the violence. The same president who had won the White House by employing racially loaded rhetoric, from spreading the "birther" lie about Barack Obama to slandering Mexican immigrants as "rapists," was all of a sudden thrust into the position of calming a nation terrified by racist thugs on the march in Virginia.

There is really no other way to put it except to say that in the moments that followed, Trump failed to ease the public's concerns. In his first remarks on the violence in Charlottesville, he appeared to blame both the white supremacists and the counterprotesters equally.

"We condemn in the strongest possible terms this egregious display of hatred, bigotry and violence on many sides, on many sides," Trump said. "It has been going on for a long time in our country—not Donald Trump, not Barack Obama. It has been going on for a long, long time. It has no place in America."

His "many sides" comment was not an accidental slip of the tongue. If you go back and watch the video, Trump pauses dramatically and repeats the words "many sides." He wanted to make it clear that, as far as he was concerned, there was blame to go all around, never mind the fact that there were neo-Nazis and Klan members on one of those sides.

It was jarring to hear this kind of equivocation. Had Trump made this statement as a private citizen, I'm not sure many people would

have cared. But it was surreal and disturbing coming from the mouth
of the leader of the free world. No modern president from the post–
World War II era had ever made such a statement. Trump wasn't
bringing calm to the situation, I thought. More than he had during
the campaign, he was revealing who he was. There was no base to
placate or excite in the hours after Charlottesville. This was a moment
for leadership, not more pandering.

Here we had the president of the United States failing to adequately
condemn neo-Nazis and Klansmen who had felt comfortable enough
to march across an American city, Thomas Jefferson's hometown no
less, and create a violent spectacle so heinous that, by the time it was
over, a young woman was dead in the street. It was the most disturbing moment of Trump's presidency to date, and yet, to anyone who
had followed his campaign or attended his rallies, it should have come
as no surprise. While no one could have predicted the specific horrors
of Charlottesville, the seeds of this spectacle were there during the
campaign, and in the months since his election, there was ample evidence that these newly resilient pockets of American bigotry had only
grown more empowered.

Trump's initial response to the Charlottesville tragedy immediately
resurrected other memories from his poor record on race during the
2016 campaign. There was the time when he equivocated over whether
he should reject the endorsement of former KKK grand wizard David
Duke, before finally telling reporters, "I disavow." Then there was the
controversy over his comments about the Mexican American judge
who was handling the investigation into Trump University, the then-
candidate's failed for-profit real estate business program that had
fleeced students. And who could forget Trump tweeting out an image of Hillary Clinton surrounded by a pile of money, next to which
appeared to be the Star of David? Trump's social media director, Dan
Scavino, said at the time that it was a "sheriff's star," not an attempt to
use anti-Semitic imagery.

Of course, there were also cringe-worthy moments from Trump's supporters themselves. At one rally in Kissimmee, Florida, my colleagues and I watched as two men hung a Confederate flag with "Trump 2016" printed on it. It took Trump's security about thirty minutes to convince the two men to take it down. After the rally ended, an irate Trump supporter walked up to my colleagues and gave them the middle finger, screaming, "I am a patriot! And your name is 'traitor.'" Confederate flags kept on appearing over and over at Trump rallies. There was raw hatred pouring out of these events, day in and day out on the Trump campaign trail.

Sensing the gravity of the moment, leaders from both parties immediately blasted Trump's response. To counter the bipartisan condemnation, the White House released a statement, via an anonymous official too cowardly to put his or her name to it, that shamelessly parroted Trump's disgusting reaction to Charlottesville.

"The President was condemning hatred, bigotry and violence from all sources and all sides. There was violence between protesters and counter-protesters today," the official said.

Offered a chance to do cleanup, the White House instead doubled down on Trump's comments. There was no going back. Trump had crossed a line and, in my view, permanently damaged his presidency. And he wasn't done.

———————

TWO DAYS LATER, ON AUGUST 14, TRUMP TRIED AGAIN. STUNG BY the intense criticism he had received in response to his remarks immediately following the violence in Charlottesville, he addressed the nation. I was in the pool that day, as it was CNN's day to represent the TV networks. The press gathered in the Diplomatic Room of the White House, where we awaited the president's latest comments. The story, of course, was whether Trump would strongly condemn the white supremacists behind the melee in Charlottesville, as he should have done from the very beginning. Reading from prepared remarks, he did just that:

"Racism is evil. And those who cause violence in its name are crim- inals and thugs, including the KKK, neo-Nazis, white supremacists, and other hate groups that are repugnant to everything we hold dear as Americans," he said to the nation.

Later in the day, Trump held a separate event where he called for an investigation into Chinese trade practices. Still in the pool for that afternoon, I asked him about the contrast between his remarks from earlier in the day and his initial response to what had happened in Charlottesville over the weekend.

"Can you explain why you did not condemn those hate groups by name over the weekend," I asked.

"They've been condemned. They have been condemned," he replied.

I then followed up and asked why he wasn't holding a press confer- ence on Monday, as he had promised that previous Friday, before the events in Charlottesville.

"We just had a press conference," he answered.

"Could we ask you some more questions?" I inquired.

"It doesn't bother me at all, but I like real news, not fake news," he said, and then pointed at me. "You're fake news."

"Mr. President, haven't you spread a lot of fake news yourself, sir?" I responded.

Ah, the old "fake news" line. It was back. I've learned that's become one of his "tells." Like a poker player, Trump has a tell, giving away what kind of hand he's holding. If he's screaming about "fake news," he's almost always losing. And he was losing on Charlottesville. Trump clearly didn't like the fact that he had been compelled by his advisers to revise his botched response to Charlottesville. That was as bad, in his view, as admitting a mistake. And in Trumpworld, as I've been told time and again by his advisers, you don't admit mistakes. You double down on everything, even the stuff you did wrong.

Which brings us to his third crack at commenting on the events in Charlottesville, this time at Trump Tower in Manhattan. Trump had traveled to his office tower and residence in the city to meet with some of the top officials in his administration about the need to upgrade the nation's infrastructure. Treasury Secretary Steve Mnuchin, Transportation Secretary Elaine Chao, Office of Management and Budget director Mick Mulvaney, Trump's chief economic adviser, Gary Cohn, and a new member of the team, Chief of Staff John Kelly (who had just replaced Reince Priebus), were all in attendance.

After what had occurred the day before, I traveled up to New York with the hunch that Trump would not be able to help himself and would dive back into the Charlottesville issue. As we had so often during the campaign, we gathered in the gold-plated lobby of Trump Tower to await Trump. It felt like old times. (It should be noted that his aides told us in advance that he wouldn't take any questions.) Trump came down the elevator, made some remarks about his hopes for an infrastructure bill, and before he could turn to exit the lobby, a question on Charlottesville was shouted his way by my NBC colleague Hallie Jackson, and we were off to the races.

It is still stunning to read the president's remarks from that day. As of this writing, remarkably, they remain on the official White House website. In them, Trump returned to blaming both sides for the violence in Charlottesville. And that's when I jumped in, mainly because I couldn't believe what I was hearing.

TRUMP: Yes, I think there's blame on both sides. If you look at both sides—I think there's blame on both sides. And I have no doubt about it, and you don't have any doubt about it either. And if you reported it accurately, you would say.
ACOSTA: The neo-Nazis started this. They showed up in Charlottesville to protest—

TRUMP: Excuse me, excuse me. They didn't put themselves—and you
had some very bad people in that group, but you also had people that
were very fine people, on both sides. You had people in that group.
ACOSTA: No sir, there are no fine people in the Nazis.

As you may have noticed, I didn't put my questions in question
form. That wasn't necessary in this case, and here's why. I suppose I
could have asked him, "Sir, isn't it true that there aren't any fine
people in the Nazis?" But that would have suggested that this notion
was open to debate. I'm sorry, but there aren't two sides when it comes
to Nazis. I think we have reached the point where we can state, definitively, that Nazis are bad people. It kind of goes without saying. But I
will: If you are a Nazi, you aren't a fine person. You're bad. So, yes, I
felt well within the safe bounds of reporting to state back to the president "there are no fine people in the Nazis." When it's a matter of right
versus wrong, there are not two sides to the story.

There's another point to be made here, one going back to the idea
that a different kind of president requires a different kind of press. If
a president is trying to bully his way through some tough questions,
interrupting and shouting, "Excuse me excuse me," what do you, as a
reporter, do? This is when it's probably time to throw out the old rule-
book. Trump was likely not going to candidly volunteer a comment
that there are "very fine people" on both sides had I not challenged
him. Sometimes the sparring he craves can be his own undoing;
that's when he often shows who he really is. And at that bizarre news
conference at Trump Tower, that's exactly what he did.

In responding to Trump's attacks, my thinking is you have to be
measured and choose the right moment. Opinions vary as to whether
I have met that standard, but there are very clear moments when challenging the president's thinking is the right choice. Who am I to judge
when his thought process goes off the deep end? I think that's fairly
obvious. Whether it's an attack on the press or a blatant lie about policy

or a betrayal of American principles (e.g., that Nazis are the scum of the earth), a more restrained reaction from a reporter sets a precedent that what has been said is now acceptable in our democracy. The same goes for the president's unrelenting assault on journalists in America. Yes, Trump's attacks on the press are designed, for the moment, to elicit a response. And yes, that response excites parts of his base. And yes, the Trump people sit back and say, "See? It works." And yes, some news editors say, "See, that's why we shouldn't respond." But Trump's apologists and propagandists are going to go on the attack and make our lives miserable no matter what we report. That's what they do. If we tailor our coverage to appease them, we've already lost. Their reaction shouldn't change the essential calculus that attacks on the press, if left unanswered, are just going to get worse. So, the question becomes: do you take the bait or take the knife?

More often than not, I opt for the bait, which bothers some people—both in the media and in the White House. But to those critics, I ask: does every president lie and attack the press as Trump does? No. As new presidents come along and return a state of normalcy to dealings with the news media, will there be as great a need to stand up for ourselves? Of course not. Playbooks for individual journalists and news organizations will be adjusted accordingly, as we will no longer be under attack.

After our exchange about "very fine people" that day in Trump Tower, Trump then tried to change the subject back to the grievance that drew the Unite the Right protesters to Charlottesville in the first place, the removal of the statue of Robert E. Lee. When it came to sides, guess which one Trump chose? The president said in all seriousness that somehow George Washington would be next, as if federal workers would dismantle the Washington Monument.

TRUMP: Excuse me, excuse me. I saw the same pictures as you did. You had people in that group that were there to protest the taking down of, to them, a very, very important statue and the renaming of a park from Robert E. Lee to another name.

ACOSTA: George Washington and Robert E. Lee are not the same.

TRUMP: George Washington was a slave owner. Was George Washington a slave owner? So will George Washington now lose his status? Are we going to take down—Excuse me, are we going to take down statues to George Washington? How about Thomas Jefferson? What do you think of Thomas Jefferson? You like him?

A few moments after that "very fine people" comment, Trump tried to clean up his mess by adding a bit of a disclaimer. "I'm not talking about the neo-Nazis and the white nationalists, because they should be condemned totally," he said. "But you had many people in that group other than neo-Nazis and white nationalists, okay? And the press has treated them absolutely unfairly."

The president's defenders like to point to this final comment as an exoneration of his performance on Charlottesville. I call bullshit. In my view, a president of the United States should get this right the first time. It shouldn't take four or five (or whatever number we are on) tries to get it right. Within a matter of four days, Trump had equivocated on the violence in Charlottesville, reversed himself to condemn the fascists, only to pull another about-face on the issue, basically landing where he had started, essentially siding with the white nationalists who had touched off the violence. The epic fail at Trump Tower was written all over John Kelly's face as the chief of staff hung his head in full view of the cameras.

As I told anchor Don Lemon that night on *CNN Tonight*, "I think the president showed his true colors today. And I'm not sure they were red, white and blue." This time, Trump's revolting behavior had finally rocked his own party, destabilizing his presidency. A senior GOP congressional aide told me that night that Trump's ability to govern was "diminishing." Still, the president was able to weather the storm as he often does, weakened and damaged, but still standing.

Senior officials inside the West Wing were telling reporters that they were appalled by Trump's behavior. One aide questioned why Trump was allowed to go back out in front of reporters at Trump Tower, a setting where he wouldn't be able to resist the urge to engage with reporters. The aide told me I must have known I would have a confrontation with Trump the minute he arrived in the lobby. Honestly, I didn't. But this official had assumed, as soon as he saw me, that a battle would ensue.

Two days after the Trump Tower debacle, the president found a way both to change the news cycle and to tamp down some of the blistering criticism of his handling of Charlottesville. He fired his chief strategist, a hero of the white nationalist movement in the United States, Steve Bannon. This was no small ball move on Trump's part. Firing Bannon was a huge deal. While he had come on board the Trump team toward the end of the 2016 cycle, Bannon was seen at the time as one of the key voices of the growing nationalist movement in America, having been at the helm of the ultraconservative Breitbart website. Bannon encouraged Trump to continue to rail against immigration, free trade, and journalists—indeed, Bannon had once called the press "the opposition party" and helped Trump come up with the "enemy of the people." (Note to the reader: Bannon privately loved the press and chatted with reporters on background all the time, conversations he used to knife his adversaries in the West Wing.)

Bannon's firing came at a curious, almost too-convenient moment for Trump. After Bannon was let go, one White House official told me that the plan inside the West Wing had been to oust the conservative firebrand two weeks prior to his forced departure. That would have coincided with the hiring of John Kelly, who was already imposing discipline on Trump's chaotic operation and cleaning house, having dispatched with Anthony Scaramucci. Whereas Priebus had an open-door policy, allowing Trump's buddies to visit him whenever they wanted, Kelly was restricting access to the usual suspects. This was not good for Bannon, who had plenty of enemies inside the White House. Trump hated the perception that Bannon was the real brains behind the scenes inside the White House. Republican strategists suspected that Bannon's firing was a kind of emergency vaccination for the poisonous atmosphere Trump had created.

"White House Chief of Staff John Kelly and Steve Bannon have mutually agreed today would be Steve's last day. We are grateful for his service and wish him the best," Sarah Sanders said in a statement.

Bannon let it be known that he felt betrayed, going as far as to tell *The Weekly Standard* that Trump's presidency was "over."

There was almost one other high-profile departure in the days after Trump's remarks on Charlottesville. The president's top economic adviser, Gary Cohn, who is Jewish and was at Trump Tower for that disastrous news conference, told the *Financial Times* on August 25, about two weeks after the neo-Nazi violence that led to the murder of Heather Heyer, that he was under "enormous pressure" to leave the administration.

"I have come under enormous pressure both to resign and to remain in my current position. As a patriotic American, I am reluctant to leave my post as director of the National Economic Council because I feel a duty to fulfill my commitment to work on behalf of the American people. But I also feel compelled to voice my distress over the events of the last two weeks. Citizens standing up for equality and freedom can never be equated with white supremacists, neo-Nazis, and the KKK. I believe this administration can and must do better in consistently and unequivocally condemning these groups and do everything we can to heal the deep divisions that exist in our communities. As a Jewish American, I will not allow neo-Nazis ranting, 'Jews will not replace us' to cause this Jew to leave his job. I feel deep empathy for all who have been targeted by these hate groups. We must all unite together against them," Cohn told the *Financial Times*.

It was an extraordinarily candid takedown of Trump's response to Charlottesville. It was rare to hear a current White House official criticize any sitting president in this fashion. Sure, officials leave and say all sorts of things. But typically, White House staffers bite their lip when it comes to criticizing the boss. Cohn's candor was striking. He told the *Financial Times* that his decision to stay was not influenced by Bannon's firing, and in another stark admission, he suggested that others in the administration, namely, Deputy National Security Advisor Dina Powell, were struggling with how to react to Trump's inadequate response to the frightening rise of white supremacy in America.

"This is a personal issue for each of us—we are all grappling with it—this takes time to grapple with," he said.

My colleagues Sara Murray with CNN and Maggie Haberman with the *New York Times* were both reporting that Cohn strongly considered resigning in the aftermath of Charlottesville. But one source told Murray that Cohn did not really come close to stepping down. Once again, in the hall of mirrors of the Trump White House, the truth seemed elusive. A senior White House official later scoffed at the notion that Cohn was serious about resigning. "Some people were trying to make themselves look good at the country club," the official deadpanned. Was Cohn just trying to save his reputation by speaking out against Trump? The following March, he would leave the administration after losing a major battle with Trump over his plans to impose tariffs on key U.S. trading partners. So, he felt it necessary to leave over a trade dispute but not over Charlottesville? That's puzzling.

As it turned out, Bannon's firing was the only significant departure to come in the fallout after Charlottesville. Stop for a moment and think about that. It is stunning. Almost two years after the events of

Charlottesville, a key question remains: what would have happened to Trump's presidency had other officials searched their consciences and resigned in protest over the president's remarks? Wouldn't that have been a powerful message to send to the country and the world? We will never know, because it didn't happen.

Likewise, most Republicans outside the administration, nearly united in their cowardice, stood firm in their refusal to confront the president. This sad chapter only reinforced the recognition that the Republican Party, the party of Lincoln, had become Trump's latest real estate acquisition. As so many GOP strategists have privately conceded to me, in latching on to Trump, their fellow Republicans were compromising their own principles. While this had been true for months, Charlottesville etched it in stone. The rhetoric and behavior exhibited by the president and too many of his supporters, and quietly accepted by too many Republicans during the campaign, during the transition, and during the Trump administration, had finally been realized in horrific Technicolor.

An inescapable lesson from the rise of Trump is that hatred left unchecked and unchallenged, even in the twenty-first century, can have terrible consequences. Over the first eight months of Trump's administration, Republicans had shown time and time again that they were willing to abdicate their role as a check on the president, and once again, that left the media in this vacuum. For all our mistakes, it was moments like Charlottesville that reminded me of the role we in the press had to play.

The stakes were indeed high, and growing higher by the day, particularly because Trump spent the next weeks and months trying to rewrite the history we had all just lived, as he began to gaslight the public about Charlottesville. In a fiery speech at a rally of supporters in Phoenix on August 23, around the time Cohn told the *Financial Times* he had come under pressure to resign, Trump lied about his initial Charlottesville remarks. And not surprisingly, he blamed the media for misreporting what he had said. Trump's ladder out of the hell he had created for himself, once again, was his continuing war against the press.

"So the—and I mean truly dishonest people in the media and the fake media, they make up stories. They have no sources in many cases. They say 'a source says'—there is no such thing," Trump told the crowd in Phoenix. "But they don't report the facts. Just like they don't want to report that I spoke out forcefully against hatred, bigotry and violence and strongly condemned the neo-Nazis, the White Supremacists, and the KKK."

Trump, as he is prone to do, was projecting, accusing the media of misreporting what had happened when, in fact, it was he who was misleading the public. He then attempted to rewrite history as he recalled his version of events from August 12.

"So here's what I said, really fast, here's what I said on Saturday: 'We're closely following the terrible events unfolding in Charlottesville, Virginia'—this is me speaking. 'We condemn in the strongest, possible terms this egregious display of hatred, bigotry and violence.' That's me speaking on Saturday."

Notice anything missing? Trump completely left out the fact that he said "many sides" were to blame for what had happened in Charlottesville. He also said that on that Saturday. Had his response been flawless, why did he leave that out?

Later on, in September, on a flight aboard Air Force One, after viewing hurricane damage in Florida, Trump again defended his handling of the violence in Charlottesville. Even after a few weeks of reflection, he had not changed his mind on what had happened. He stayed true only to the creed of Trumpworld: admit no mistakes. When pressed on the errors of his ways, Trump predictably doubled down again. He insisted that the anti-fascist protesters in Charlottesville were also to blame for the violence.

"You look at really what's happened since Charlottesville, a lot of people are saying and people have actually written, 'Gee, Trump might have a point.' I said, 'You've got some very bad people on the other side also,' which is true," he told reporters.

In October, Senator Sherrod Brown, an Ohio Democrat, made some news on CNN by accusing members of the White House of having sympathies for the alt-right. Brown was echoing a broadside from Democratic congresswoman Frederica Wilson, who, after a fight with John Kelly over Trump's treatment of a widow of a fallen soldier, had slammed the White House as being full of white supremacists.

"I agree that Steve Bannon is a white supremacist and Stephen Miller seems to be. And I know that studies have shown that they have their allies sprinkled around the White House," Brown told CNN's Dana Bash.

The Brown interview got under the skin of top officials inside the White House. One top official, principal deputy press secretary Raj Shah, actually vented about the interview to me. He had called me back to his office, as Spicer had done before, to complain about Brown's interview on CNN. A bit more good-natured than Spicer, Shah tried to laugh off the accusation from Brown that white supremacists worked in the West Wing.

Shah, who is Indian American, shouted out to one of his aides, "Are you a white supremacist? Any white supremacists around here?"

He was joking, but it was an odd response, to say the least. I remember walking away from that meeting thinking, What the hell? I don't think Shah was trying to blow off the horrors of white supremacy. Nor do I think he was trying to excuse Trump's behavior. It was more an attempt to accuse the other party of going overboard in its criticism of Trump. Still, I couldn't believe what I had just heard. I kept thinking, How do you joke about white supremacists while working inside the White House?

None of this was normal.

A senior White House official defended Trump's response to Charlottesville, insisting pretty passionately that the president had been unfairly maligned over his response.

The official asserted Trump's "very fine people" moment over-shadowed other instances when he stated that he condemned Nazis.

"I wouldn't be here in the first place if I thought Donald Trump was a racist. There would be no reason to be here," the official said.

I then asked the official whether that could be stated on the record.

"I don't want to say that on the record," the official replied.

The stain on Trump's presidency left by his response to Charlottes-ville never did come out in the wash; nor should it have. Moments that reveal character on that scale tend to leave an indelible mark on us all—for better or, in this case, for worse. As disgusting, sleazy, and appalling as the remarks captured in the *Access Hollywood* tape had been, Trump's handling of Charlottesville felt worse. It felt un-patriotic and un-American. Until Charlottesville, some of Trump's language had been coded through the alt-right's dog whistles about immigration—birtherism, the wall, the Muslim ban, the list goes on. But now, because it had been framed by his equivocation over hate groups such as the KKK and neo-Nazis, a new reality was upon us, one that his critics said exposed the president's racism.

In the aftermath of that moment, I felt a profound shift in how this White House had to be covered. Because of how journalists have been taught their craft for decades, we have long been obsessed with the idea of balance; that both sides deserve equal skepticism. While it's one thing to say this about health care reform or tax policy, Charlottes-ville revealed that it's entirely different when you're talking about neo-Nazis and white supremacy. When it comes to the KKK, there is no balance, the other side does not get equal treatment. The risk is too great to pretend that such groups are anything but what they are—racists.

Purists in the field of journalism and academics opining from the safety of the classroom can lament the downfall of neutrality. But neutrality for the sake of neutrality doesn't really serve us in the age of Trump. And indeed, we can always look back to previous administrations when it became absolutely necessary for reporters to step out of their roles as objective arbiters of the truth. Walter Cronkite of CBS told the American people the truth about Vietnam (that it could not be won), enraging Lyndon Johnson. The *Washington Post* and the *New York Times* exposed Nixon's secret bombings of Laos and Cambodia with the release of the Pentagon Papers, in defiance of Richard Nixon, who also tangled at times with Dan Rather, over Watergate. Reagan had Sam Donaldson shouting across the South Lawn of the White House when "the Gipper" didn't want to take questions. The press called out Clinton's lies about Monica Lewinsky, and so on. Conversely, I think it can be fairly argued that the press failed the American people in the run-up to the Iraq War, when we allowed the George W. Bush administration to mislead the public into a costly conflict based on weapons of mass destruction that didn't exist.

Yes, the perils have indeed been high for the press countless times, and yet there's no denying that even with that historical perspective, there was a sense that with Trump's latest remarks, we were at a profoundly dangerous moment—for everyone. After Charlottesville, I think more members of the press began a more dogged pursuit of what was right, and that meant telling the truth, as painful as it was. That doesn't mean that everyone started getting it correct all the time, but reporters grew more comfortable adopting honest assessments of Trump's words and behavior, less fixated on catering to the media referees scoring whether we gave both sides equal time. We don't exist just to tell the truth. We have to tell the truth, even when it hurts.

8

"We Reap What We Sow . . ."

One inescapable lesson from the first two years of the Trump administration is that Republicans have shown time and time again that they are willing to abdicate their role as a check on the president in order to advance their policy agenda. This would become all the more apparent in the wake of Charlottesville, when rather than challenge a president who had just equivocated over the rise of neo-Nazis in an American city, much of the GOP stayed loyal to Trump. After Charlottesville, there were other off-ramps available to Republicans. But in most cases, the party of Lincoln, Eisenhower, Reagan, and the Bush family, by and large, was all too willing to look the other way.

Sure, some high-profile Republicans publicly criticized Trump. In the fall of 2017, Bob Corker referred to the White House as an "adult day care center" after Trump criticized the Tennessee senator's handling of the Obama-era Iran nuclear deal. Corker even went as far as to tell a group of reporters that three key administration officials were essentially the ones preventing the country from going off the rails.

"I think Secretary [of State] Tillerson, Secretary [of Defense] Mattis, and [White House Chief of Staff] Kelly are those people that help separate our country from chaos," he said.

Still, Corker and other prominent GOP Trump critics, such as Arizona senator Jeff Flake, preferred to wage a war of words with the president than do much of anything to derail his presidency. In their defense, the Senate majority leader, Mitch McConnell, was not about to let them subvert Trump's agenda in any meaningful way.

House Speaker Paul Ryan also had his concerns with Trump's rhetoric and behavior. But Ryan, who, I'm told, spoke with Trump more often than the public ever really knew, registered his complaints privately. Ryan, a source close to him told me, did not want to create other distractions for the GOP by getting into public spats with the president. What was the point of that? Ryan thought.

But the party faced one of its more critical tests in the fall of 2017, with Trump's disastrous endorsement of Alabama Republican candidate Roy Moore for the U.S. Senate. Had the accusations of sexual misconduct against Moore never come to light, it's almost certain he would be sitting in the Senate today. As we all now know, Moore almost won the seat, thanks to Alabama's bright-red conservatism but also to Trump, who will go down in history with the dubious distinction of throwing the full weight of the presidency behind a candidate facing allegations of child molestation. While Charlottesville was a jarring experience for so many Americans, who simply could not fathom a president waffling over white supremacists rioting in a U.S. city, the Moore campaign proved that Trump could deliver one unimaginable blow after another to the nation's consciousness. As was often the case during Trump's first two years in office, some in the GOP disagreed with him over his endorsement of Moore, yet there was no accountability for Trump. At Corker's so-called White House day care center, you might say, there were seemingly no adults in the room willing to take on the president.

On November 9, 2017, the *Washington Post* broke the story alleging that Moore, while a thirty-two-year-old assistant district attorney in Alabama, had molested a fourteen-year old girl, an accusation the

GOP Senate candidate blasted as—you guessed it—"Fake news." In addition to that allegation, the *Post* had found other women who said that, when they were in their teens, Moore asked them out on dates and made other appalling, untoward advances. Following the bombshell in the *Post*, much of the GOP establishment immediately abandoned Moore, who had beaten Trump-supported sitting Republican senator Luther Strange in the primary.

The Moore story exploded toward the end of Trump's eleven-day trip to Asia, in the fall of 2017. Having traveled on a number of these excursions, I can tell you that they are almost always interrupted by news back home, and not in a good way. It happened to Obama, and with the Roy Moore scandal, it was happening to Trump. On November 11, Trump tried to sidestep questions from reporters about the Moore story while on Air Force One.

"Honestly, I'd have to look at it and I'd have to see. Because, again, I'm dealing with the president of China, the president of Russia. I'm dealing with the folks over here," he told reporters. "I haven't been able to devote very much time to it."

What's astounding is that some in the GOP were giving Trump every opportunity he needed to abandon Moore. On November 13, Colorado senator Cory Gardner, head of the National Republican Senate Committee, recommended that Moore be expelled from the Senate should the Alabama Republican win the race.

"I believe the individuals speaking out against Roy Moore spoke with courage and truth, proving he is unfit to serve in the United States Senate and he should not run for office. If he refuses to withdraw and wins, the Senate should vote to expel him, because he does not meet the ethical and moral requirements of the United States Senate," Gardner said in his statement.

Yet, once Trump and his team had returned to the White House from their foreign trip, it became evident they had other plans. The wheels were in motion for the president instead to do the unthinkable:

not only endorse Moore but also campaign for him in the Alabama election. At a press briefing on November 16, Sarah Sanders did not rule out the possibility that Trump could hit the trail for an accused child molester.

"Do you think he's a creep?" I asked Sarah at the briefing.

"Do I?" Sanders responded. "Look, I don't know Roy Moore. I haven't met him in person, so I wouldn't be able to respond to that."

Five days later, Trump disregarded the condemnations of Moore's behavior coming from his own party and signaled that he would back the GOP contender.

"He denies it. Look, he denies it," Trump said of Moore. "If you look at all the things that have happened over the last 48 hours. He totally denies it. He says it didn't happen. And look, you have to look at him also."

As the race between Roy Moore and his Democratic challenger, Doug Jones, tightened, Trump finally made the decision to endorse the GOP candidate. In an attempt to lure more Republicans to adopt his way of thinking, he said that Moore could be counted on to support the GOP tax-cut package that had been making its way through Congress. In December, Trump would take his support one step further, holding a rally in Pensacola, Florida, a city on the state's panhandle, where local TV coverage of the event would be seen in Mobile, Alabama. The president, perhaps a bit too embarrassed actually to campaign for Moore in Alabama, was doing the next best thing.

"We can't afford to have a liberal Democrat who is completely controlled by Nancy Pelosi and Chuck Schumer. We can't do it," Trump told the crowd in Pensacola. Never one to hold back, he would go on to poke fun at one of the women who had accused Moore of sexual misconduct.

In the end, Trump's craven endorsement was not enough to pull Moore across the finish line. It was a humiliating defeat for Trump, who could hear the "I told ya so"s coming from Congress, where more experienced operatives had been proven correct about Moore's chances. A source close to Trump offered a candid assessment of the damage done to the president's standing.

"It's devastating for the president. . . . This is an earthquake," the source told me.

The Alabama race demonstrated vividly that Trump could be beaten, even in one of the most conservative states in the country. He had disregarded the wishes of his own party, thinking somehow that he had the Midas touch every time he entered the fray. But the voters, even in deep-red Alabama, had their limits.

GOP operatives across Washington, especially in the Senate, were furious with Trump's decision to embrace an accused child molester. Yes, before the Alabama race, they had feared Trump—incumbent GOP lawmakers and their political teams constantly worried about the prospect of Trump riding into their states or districts to back a more conservative rival during the primary process. That had kept these members and the rest of the party in line, to some extent. The Moore debacle shattered that, revealing that there was in fact a risk to being too closely tied to Trump, particularly in swing districts in the House, a key battleground for the upcoming 2018 midterms. With Moore, Trump had been amateurish and reckless, and more than a few GOP operatives were beginning to think they could all pay a price for that when the midterms rolled around.

Indeed, it was also another gut-check moment for the people around the president. As with Charlottesville, though, there were no mass resignations. The president's aides kept right on whistling past the graveyard. All this was baffling to me. If the Moore allegations don't disgust you, nothing will. But, for Trump, a Senate seat was more important, obviously, than doing the right thing. Much of the White House team around him apparently agreed.

As destructive as the Roy Moore debacle had been for Trump and the GOP, the Republicans were able to steady themselves just days later with the passage of a massive tax-cut package that delivered a tremendous windfall for Wall Street and wealthier Americans. Moore's vote wasn't needed after all; the bill passed anyway. The tax cuts represented one of the largest transfers of wealth from one generation to another. As deficits began to skyrocket in 2018 and into the next decade, the Millennials and younger generations would sink deeper into debt.

On December 20, 2017, roughly one week after Moore's loss, nearly the entire Republican Party in Congress gathered on the South Lawn of the White House to heap praise on Trump and celebrate the passage of the tax-cut plan. There was no mention of Trump's endorsement of an alleged child molester. I remember being struck by the rather emotional statement delivered by Utah Republican senator Orrin Hatch, the former chairman of the Senate Finance Committee, who all but described Trump as the second coming of Lincoln:

"All I can say is that God loves this country," Hatch said. "We all know it. We wouldn't be where we are without Him. And we love all of you. And we're going to keep fighting, and we're going to make this the greatest presidency that we've seen, not only in generations, but maybe ever."

The greatest presidency ever? I remember asking myself. Trump had just endorsed Roy Moore, only months after equivocating over the white supremacist violence in Charlottesville amid a constant campaign of demonizing immigrants—that assessment seemed a stretch.

The South Lawn celebration's coming on the heels of the Moore debacle was stunning. In a presidency littered with news-making events, this bit of political pomp barely registered for many, but as I sat there watching, I felt it was a key moment in the Trump presidency, cementing in my mind one of the important aspects of the curious relationship between Trump and the rest of the Republican Party. Portions of the GOP, it seemed, were willing to compromise themselves in favor of achieving long-term party goals. If you wanted your tax cuts, you had to swallow Trump's highly questionable behavior. Same thing if you wanted conservative judges. Trump and the Republicans may not believe in compromising with Democrats, but there was compromising going on inside their own party. They were horse trading, all right. The party was achieving a few of its policy goals in exchange for looking the other way.

In nearly all the episodes of Republican inaction, a familiar pattern would emerge: Trump would take things too far, and much of the GOP would do little or nothing to challenge his behavior. That dynamic is principally why the press found itself, over and over, in Trump's crosshairs. GOP members of Congress had largely given up on calling the president out on his behavior, which meant that task fell to us reporters.

This was one reason it became harder and harder to keep up the faux collegiality of such formalities as the annual White House holiday party for the press corps. It was during the Roy Moore saga that CNN had announced it would not attend this reception, and after being called "fake news" and the "enemy of the people," we had good reason to decline the invitation.

"In light of the President's continued attacks on freedom of the press and CNN, we do not feel it is appropriate to celebrate with him as his invited guests," a network spokesperson said.

Sarah Sanders, who can work in a dig at the press while brushing her teeth, couldn't resist poking CNN in the eye. **Christmas comes early! Finally, good news from @CNN,** she tweeted at the time.

Declining the invitation was a good call for CNN, even if some of our colleagues in the press believed we were playing into Trump's hands. My sense of it was that we couldn't criticize Trump's demonization of the press while drinking eggnog and posing for pictures with him. Others in the press were comfortable doing this; I was not. Such photos could easily be released and posted on social media, thus sending the wrong message: enemies of the people by day, drinking buddies at night.

As if to confirm that we had made the right decision, the White House made a point of not inviting certain reporters to the reception (not exactly in keeping with the holiday spirit). April Ryan, of American Urban Radio Network, was on the Trump naughty list. How could I attend a White House holiday reception to which April, in obvious retaliation for her coverage, hadn't even been invited? But this is how the White House played the game. By inviting some outlets and not others, Trump was encouraging media organizations to make a choice: to show solidarity either with the White House or with their fellow journalists. It was pure divide and conquer, even at Christmastime.

"They have a disdain for me," April said about the snub to the *Washington Post*.

It was a terrible development in relations between the press and the White House. The holiday reception for the press was canceled altogether in 2018, ending a tradition that had gone on for decades under Republican and Democratic administrations alike. I had taken my own children to these events when Obama was in the White House; so had many other journalists. It was a small way to repay our kids for enduring the headache of having a parent working in the White House press corps.

————

OVERLOOKING A ROY MOORE ENDORSEMENT IN EXCHANGE FOR TAX cuts certainly demonstrated that Republicans enjoyed reaping the benefits of having Trump in the White House. But there were many in the GOP who initially turned down the idea of crafting policy in the administration. Part of the problem was that so many Republicans had been deeply critical of Trump during the campaign. Most of these "Never Trumpers" had been cast aside as insufficiently loyal, and disqualified from working at the White House. This meant that many of the people willing to work for Trump were inexperienced in running a government. Several solid GOP operatives who were Trump critics from the campaign, such as political strategist R. C. Hammond, did join the Trump administration, but most have since left for the private sector. Few, if any, openly die-hard Never Trumpers ended up working inside the White House, because the environment favored Trump loyalists and those who would always have the president's back.

The staff woes of the Trump White House reached their lowest point during the Rob Porter saga. Porter was the personal staff secretary to the president, a coveted position in any administration. Wherever Trump went, Porter was almost always close behind, preparing documents for him to sign and keeping him on schedule. It's an important job in any White House, certainly not a position you hand out to just anyone. That was made all too clear when the British tabloid the *Daily Mail* first broke the news about disturbing allegations of marital abuse leveled against Porter. Trump, who liked to brag that he hired only the best people, obviously had a major problem on his hands in Porter: despite accusations from two ex-wives that he had beaten them, the White House aide had been authorized to work closely with the president of the United States.

Strangely, Porter announced his resignation in a statement that seemed to acknowledge the allegations while also denying them. Despite that giant red flag, the White House Press Office still thought it was a good idea to produce testimonials praising the staff secretary, including one from the chief of staff, General John Kelly, who described Porter as "a man of true integrity and honor." It was a major blunder that most press offices at the city or state level would have avoided.

Part of the reason the Porter scandal was so devastating for the White House was that the staff was frozen in just how to handle the embarrassing revelations. As many of us in the press were already aware, Porter at that time was dating a key staffer inside the West Wing, Hope Hicks, Trump's glamorous communications director and one of the "originals" from the campaign. Hicks could be shy around certain reporters, but she had no problem drawing attention to herself. A former model, she often dressed more like a political spouse than a press aide, and was often snapped wearing designer clothes and expensive sunglasses as she descended from Air Force One on official trips with the president. It was no secret that she was seeing Rob Porter. During Trump's trip to Asia in the fall of 2017, I ran into both of them while on a hike in Vietnam in between Trump events. Hope was showing off her Lululemon attire while Rob was sporting a Harvard T-shirt. They didn't have any Vietnamese money on them and were trying to figure out how to pay the admission fee to hike around a touristy site outside Da Nang. White House staffers were aware of the couple's cozy relationship, which added to the difficulty of simply kicking Porter to the curb. He was Hope's boyfriend, after all.

But Porter had other allies in the White House.

"There certainly was a clique around" Porter, a senior White House official told me. "A protective clique."

Part of the reason for that "protective clique" was that so many people inside the West Wing saw Porter as a rising star in Trump-world. Porter had big plans, the official told me.

"Here's a guy who thought he was going to be on the Supreme Court one day," the official said.

But this official insisted Porter destroyed all of that himself, in part, by not coming clean when confronted by top White House officials about the allegations. He lied to everybody about his past, the senior official told me.

"The president was literally shocked" when he learned the truth, the official added.

The Porter saga was a useful window into just how far the Trump

White House was willing to go to fill its ranks with loyalists. As it turns out, Porter lacked the full security clearance that seemed vital for a job that included the handling of classified documents for the president. Instead, he was working with a temporary security clearance. He was not alone in this category. One week after Porter's resignation, I broke the news that well over a hundred staffers at the White House, including some senior officials, were working with only temporary security clearances. This was disturbing one full year after Trump was elected president. Ivanka Trump, Jared Kushner, and Rob Porter were all on the list we obtained of West Wing aides who lacked full clearance. If there was a silver lining to the Porter saga, it was that the White House had to start addressing what was a pretty embarrassing lapse in security. But other dramatic changes were on the way.

Three weeks after Porter resigned, Hicks stepped down. Hope's resignation was no small thing. Outside the Trump family, she had come to understand the president better than anyone in the West Wing. She was a fierce Trump defender behind the scenes, often becoming emotional with reporters who doubted Trump's sincerity in his promise to "Make America Great Again." We just didn't know the real Trump, she continually told us. Trump had complete trust in Hicks, frequently putting her on the phone with reporters to praise or critique stories he didn't like. She was an extension of the president, practically part of the Trump family. One clear sign of her status in the Trump White House was that she could often be found in the residence, a privilege not granted to most other staffers.

Others embroiled in the Porter saga, such as Chief of Staff John Kelly, would stay on, but badly damaged. Kelly confided to other officials in the White House that he felt he had been unfairly blamed for the Porter fiasco. But there were serious questions inside the West Wing as to how long the chief of staff was aware of the problems with Porter's background check. (Indeed, Kelly had discussed with the president whether he should resign.) The accomplished retired general, it appeared, lacked the political skills needed to run the White House, especially one as chaotic as this one. He couldn't see the error of praising Porter even as the aide was facing allegations of marital abuse. The general did walk back that statement in which he gushed about Porter's character, but it took hard evidence to change his mind. As soon as he saw one of the photographs published in the *Daily Mail* depicting one of Porter's ex-wives with a black eye, we reported, Kelly then decided he could no longer defend a young staffer he clearly liked.

The chief of staff tried to bring military-style discipline to the West Wing, keeping lists of items on note cards that we could occasionally spot him carrying from one event to another. He was exasperated with Trump's antics, frequently clashing with the president behind the scenes as he tried to curb his erratic behavior. His efforts to clamp down on Trumpworld did not always go over well with the president, but Trump, who enjoyed surrounding himself with generals in the early months of his administration, found a kindred spirit of sorts in Kelly. Also appealing to Trump, no doubt: the "chief," as Kelly was called behind the scenes, was a hard-liner on the issue of immigration dating back to his days as secretary of homeland security. Still, with the Porter fiasco, Kelly had become vulnerable to the more troublesome forces of Trumpworld. The same people who had been iced out by him after he restricted access to the West Wing were now whispering to reporters that the general's days were numbered. And as if that weren't enough, the "Corey stories" were back in the news: palace intrigue articles mentioning Lewandowski as being back in the mix to take over as chief of staff were plaguing Kelly, just as they had Reince Priebus when he was on thin ice.

A former senior White House official insisted to me that Kelly shouldered too much of the blame for the Porter fiasco. As this official explained, White House counsel Don McGahn knew a lot more about Porter's background than he revealed to Kelly as the scandal was unfolding. Kelly was initially unaware that McGahn had been talking to people with direct knowledge of Porter's abusive past. To protect

McGahn, Kelly "fell on his sword," this official said. Trump "knew the fuck-up was on McGahn," the official added.

This wasn't the first time McGahn was aware of damaging information but kept it from others. He was also aware of National Security Advisor Michael Flynn's contacts with the Russian ambassador Sergey Kislyak, a senior White House official told me. There wasn't anything malicious about McGahn keeping these secrets to himself, the official insisted. Just how he operated.

Why would Kelly take a bullet for the White House counsel? McGahn, who has since stepped aside, had greater influence inside the West Wing than the public fully understood, this former senior official explained. As soon as the general was named chief of staff, McGahn and chief strategist Steve Bannon went to Kelly to push for the departures of Ivanka Trump and Jared Kushner, who had become their own power center, removed from the rest of the staff. Recruiting the outgoing chief of staff, Reince Priebus, McGahn and Bannon appealed to Kelly "to send the kids home," the official told me. The "cabal," as this official called McGahn, Bannon, and Priebus, tried to recruit other top aides to join the rebellion. The factional infighting was part of the reason Kelly had been brought in from the Department of Homeland Security. Rather than unseat Trump's own family members, he tried to keep the peace, as part of his mandate to bring order to the disorderly West Wing. Still, Kelly and McGahn formed close ties and became "inseparable," the former senior official said, maintaining the counsel's position as a power player behind the scenes.

Jared and Ivanka were their own source of management turmoil inside the West Wing, multiple former senior White House officials told me. Getting rid of the "kids" was a running "theme" from the early days of the administration, one of those former senior officials said. Another former senior official went further, blaming Jared and Ivanka for most of the president's bad decisions.

"They aren't part of the problem. They *are* the problem," the ex-official said. "The railhead of every bad decision is Jared and Ivanka," the official added, pointing to the firing of James Comey as exhibit A.

"They are also grifters," the official continued, commenting that the president's daughter and son-in-law were essentially pretending to know what they were doing. Yet, they wielded enormous power. "They are the chiefs of staff," the official added.

But Kellyanne Conway defended Jared and Ivanka to me, blaming the revolt against "the kids" on aides who wanted the couple out of the way to advance their own agendas.

"Some folks probably did. But those folks are gone," Conway told me. "No wonder they wanted them to leave; the dearly departed regarded Jared and Ivanka as obstacles more than colleagues," she added.

Indeed, Kelly's predecessor, Priebus, was so frustrated about his lack of influence inside the West Wing that he would go on to tell people he was just the "chief of stuff." A former senior White House official explained why Priebus felt this way. Anytime Priebus was locked in a heated debate with Jared over a particular policy, he often felt he was in a losing position. Reince knew he was disposable. The kids were not. So, in those arguments behind the scenes, he always felt the kids were automatically in a winning position.

Kelly was also miserable in his command position, a feeling he sometimes revealed in his public appearances. "I did something wrong and God punished me," he joked at an event honoring the Department of Homeland Security.

Kelly didn't hide his agony with White House aides, often venting with the first person he saw after meeting with Trump in the Oval Office. "He was not covert about his frustration," that former senior official told me.

Still, for Kelly, the Porter story was a devastating blow to the general's standing in the White House. "Everything went downhill pretty fast" for Kelly after that, the official added. As several outlets, including

The empty picture frames in the hallway connecting the Upper and Lower Press areas of the West Wing on the evening of January 19, 2017. Photographs of the Obama family were removed to make way for pictures of Trump and his family.

The Trump campaign press corps during the early morning hours of Election Day 2016. Trump was not available to take a photo with his press corps, so the reporters covering his campaign brought out a cardboard cutout for the picture.

President-elect Trump, Mitt Romney, and incoming White House chief of staff Reince Priebus *(with back to camera)* having dinner at Jean-Georges inside the Trump International Hotel in New York City on November 29, 2016. Romney met with Trump for dinner to discuss the idea of becoming secretary of state.

This photograph was taken during a live report outside Trump Tower on the evening of November 9, 2016. My crew and I were surrounded by a large crowd of protesters who were demonstrating against the election of Donald Trump as president.

A photo from the North Lawn of the White House on the evening of Inauguration Day on January 20, 2017. Trump responded to a question from CNN as he made his way back to the reviewing stands to watch the Inaugural Parade.

White House press secretary Sean Spicer in the Briefing Room on January 21, 2017, when Spicer told reporters that President Trump had "the largest audience to ever witness an inauguration, period, both in person and around the globe," a claim later found to be false.

As the son of a Cuban immigrant, and knowing of my dad's experiences, I have always thought of immigration as one of our most important issues. This is my dad and me when we visited Cuba in December 2016.

President Trump visiting the USS *Gerald R. Ford* aircraft carrier in Newport News, Virginia, on March 2, 2017. Later in the day, Attorney General Jeff Sessions announced his recusal in the Russia investigation.

The tweet from @realDonaldTrump when he referred to the news media as "the enemy of the American People" on February 17, 2017.

Donald J. Trump ✓
@realDonaldTrump

The FAKE NEWS media (failing @nytimes, @NBCNews, @ABC, @CBS, @CNN) is not my enemy, it is the enemy of the American People!

2/17/17, 4:48 PM

I met with Israeli CNN viewers in Jerusalem, Israel, on May 22, 2017.

I am among the group of reporters asking questions in the White House Briefing Room on June 28, 2017, after televised coverage of these news conferences was suspended by Press Secretary Sean Spicer.

Sean Spicer, as drawn by D.C. courtroom sketch artist Bill Hennessy, after televised coverage of press briefings was banned. *(Courtesy of William J. Hennessy Jr./ CourtroomArt.com)*

At Trump Tower on August 15, 2017, the president answers questions about his response to white supremacist violence in Charlottesville, Virginia.

President Trump and North Korean dictator Kim Jong Un address the press at the summit in Singapore on June 12, 2018. With the president are White House Press Secretary Sarah Sanders, National Security Adviser John Bolton, Chief of Staff John Kelly, and Secretary of State Mike Pompeo.

President Trump receives a FIFA World Cup soccer ball from Russian president Vladimir Putin at the summit in Helsinki, Finland, on July 16, 2018.

Here I join the press corps at a Trump rally.

Standing with Trump supporters at my back at a rally in Columbia, South Carolina, on June 25, 2018.

Posing with Trump supporters on the campaign trail for South Carolina governor Henry McMaster.

Being heckled at a Trump rally in Tampa, Florida, on July 31, 2018.

CNN anchor Wolf Blitzer and me in Buenos Aires, Argentina, during the G20 summit on December 1, 2018.

President Trump calling me a "rude, terrible person" and "the enemy of the people" at a White House news conference on November 7, 2018. *(AP Photo/Evan Vucci)*

Giving my statement after my White House press credentials were restored by a federal judge on November 19, 2018.

CNN, reported, Kelly had talked to Trump about whether he should resign, but the president, knowing Kelly wasn't fully responsible for what had happened, decided to keep the general on board.

With the Porter fiasco, the press office had botched its response as well. Under the circumstances at play in the whole saga, a competent press shop would never have contemplated releasing a favorable statement about an employee credibly accused of spousal or other abuse. A statement from a competent press shop would likely have read, "Rob Porter is leaving the White House. His final day was today." Kind of the way they gave Steve Bannon the boot.

I pressed Raj Shah, the deputy press secretary, who was filling in for Sanders in the Briefing Room that day, on that very question.

ACOSTA: How can the White House Chief of Staff, how can the Press Secretary, how can this White House still be standing behind him when Mr. Porter appeared to be acknowledging that he had this past?

SHAH: I think it's fair to say that we all could have done better over the last few hours—or last few days in dealing with this situation.

My sources told me at the time that Trump hated that statement from Raj. In Trumpworld, this was a violation of the rules: you never admit a mistake.

What happened with Porter added up to be much more than a failure on the part of Trump's staff. The code of ethics of the Trump White House had revealed itself yet again, as the president fell back into a familiar pattern. When it comes to allegations of sexual misconduct, Trump almost always stands with the accused and not the accuser. He had done this before; he would do it again. Speaking to reporters, Trump expressed sympathy for his former staff secretary, noting that Porter had proclaimed his innocence.

"He also, as you probably know, says he's innocent and I think you have to remember that," Trump said. "He said very strongly yesterday that he's innocent so you have to talk to him about that, but we absolutely wish him well, he did a very good job when he was at the White House."

That statement, siding with Porter, was another reminder of just how Trump didn't seem to understand the president's role of providing moral leadership in a situation like this. This would not have been tolerated at a Fortune 500 company, and yet it was happening at the White House.

All this was exacerbated, of course, by the fact that Trump lacked a top-flight press shop. But as I've said before, there wasn't much of a choice. Too many Republicans in Washington simply wouldn't (and won't) work for Trump. I could name names here, but I won't. That would be wrong. But privately, a good number of well-known Republican operatives have told me they could never serve in the Trump administration. Others tried it and walked away, viewing the situation as unworkable. That left Trump with a lot of folks who, under normal circumstances, wouldn't have been working somewhere as important as the White House.

But the staff is not the story here, and this is key. This is why I keep coming back to what a top GOP congressional aide told me during the 2016 campaign. The staffer, who shall remain anonymous, sounded almost helpless watching from the sidelines as Trump vanquished a field of sixteen establishment candidates to win the party's nomination.

"Our top candidates are just playing into people's worst prejudices rather than rising above them. And so this is what we get. The bubble will crash at some point," the aide said, worrying that Trump would ultimately leave the party in "tatters."

"We reap what we sow," he added.

In the early days of the administration, it was equally revealing to listen to the GOP officials who had been on the inside. Former administration officials described to me scenes of unbelievable incompetence—agency after agency staffed with young, inexperienced aides who came into the administration from the Trump campaign with little or no government experience.

Many inside the party told me they were concerned Trump had no real moral compass. In less than six months, he had aligned himself with white supremacists, supported an alleged child molester, and defended an accused wife beater. Some in the party may have wrestled with these demons, but Donald Trump did not.

ONE OF TRUMP'S POLICIES THAT MOST REPUBLICANS QUICKLY ADopted as their own was his stance on immigration. Gone were the days of George W. Bush's moderate ideas on the issue, such as a path to citizenship for the nation's undocumented immigrants living in the shadows. Trump had made his vow to crack down on immigration as a cornerstone of his campaign, in ways that took the Republican Party by surprise. Once in office, he wasn't about to let up in his approach to the subject, including his hate-filled, extremist language. The GOP largely followed Trump's lead.

In January 2018, Trump began to reveal what was at the heart of his immigration agenda. During a closed-door meeting with Democratic and Republican lawmakers, he made the ugly remark that he didn't want immigrants coming into the United States from Haiti and certain countries in Africa, nations he referred to as "shitholes." According to Illinois Democratic senator Dick Durbin, who was at the gathering, Trump said he would rather have immigrants come in from places like Norway. So, naturally, during an event in the Oval Office, I asked Trump about his remarks. That was when he told me to get out.

"Did you say that you wanted more people to come in from Norway," I asked him on January 16, 2018.

Trump then told a whopper to the reporters gathered in the room. "I want them to come in from everywhere. Everywhere," he responded.

Give me a break, I thought. That's definitely not true. So, I followed up with the question that was on everybody's mind.

"Just Caucasian or white countries, sir? Or do you want people to come in from other parts of the world? Where there are people of color?" I asked.

"Out," Trump responded, ordering me to leave the Oval Office. Adding to the chaos, White House aides were shouting right in my face to drown out my questions.

Moments later, Trump moved on to another event, in the Roosevelt Room of the West Wing, where I again attempted to ask him about his immigration comments. This time, however, a few of Trump's aides stood right in front of me and began shouting in my face to drown me out. It was an absurd scene straight out of a totalitarian country like China, not the United States. Imagine trying to ask a question in that kind of environment. I have covered elected officials from city hall to the White House. That's never happened before.

My questions clearly angered Trump and his allies. An adviser who is close to the president texted me in protest: "Haiti is a shithole."

Truth be told, I struggled for a bit over how to relay the "shithole" story to viewers. Then the executive producer of CNN's *Situation Room*, Jay Shaylor, got in my ear about a minute before my live shot to inform me that, yes, I could say the word *shithole* on CNN. So, I did. Minutes later, the show's host, Wolf Blitzer, declined to say "shithole," reminding me once again that Wolf is one of the most decent people in our business, a true gentleman.

As for the Trump staffers screaming in my face, it's one part of the job in Trumpworld that clearly fascinates everybody. People continually ask me, "Who are those people screaming in your face when you're trying to ask a question?" Some of them are perfectly nice and friendly; others are not. Take Katie Price, a former makeup artist who once worked at CNN. She made a name for herself in the White House as the loudest screamer of them all. When you watch video of reporters gathered around the president in the Oval Office or the Cabinet Room trying to ask questions, Katie is the wrangler who can be heard shouting over all the voices of reporters in the room. It's kind of impressive, in a sick and twisted way.

"Time to go, guys!" she'd shriek. "No questions!" she'd yell, inches away from our ears. "Let's go, Jim. Time to go!"

Posing a question to the president with wranglers screaming in your ears is quite an experience for a White House reporter. It's a bit like being the umpire at a baseball game and having the most unruly, drunken fans in the stands shouting directly in your face. Try calling balls and strikes in that kind of environment. I don't blame Katie. How would she have known any better? Besides, her shrieks made her a Trump favorite. An administration official told me Trump loved the way Katie yelled at us, at one point remarking to aides that she should be deputized in his battle against illegal immigration.

"I should send her down to the border," he would say of her, according to the official. Katie, Trump thought, would scare the migrants away.

I once asked Katie how she became one of Trump's favorites. "He likes how I can be both assertive and professional," she told me at one of his rallies.

But I digress. Like Charlottesville and Roy Moore, the "shithole" controversy was hardly the end of the cavalcade of cringe-worthy moments at Trump's White House. Almost like clockwork, more episodes occurred, ranging from the disturbing to the depressing.

Immigration, it seemed for Trump, was the issue where he excelled in finding new ways to turn this reporter's stomach.

Consider Trump's handling of the millions of young Americans brought into the country illegally by their parents but protected under the Deferred Action for Childhood Arrivals program known as DACA. A life-saving initiative launched by the Obama administration,

DACA was designed to prevent children from being deported back to countries where they would essentially be foreigners. The DACA recipients, also known as Dreamers, are kids, teenagers, and young adults who attend our schools and colleges and, in some cases, serve in our military. During the Obama administration, they were able to live in the United States, largely without fear of deportation—which is good, because many of these DACA kids don't even speak the language of their country of origin. They are, for all practical purposes, American.

Back in September 2017, Trump had decided to end DACA as part of his crackdown on immigration. Now, it should be noted that about a year later, in November 2018, an appellate court decision kept the system on life support—as of this writing, the Supreme Court has not yet heard the case—but up until that relief at the appellate level, for a good year, those Dreamers were living in fear of deportation. On April 1, 2018, Trump ratcheted up that fear. As he was heading into Easter Sunday services in Florida, he blamed Democrats for the failure to pass legislation in Congress to protect the Dreamers. The truth, of course, is that for years, both parties in Congress had failed to address the problem. And in any case, it was he who had terminated the DACA program.

@realDonaldTrump
Border Patrol Agents are not allowed to properly do their job at the Border because of ridiculous liberal (Democrat) laws like Catch & Release. Getting more dangerous. "Caravans" coming. Republicans must go to Nuclear Option to pass tough laws NOW. NO MORE DACA DEAL!
8:56 AM–Apr 1, 2018

Looking back now, one easily sees how much of this was just his typical bluster. But at the time, his tweet sent shockwaves through the immigrant community. If Trump had closed the door on solving DACA, a program he had eliminated six months earlier, these young immigrants would be at risk. The DACA kids could be sent back to their countries of origin. Families would be ripped apart.

One day after Trump made these comments, he hosted the Easter Egg Roll at the White House. As is customary, the press was invited to cover this event. Now, the expectation among White House staffers is that we reporters will stay dutifully on the sidelines, taking our pictures and keeping our mouths shut. But with his DACA tweet, Trump had rolled out his own Easter surprise. We had no idea if he was serious about pulling the plug on the Dreamers, but we meant to find out. After all, it had been his decision to go on the attack on this issue on Easter Sunday, and our feeling was, If *he's* not going to relent on an occasion like this, then why should the press? So, needless to say, watching kids roll Easter eggs was not exactly what I had on my mind that day.

Easter Bunny or no Easter Bunny, the president had struck fear into the lives of millions of immigrant families and the people whose lives they touched. DACA kids aren't just a bunch of numbers in a graphic on the nightly news. They have parents, grandparents, brothers, sisters, teachers, principals, friends, classmates, coaches. The very least Trump could do was give a broader explanation of what he planned to do about the Dreamers.

As we entered the South Lawn, the White House press wranglers were waiting for us. One of them, Caroline Sunshine, took a special interest in where I was standing for the event. Caroline had just come on board at the White House. Prior to joining the administration full time, she had worked as a White House intern. Before that, she had gained notoriety as a teen star on the Disney Channel.

"Acosta!" she yelled. "This way," and she ushered my photographer and me to the area where the press pool was positioned.

Great, I thought. This is perfect. She had moved me into the press pool area, much closer to where the president would interact with the kids, and possibly within earshot of a question.

But CNN wasn't in the pool that day, which meant she had accidentally placed me in a better spot than where I was supposed to have been corralled. A mistake that would be exploited!

Then I heard her call my name again. "Acosta!" Apparently, somebody had told her I wasn't in the pool that day, and so I was moved to a different area, where the print reporters were allowed to stand—not as close to where I thought the president would be, so I was disappointed.

But then I was moved *again*. A separate wrangler, Annie, was now in charge. "Jim, you're not supposed to be in here," she said to me and dispatched me to an even less desirable press area, where, truth be told, I should have been sent in the first place.

All this was starting to crack me up. What on earth is with these people? I thought. But I knew the reason. I had become such a pain in the ass that I warranted individual attention.

Then the moment arrived. Trump had delivered his remarks at the Easter Egg Roll and was starting to move into the crowd. This was my moment. As it turns out, despite the wranglers' best efforts, I had ended up in the perfect spot. It was a pretty clear example of an inexperienced press shop working in my favor, and putting Trump in a less-than-ideal situation.

Near where I was now standing, several children were seated at a table coloring away, the tabletop covered with adorable Easter Bunny drawings. And Trump walked right over to them and took a seat at the table . . . about ten feet away from me.

Fixated on blocking me from trying to shout a question to Trump, the wranglers had moved me three times, but the third time was the charm, at least for me.

Then another stroke of luck came. While the children sitting among the president were working with their boxes of crayons, the music piped into the festivities suddenly stopped. It was fairly quiet.

"Mr. President," I called out, "what about the DACA kids? Should they be worried about what's going to happen to them?"

"The Democrats have really let them down," he said. "They really let them down. They had this great opportunity. The Democrats have really let them down. It's a shame. And now people are taking advantage of DACA and that's a shame."

Trump, of course, was rewriting history. *He* had ended the DACA program. *He* had dashed the hopes of hundreds of thousands of Dreamers. It was just like the Oval Office encounter on the "shithole" countries: once again, he was lying. A follow-up question was required.

"Didn't you kill DACA, sir? Didn't you kill DACA?"

Trump did not respond. Pursing his lips in disgust, he went back to chatting with the children, who probably wondered what these adults were talking about. But his silence was clear. He didn't have a response.

Why did I ask that second question about Trump killing DACA? Well, to be blunt, it would have been journalistic malpractice simply to let the president get away with the blatant lie that the Democrats were to blame for ending DACA. Trump had terminated the DACA program back in September 2017 with a statement that spoke volumes:

"We must also have heart and compassion for unemployed, struggling and forgotten Americans," Trump had said, referring to the country's nonimmigrants. It was another example of him pitting one group of people against another. In Trump's worldview, it's the immigrant community versus native-born American citizens.

The fact that Trump responded to my question at the Easter Egg Roll at all should surprise no one. He often can't help himself—which is great if you're a White House reporter. And for some reason he particularly can't seem to help himself around me. I'm not bragging, but for all the times I've been advised not to take Trump's bait, it should be noted that he himself finds my questions, my bait, hard to resist, too. I suppose this is part of the reason some reporters just can't get enough of covering this guy. Sure, Trump has endangered reporters with his "enemy of the people" rhetoric, but his impulsiveness around the cameras also makes him extremely accessible. Some reporters like the idea of the access and ignore Trump's taunts and threats. After all, it's a byline-rich environment.

As for the Easter Egg incident, Trumpworld was not pleased. His 2020 campaign manager, Brad Parscale, demanded that my press credentials be pulled, a foreshadowing of events yet to come.

Maybe it is time for Jim Acosta to get a suspension for breaking protocol. He continues to embarrass himself and @CNN. Pull his credentials for each incident, Parscale said in a tweet, with a link to a story in the Daily Caller.

Just doing my job, which is protected by the First Amendment of the Constitution. You might want to give it a read, I replied on Twitter.

I understand why Parscale posted his tweet. He was channeling the frustrations inside the White House, and from Trump specifically, that reporters were asking questions that interfered with the president's message of the day. I totally get that. But asking questions of the president at photo opportunities is a long-standing practice inside the White House.

Needless to say, this was not how Trump's apologists and propagandists in conservative media saw things. Sebastian Gorka, a former White House official turned Republican analyst on Fox News, tweeted, **Despicable. @Acosta is a self-aggrandizing activist hack.** That's rich. He's as cartoonish as Washington hacks come.

The conservative blog *Power Line* referred to me as "Resistance man Jim Acosta" and as the "grandstanding clown who covers the White House of CNN."

Another right-wing blog, *RedState*, wrote, "Acosta has no regard for time and place because, to him, every time and place is one for self-aggrandizement. . . . Either way, CNN continues to send Acosta to the White House despite his obvious flaws and agenda, which means that CNN is continuously endorsing his behavior."

The Gateway Pundit, another conservative site devoted to criticizing the mainstream media, offered up the headline "CNN's Jim Acosta Gets SAVAGED for Yelling at Trump While He Was Coloring with Children at White House Easter Egg Roll." The article's contents, however, don't live up to the hype, merely referring back to Parscale, Gorka, and the Daily Caller article. These sites are all part of the same ultraconservative echo chamber that, for all intents and purposes, serves as Trump's propaganda machine. These were the same guys who were giddy with fanboy excitement when I pressed Obama on ISIS, asking him, "Why can't we take out these bastards?" They may not remember, but I do.

In a sign of things to come, all that hostility from the conservative movement over my work at the Easter Egg Roll appeared to inspire an outbreak of violent and threatening language on my social media and email accounts. Ever since the 2016 presidential campaign, I'd been subjected to threats and disgusting comments on social media, a fact of life for just about every reporter covering Trump these days. After the Easter Egg Roll, though, the death threats and other suggestions of violence started pouring into my Facebook, Instagram, and Twitter accounts in numbers I had never seen before.

One disturbed person sent an email to me that was so appalling that it cannot be published in its entirety here. The message was forwarded to CNN security. To explain how the stakes had changed for reporters covering the Trump White House, I talked about this email during a private meeting at a CNN management retreat in April 2018. Former ABC News White House correspondent Sam Donaldson came to speak to the crowd and explain that my shouted questions were part of a long tradition of covering American presidents. CNN president Jeff Zucker put the threatening email up on a giant screen so other managers could see some of the hazards of the White House beat.

Date: April 3, 2018 at 9:26:17 AM EDT
To: Jim Acosta
Subject: You

You truly a scumbag . . . maybe some of us will find out where . . . you
have the couth of a cockroach. You are not a journalist, you're a carnival
barker.

The violent part of that email has been removed from the message,
but you get the point. Think of the worst possible death threat you can
imagine. It was that bad.

For years, I'd been getting threats through social media. In that time,
I'd seen a lot of disturbing things, the vast majority of which I was able
to push aside. But the longer Trump was in office, the harder it became
to ignore the reality that the threats were getting more disturbed. By
this point, Trump had been attacking and threatening the media from
the White House for over a year, and the effects of those attacks were
clear, not in how our coverage had changed, but in the ever-increasing
amount of hateful comments we received. The violent messages flow-
ing into my social media accounts were becoming more intense. While
my hope was that these threats would remain in the relatively harmless
world of Twitter and Instagram, a part of me began to fear that they
would soon become a real-world problem as well.

Arguably worse than Trump's fearmongering over DACA or his
support for people such as Roy Moore and Rob Porter was the cruelty embedded in his administration's "zero-tolerance" policy at the
border, which officially launched in spring 2018. Time and time
again with this administration, everything kept coming back to
immigration and the White House's continued demonization and
punishment of people entering this country out of desperation.
With people such as Stephen Miller pulling the strings behind
the scenes, each month seemed to reveal an increased willingness

on the part of the Trump administration to formulate policy on a foundation of ultra-nationalist ideas, with fear used to build a case for actions. The travel ban had been about Muslims of course, but "zero tolerance" was about people from Latin America. As I said before, remember the three *M*'s: the Mexicans, the Muslims, and the media. Like so much under Trump, with each month, things grew more concerning. Still, in many ways "zero tolerance" felt like the culmination of many of the racist ideas that had shaped both the Trump campaign and his first year in office.

Homeland security secretary Kirstjen Nielsen was one of several top administration officials who tried to dance around this reality. She lied to the American people when she said the Trump administration did not have a family-separation policy. But as has been noted count-less times, Attorney General Jeff Sessions confirmed the existence of such a policy when he issued a verbal warning to migrants in May 2018, saying that immigrant children could be separated from their parents at the border.

"If you are smuggling a child then we will prosecute you, and that child will be separated from you as required by law," Sessions told law enforcement officials at an event in Arizona.

Incredibly, Nielsen continued to deny on multiple occasions that the administration had a family-separation policy. **We do not have a policy of separating families at the border. Period,** she tweeted in June 2018, after Sessions made his comments. Nielsen was contradicted by memos sent to officials in her own department, including her, detailing just how the separations would be handled. The memos, obtained by two government watchdog groups, revealed that the department indeed had a family-separation policy.

Trump himself reversed course on the policy in June 2018, when he issued an executive order purportedly to put a stop to the separa-tions. But that was only after the horrors of the policy were brought to the attention of the American people. Later, in August 2018, Ivanka

Trump described the awful sight of families being broken up as a "low point" for the administration, but it was worse than that.

There were other top officials inside the West Wing who were also horrified by the "zero tolerance" policy.

Kellyanne Conway is one of the few officials who admitted to me on the record that the family separations were simply contrary to her religious beliefs.

"As a mother, as a Catholic, as a person of conscience, I don't want children ripped from their parents," she said with some regret.

"I also don't want those parents lied to by smugglers and embarking on the perilous, treacherous journey to the border where the smugglers and coyotes take your money and promise you lies," she added, returning to the West Wing talking points.

But the zero-tolerance policy should not have come as a surprise to Ivanka or to the rest of the country. Consider the variety of ways in which the president has characterized immigrants with his nativist rhetoric. He has referred to sanctuary cities that shield undocumented immigrants from deportation as a "breeding concept." Trump has repeatedly characterized the undocumented as being teeming with members of the violent gang MS-13, once tweeting in 2018 that Democrats "don't care about crime and want illegal immigrants, no matter how bad they may be, to pour into and infest our Country, like MS-13."

Now a shameful stain on U.S. history, Trump's family-separation policy resulted in the splitting up of more than two thousand children and their migrant parents. Some of those children were likely orphaned by the Trump administration's zeal to halt migration across the border. An inspector general's report later found that the administration never really had a firm handle on the actual number of separated children. The total is likely much higher than the government has admitted.

In April 2019, a court filing from the Trump administration estimated it could take one to two years to locate thousands of immigrants who were separated by U.S. authorities at the border.

Thinking about my own father's story of coming to America as a Cuban refugee, it was difficult to keep my emotions in check as I considered the human costs of such a grotesque policy. Can you imagine being a child in a family that has handed over its life savings to a smuggler only to reach the border and have the U.S. government tear them apart? Take it one step further. Picture yourself as a child locked in a jail-like setting, as many of these young migrants have been, caged up with other kids. Still, in the eyes of the U.S. government, you are as much a criminal as your mother who, yes, broke the law by taking you across the border. Now continue to see yourself through this child's eyes. You are waiting in this facility for days, weeks, maybe months, all the while wondering if you will ever see your mother again. You're just a kid, wondering when this government-imposed child abuse will end. Would we do this to these children if they were white?

I had been told by sources both inside and outside the administration that the White House saw these harsh tactics as a "deterrent" to illegal immigration. The thinking was that once word of this horror show at the border made its way to Mexico and Central America, migrants would think twice about fleeing to the United States. Of course, what those officials didn't understand was that they were criminalizing desperation. These families were often escaping far worse conditions in gang-infested communities. Given the choice between possible separation at the border or death at home, where is the deterrent?

I've been to the border for several assignments on the immigration issue over the course of my career. Never in my life have I seen the "invasion" of migrants Trump so often talks about. Instead, what we face at the border is a massive humanitarian challenge worsened by a U.S. policy in Latin America that has been adrift for decades. Our drug war south of the border has made the violent illegal narcotics trade wildly profitable in Mexico and across Central America. Exactly what we should all do about that ineffective policy is a debate for another book. But I will pass along what law enforcement officials have relayed to me about their experiences on the border. In many cases, they are seeing women and children, once they set foot on U.S. soil, walking right up to border patrol agents for help. Many of them aren't looking to evade the agents. They *want* to be arrested. They want to file for asylum because they've placed their hopes in the promise of America. That's the background I brought into the White House Briefing Room in June 2018, when I pressed Sarah Sanders on the morality of the zero-tolerance policy.

It was on this same day that former attorney general Jeff Sessions had defended the administration's policy by citing the Bible, paraphrasing the scripture that reads, "[O]bey the laws of the government because God has ordained them for the purpose of order." That, of course, is not how the law works in the United States. That would mean the government could devise any kind of policy and point to the Bible and order citizens to "obey." That's not much of a legal justification given the separation between church and state embedded in the Constitution.

So, I asked Sarah Sanders, the daughter of a Baptist preacher turned governor, to weigh in on what Sessions had said.

"Where does it say in the Bible that it's moral to take children away from their mothers?" I asked.

Sanders replied that it is "very biblical to enforce the law. That is actually repeated a number of times throughout the Bible." I pressed her further on this line of thinking, wondering where in the Bible it justified the separation of children from their parents. Clearly frustrated, Sanders fired back: "I know it's hard for you to understand even short sentences."

Rather than answer the question, she went on the attack, a clear sign she had lost the argument. It was all but an admission that she couldn't defend the policy in her own wheelhouse. If the daughter of a minister can't explain how it's morally defensible to rip kids away from their parents, then probably nobody can.

The next day, I got a call from Sanders. It was a bad connection, and I was in a sketchy area for cell reception, but I could make out that she was apologizing for her comment at the briefing.

"It was the heat of the moment," I replied.

Listen, I don't regret posing the question. I'd do it again and again. Truth be told, I was badgering other officials in the administration about the policy. (These guys never wanted to be quoted on the record.) One of them told me the administration would prefer to detain the families together, but that the detention facilities for adults were not suitable for children. Therein lay the problem: if you detained the parents, you had to separate the kids, the official said. The problem for the government, in some cases, was that once the families were separated, the government occasionally had trouble keeping track of it all. Kids went one way; parents went another. Most times they would be reunited. But there were incidents when it didn't happen.

Keep in mind that the entire family-separation policy was driven by Trump who had said he wanted to end "catch and release," the practice of allowing border crossers to be released before a hearing. Trump insisted that only a small percentage of those released would subsequently appear in court for their hearing. Yet the Justice Department's own data say otherwise, noting that the vast majority of migrants actually do show up for their court date. In short, Trump was exploiting a negative, and false, stereotype that migrants come into the United States only to melt into American society before mooching on the nanny state or committing crimes against law-abiding citizens. He was also willfully ignoring a number of studies clearly showing that immigrants, legal and undocumented, commit crimes at lower rates than native-born Americans.

As for my question to Sarah Sanders at the briefing, it was well within the bounds of fair reporting in the Trump era. Again, less pointed queries are likely to be met with more obfuscation and lies. When it comes to family separations, though, I'm sorry, but you have to hold their feet to the fire. I've said it before and I'll say it again: there are not two sides to a story when it is a matter of right versus wrong. Separating kids from their parents is just wrong. The White House finally backed down only after the press exposed the policy as the horror show it was.

When the history of the Trump administration is written, I have every confidence that its zero-tolerance policy will be remembered for its inhumanity maybe more than any other Trump policy. What made it so deeply troubling, even more than the repulsiveness of the policy itself, was the knowledge that, if the administration hadn't been challenged by journalists and activists on this issue, it's very likely that most Americans would never have learned of this practice. Never mind my questions in the White House Briefing Room. Think of all the terrific reporting coming from my colleagues in the field, who were down on the border, talking to the migrants about missing children or missing parents. If ever there was a case for a robust and healthy media scrutiny of governmental policy, this was it. In exposing the family-separation policy, the free press in America lived up to its promise of holding our leaders accountable. Journalists had filled a void left by the GOP-led legislative branch of government, which was unwilling to fulfill its oversight duty when it came to Trump's border madness.

While Charlottesville had pulled back the curtain on just how far Republicans were willing to go in their acceptance of the president's worst instincts, it was becoming increasingly clear that what had happened in Virginia was just a starting point. At the border, Trump was beginning to leave a legacy of cruelty that would be hard for the GOP to live down, and impossible for the country to forget. History won't soon forget what happened to the migrant children. Those kids will have good reason to doubt America's greatness.

9

Dictators over Democracies

Radical as much of Trump's domestic policy had been at times through his first eighteen months in office, his foreign policy was where the tectonic shifting was possibly more lasting, with the potential to damage American alliances for the foreseeable future. While this alienation of our closest allies had been going on since Trump first took office, it was in the summer of 2018 when we saw the culmination of his foreign policy in his first summit with Kim Jong-un, the North Korean dictator: America was now a country that was not only comfortable with dictators, but friendlier to them in some cases than we were to our closest allies.

This had the effect of fundamentally altering the foreign policy approach that had been pursued by both Democrats and Republicans since the beginning of the post–World War II era. It didn't take a genius to figure out that Trump's moves were of great concern to some of the most experienced diplomatic and national security personnel in and around government. Even within the Trump administration, national security officials have found the president's embrace of authoritarian regimes alarming, which explains the torrent of leaks of the president's phone calls and his interactions with world leaders.

"It doesn't make a difference if you're a Republican or a Democrat," one former Trump national security official told me privately. Cozying up to the likes of Russian president Vladimir Putin while elbowing aside longtime allies such as Germany's Angela Merkel is simply something a U.S. president shouldn't do. This official told me he honestly couldn't figure out whether Trump was fully committed to advancing U.S. interests. Long before Special Counsel Robert Mueller completed his investigation, this official confessed he really wasn't sure why Trump was so cozy with Russia's Vladimir Putin.

"I can't answer that question," the official told me, in what felt like an unbelievable admission from someone in the national security realm. "I really don't know."

With the world in a constant state of Trump news overload, you will be forgiven if you've forgotten the early antics of the president's first few weeks in office, when he would hop on the phone with foreign leaders, leaving those heads of state in something of a state of shock over his unconventional way of doing business. That official I just mentioned said that he and others were almost constantly rattled by Trump's behavior in dealing with his foreign counterparts. For example, there were the conversations Trump had with the Australian prime minister and the Mexican president, which were revealed less than two weeks after he entered the Oval Office. Trump unloaded on Prime Minister Malcolm Turnbull about an Obama administration agreement to take in refugees from Australia, and he complained about immigration, of course, to Mexico's president, Enrique Peña Nieto.

Trump hated the leaks. They fueled his conspiracy theories about being the victim of a "deep state," referring to a group of unelected officials actually in control of a government—a fear that his close advisers, including Steve Bannon, egged on behind the scenes. Having covered the White House for six years, including two years under Trump, I have never come across any evidence of a "deep state." What

I have come across—and this should encourage every American—are officials who have occasionally helped us reporters understand what is going on inside the government. They are dedicated public servants, folks who come forward with information that is vital to meeting the public's expectation that we have good government.

As much as I have seen obvious flaws in some members of the Trump team, I would be remiss if I didn't report on the sizable number of officials in government who have attempted to help me and count-less other reporters as we've grappled with the overwhelming task of covering Trump. (We can't name them of course. Trump would run them out of town on a rail.) There were instances, yes, when Trump officials relayed information to reporters to exact revenge on rivals inside the White House. But those were usually the political folks in-side the West Wing backstabbing one another over turf. We did our best to sort through some of that nastiness, and not just blurt it out on the air, unedited. But there were other officials who understood our need to get to the bottom of the president's agenda, shining a light on some of Trump's provocative conversations regarding policies and with world leaders that alarmed veterans in both the national security and domestic policy realm.

When they found the occasional whistleblower, the Trump peo-ple swept many of them out of their official positions as best they could, but they couldn't find them all. Whether they are still in place or have moved on, it should be noted that countless officials, who will go nameless here of course, deserve our gratitude. It's not an easy thing, during any administration, to go to a reporter with sensitive information about what's happening inside the White House. Trump likes to blast these anonymous sources as phony and "fake news," but I'm here to tell you, and President Trump knows this: these sources are as real as you and me.

Adding to the anxiety, particularly among national security staffers, Trump would occasionally bounce some pretty outlandish ideas off just about anyone in any setting. The same former national security official told me Trump talked up the idea of carrying out a military strike on Venezuela with participants at the United Nations General Assembly in September 2017.

"The Chief of Staff told him it was not a good idea. The National Security Advisor told him it was not a good idea. He's talking to foreign leaders and he keeps bringing it up," the official said about Trump's fixation on Venezuela at the United Nations General Assembly.

This was the same meeting of the UNGA where Trump was already ridiculing North Korean dictator Kim Jong-un as "Little Rocket Man." It was around this time, the official said, that Trump was also sounding out the idea of launching some kind of military action against North Korea. What disturbed some of the aides around him, the official added, was that the president seemed incapable of being discreet about such sensitive matters.

"He doesn't have a filter of that sort," the official said.

Trump seemed intrigued by the idea of giving North Korea a "bloody nose," a small-scale strike that would send a message of strength to Kim. Just about all Trump's advisers at the time, the official said, cautioned against it, as the North Korean dictator could very well launch a counterstrike at South Korea, potentially triggering a larger war, with massive unintended consequences.

"He was told all hell would break loose," the official said.

In October 2017, while viewing the damage in Puerto Rico left by Hurricane Maria, Trump continued to vent about Kim. Sources inside the Puerto Rican government told me the president seemed less interested in the storm's aftermath than in the tempest brewing between the United States and North Korea over dictator Kim's nuclear weapons program. Trump had been beating his chest for weeks, warning Kim of "fire and fury."

Meeting with Puerto Rican governor Ricardo Rosselló, sources told me, Trump boasted of his "nuclear football," the briefcase used by American presidents to initiate a nuclear attack. Summoning the aide carrying the football to approach, so the governor could have a closer look, Trump told Rosselló that he was going to use it on Kim if he stepped out of line. Rosselló, the sources said, thought Trump was "fucking crazy." After Trump failed to appreciate the level of devastation left by Hurricane Maria in Puerto Rico—at one point infamously tossing rolls of paper towels to storm survivors—Rosselló was no longer worried just about the future of his island. Now he was suddenly fearful of Trump's handling of arguably the world's most sensitive national security crisis.

When I interviewed Rossello about this in March 2019, he wouldn't elaborate on what Trump said. At the time of the interview, his team was being bullied by White House officials who were threatening the governor's aides after Rossello criticized Trump for accusing the Puerto Ricans of wasting disaster relief money.

"Your governor is fucking things up," the aides quoted White House adviser Peter Navarro as saying during the meeting.

"If the bully gets close, I'll punch the bully in the mouth," Rossello told me.

As for Trump's comments about using the nuclear football on Kim, Rossello would only say "there were other topics that were being discussed, and my view is that the sole focus of that trip should have been on Puerto Rico.

"He was talking about a whole host of other issues, but I would rather leave those conversations internal," the governor added.

Later, in January 2018, Trump repeated much of this braggadocio when he boasted on Twitter that his nuclear arsenal was larger than Kim's: **Will someone from his depleted and food starved regime please inform him that I too have a Nuclear Button, but it is a much bigger & more powerful one than his, and my Button works!** he tweeted.

Needless to say, all this rhetoric was highly unnerving to America's closest allies. One of the side effects of my clashes with Trump was that I had become of interest to some of the embassies around Washington. Ambassadors and their staff were seeking to invite me over, mostly for off-the-record discussions, to get a sense of what I knew about Trump. The conversations almost always boiled down to questions about Trump's mental state: "What's he really like?" "Is he unstable?" As I have told countless people, U.S. citizen and non-U.S. citizen alike, I don't have an answer to that question. I'm not a psychiatrist. Trump's behavior is, to put it mildly, outside the spectrum of what we have come to expect from an American president. But I also thought Trump was more crazy like a fox.

It was on this particular occasion, over drinks at the embassy of a key U.S. ally, that it was disclosed to me that there were concerns about whether Trump could initiate a sudden launch of America's nuclear arsenal. This became a story for me, which I wrote, along with my colleague Pentagon correspondent Barbara Starr. Multiple sources told us that these concerns had been raised with members of Congress. Senate Foreign Relations Committee chairman Bob Corker, a frequent Trump critic, eventually held a hearing on the presidential authority to launch nuclear weapons. I won't go too deeply into how such launches are authorized, but the president cannot simply push a button on his desk and fire missiles across the globe. Still, as we reported at the time, at least one NATO partner country raised concerns with members of Congress about the president's command of the U.S. launch system. A diplomatic source from the country whose embassy I visited that day said that they became more comfortable following a U.S. government briefing on the subject. Members of the administration tried to allay their fears by explaining that the existing launch process had sufficient checks in place to discourage Trump from doing anything rash. But none of this is really comforting, is it?

Still, Trump continued to raise alarm bells on the world stage with his abnormal behavior right into 2018, when it was disclosed to me in May that Trump had clashed over the phone with Canadian prime minister Justin Trudeau. During the call, Trump and Trudeau argued over the steep and punitive tariffs the administration had imposed on Canadian steel and aluminum imports. Trump had imposed the new tariffs unilaterally—that is, without an okay from the legislative branch—citing national security reasons, something he needed to do in order to go around Congress. Senior administration officials had oddly justified the steel and aluminum tariffs to me as necessary to protect the U.S. steel industry so that—get this—there would be enough factories in the United States capable of producing the volume of military hardware needed *in the event of a Third World War.*

Yes, they actually said that. This is a good case in point for why sources sometimes go on background, to tell us things anonymously they'd be embarrassed to say publicly.

When Trudeau asked Trump how he could justify the tariffs on national security grounds, the president did not mention a Third World War; he tried a different argument, and made an erroneous historical reference (to put it mildly).

"Didn't you guys burn down the White House?" Trump asked a puzzled Trudeau.

It was a reference to the War of 1812, except Trump had his facts wrong. The Canadians didn't burn down the White House. That was the British. Canadian sources confirmed this part of the conversation to my colleague Paula Newton, who covers Canada for CNN.

After that leaked call, I'm told, Trump and his team decided that enough was enough. They began to shrink the circle of officials brought into the loop on such calls.

Since our reporting on the War of 1812 phone call, I have come to learn some of the difficulties encountered by these officials who struggled to stay abreast of Trump's conversations with other world leaders. One serious complication, according to a well-placed administration official, was that Trump preferred to conduct these calls from inside the Executive Residence of the White House, which was off-limits to many staffers. So, some officials, rather than being in the room with the president, would have to monitor the calls from the Situation Room, far away from Trump. That's a problem, as such officials are often needed in the room to guide the president through complicated issues on a phone call with a foreign leader, not something you can do if you're in another part of the White House.

And when it comes to our neighbors and allies, Trump is not only skeptical of them but also downright hostile—curious behavior for any government official, but positively baffling for the sitting U.S. president.

PERHAPS MOST STRIKING ABOUT TRUMP'S APPROACH TO FOREIGN policy was not just whom he attacked, but also whom he cozied up to. In retrospect, it should come as no surprise, given the president's treatment of the free press and his willingness to interfere with the independence of the judiciary, that Trump befriended some of the most notorious autocrats and human rights violators in the world.

Around the time of Putin's reelection in March 2018, I was told, Trump wanted to send the Russian president a news clipping, signed by him, to wish him good luck.

"Vladimir, you're going to do great," Trump was going to tell Putin, according to an administration official who saw what happened and then raised the concern with other aides.

"Other people were aware," the official said.

It was something Trump used to do during his campaign for president: mail off a news article to a reporter, as a way of saying he liked the piece. Trump's oversize squiggly signature would be scrawled across the clipping. That Trump wanted to make the same gesture to Putin worried some West Wing aides. The official who told me about this said it's not clear whether Trump ultimately sent off the clipping to the Russian president.

Still, as has been reported, Trump ignored the warnings of national security officials when they urged him not to congratulate Putin during a phone call between the two leaders after the Russian president was reelected to a fourth term in office, as the election was essentially a sham. The phrase "Do not congratulate" was written on briefing materials that Trump apparently had not read or disregarded altogether. A senior administration official confirmed for me the "Do not congratulate" story, first reported by the *Washington Post*.

Trump routinely confounded his own national security team with this sort of behavior. That same former member of the team told me it wasn't clear if any of this was proof that Trump had been "compromised" by the Russians, but the official couldn't rule out that possibility, a disturbing bit of analysis from someone who had worked so closely with the president. Still, the official said, it could also be that Trump can't control his impulses. Either way, it's a stunning admission from a top official who worked in the Trump administration.

The same official said that Trump's unpredictability often made life miserable for top officials in the West Wing, mainly Chief of Staff John Kelly, who could be overheard outside the Oval Office asking other staffers, "You didn't leave him alone, did you?"

Kelly was kidding, a separate senior White House official explained, acknowledging the chief of staff often joked about his unhappiness with Trump.

"He didn't disguise the fact that he didn't always like his job. He has a very dry sense of humor," the senior official explained.

It goes without saying that what most puzzled and worried national security officials inside the administration was Trump's coziness with Russian president Vladimir Putin. There was just something strange about how, despite the heightened scrutiny of his relationship with Russia and the investigations surrounding him, Trump never criticized Putin, and in fact he pursued policies that benefited the Kremlin, often over the interests of the American people. Yes, the Trump administration finally imposed sanctions on Moscow, but it did so, for all intents and purposes, because it was forced to take action by Congress. A question posed time and again at Trump press conferences and at White House briefings was why the president just couldn't bring himself to agree with the U.S. intelligence community's conclusion that Russia had interfered in the 2016 election.

As we traveled the world with Trump on his tumultuous foreign trips, the president would all but toe the Kremlin line on a variety of issues. Take NATO, for example. Again, much of this dates back to the campaign, when Trump would refer to the decades-old alliance as "obsolete," but he continued this baffling behavior as president. When we got to Belgium in May 2017, for a meeting of NATO in Brussels, Trump was beating up on the alliance again. One of the key questions of that trip was whether he would honor Article 5 of the NATO charter, which states that an attack on one member country is an attack on all members of the alliance. The one and only time that article was put into action was after 9/11, when NATO countries joined forces and went to war against the Taliban and al Qaeda in Afghanistan. For starters, there should never be a conversation about whether a U.S. president will honor Article 5. The mere mention of that all but invites Putin to meddle in the affairs of NATO's smaller member states, such as those in the Baltic region. Trump had suggested during the campaign that his commitment to Article 5 might hinge on whether members of the alliance were meeting their financial commitments to the organization and devoting 2 percent of their GDP to defense spending. Some countries were falling short in that regard.

Trump tried to sell this squishiness on NATO in populist terms during a speech at NATO headquarters in Brussels, as he heaped criticism on U.S. allies.

"Twenty-three of the twenty-eight member nations are still not paying what they should be paying and what they are supposed to be paying for their defense. This is not fair to the people and taxpayers of the United States," he said in his speech.

He never explicitly restated America's commitment to Article 5 during the course of his remarks. Secretary of State Rex Tillerson later told reporters that Trump was still on board with that key pillar of the NATO alliance. But was he? As Trump might say, "Who the hell knows?" Privately, national security officials were growing increasingly worried about Trump's true intentions. And diplomatic officials with NATO and at foreign embassies in DC with whom I spoke were beginning to wonder whether Trump could be counted as a friend when it came to European stability. Nobody could figure out what it all meant, but it was concerning, administration and diplomatic sources have told me. Publicly, it should be noted, NATO's secretary general Jens Stoltenberg has said Trump's tactics have prompted some countries to increase their defense spending.

The pattern continued, as we all remember, during Trump's meeting with Putin in Hamburg, at the G20 summit in July 2017. Trump and Putin met behind closed doors for more than two hours on the sidelines of the summit. After their meeting was over, Secretary Tillerson told reporters that Trump had pressed Putin on the election interference issue. That seemed significant, we all thought. Putin, the secretary of state said, had denied the allegation. But the Russians had a different take on the closed-door discussion. Foreign minister Sergey Lavrov told reporters that Trump seemed to accept Putin's denials and even conceded that the election-meddling story had been exaggerated in the American media. That seemed believable given Trump's tirades on Twitter over the Mueller investigation. Even more troubling, the *Washington Post* reported a year and half later, in January 2019, that Trump had sought to keep notes from the closed-door meeting with Putin from being leaked and instructed his interpreter not to talk about the encounter. Add to that, Trump and Putin had a separate meeting after dinner at the same G20 in Hamburg, but that encounter wasn't even disclosed until days later. Further, Trump did not bring his own interpreter to that meeting. Video emerged of the two leaders at the dinner table from that night. Trump can be seen in the video motioning to Putin in a way that appeared to indicate he wanted to pull the Russian president aside to speak to him in private. All of this added to the speculation in the U.S. national security community that something was off with Trump's behavior. It was all so damn puzzling.

Trump and Putin had another peculiar encounter later in the year, at the Asia-Pacific Economic Cooperation (APEC) summit in Vietnam. During that November 2017 conversation, Trump said he and Putin again spoke about the continuing questions regarding interference in the 2016 U.S. election. Trump sounded almost sympathetic as he relayed how Putin had denied it all.

"Every time he sees me, he says, 'I didn't do that,' and I really believe that, when he tells me that, he means it," Trump said to reporters on Air Force One. "I think he is very insulted by it, which is not a good thing for our country."

The comment made waves all the way back in Washington. Who cares if Putin is upset about the special counsel's investigation? What's more important than getting to the bottom of a conspiracy by a foreign adversary to interfere in an American election? Both Republicans and Democrats largely agree with the refrain that Putin can have better relations with the United States when he ceases his destabilizing actions. Trump's point of view appears to dovetail more with the rhetoric coming out of Moscow than the bipartisan concerns about election integrity back in Washington. And this is precisely what worried members of his own national security team. It was one of those episodes that just seemed weird. If it had happened only once, that could be understood. But this acceptance of the Kremlin's version of events kept happening and would only get louder and more emphatic as time went on.

Trump's unusual behavior with autocrats and dictators extended well beyond his relationship with Putin. As we all saw during his trip to Asia in 2017, he cozied up to China's president Xi Jinping before jetting off to the Philippines, where he laughed it up with that country's brutal leader, Rodrigo Duterte.

In Beijing, Trump and Xi got along famously. Xi rolled out the red carpet for Trump's visit to the Chinese capital with the kind of pomp and circumstance that other world leaders have come to recognize as the way to this president's heart. In Beijing's Forbidden City, there were elegantly choreographed dances. Xi told Ivanka that her daughter had become a national obsession after she sang in Mandarin for the Chinese people. Trump ate it all up.

A senior White House official acknowledged that the two leaders have forged a close bond. For all of the criticism of the president's relationship with Putin, this official told me Trump and Xi have the real "bromance."

"What's fascinating to me is that he's much cozier with President Xi. And I can't believe that doesn't get more coverage," the official said.

Meanwhile, members of the White House press corps learned what traveling to China is truly all about. We had to be on guard at all times to prevent any kind of cyberattacks on our cell phones. As we landed in Beijing, we turned over our mobile phones and laptops, which were all placed in a metal box on our charter plane. We used burner phones and laptops instead to prevent hackers from infiltrating our devices and wreaking havoc. It's an important reminder of the liberties we take for granted in the United States. In China, there is no expectation of privacy, and there is certainly no respect for freedom of thought.

Having this kind of awareness of the importance of freedom of thought and expression is an essential American value that should be shared by any U.S. president, in my view. During a trip to China in November 2014, President Obama held a rare joint news conference with Xi. What was so remarkable about that press conference was that Xi actually took a question from an American journalist, Mark Landler of the *New York Times*. Landler pressed Xi on press access issues in China. And remarkably, after it first seemed that Xi was going to ignore the question, the Chinese leader actually answered it—not to anybody's satisfaction, except for the Chinese, but he answered it. We later learned that it took some arm-twisting from top White House officials, including Obama, to persuade Xi to take the question. It was a critical moment during Obama's trip, demonstrating the U.S. commitment to press rights around the world.

Flash forward three years to Trump's so-called press conference with Xi. The Trump team didn't do the same arm-twisting. So, there were no questions, which meant it wasn't really a news conference.

"It was at the Chinese insistence there were no questions today," Sanders told reporters.

Previous press and advance officials from both Democratic and Republican administrations complained in news accounts that the Trump team had stumbled badly. As these veterans from past administrations explained, the Chinese always gripe about questions. They never want to take questions because they can't control what American journalists are going to ask. But it's the job of the White House, including the U.S. president, to insist that the press always be allowed to do its job. That's standing up for American values on the world stage. If the Chinese want to have the American president posing side by side with their leader, an image of legitimacy and stability to send to their citizens, then they need to respect U.S. values. The problem with Trump, of course, is that he couldn't care less about press freedom.

This total lack of regard for the American press was magnified further during Trump's visit to the Philippines. In Manila, he once again demonstrated his fondness for brutal autocrats, as he praised that country's leader, Rodrigo Duterte.

"We've had a great relationship," he said at a bilateral meeting with Duterte.

After the two leaders delivered their statements, reporters attempted to shout their questions, only to be ridiculed.

"You are the spies," Duterte said, getting a chuckle out of Trump. "You are," Duterte continued. Trump laughed some more.

Duterte had good reason to dodge questions from U.S. reporters. Ever since he came into office, he has presided over a violent crackdown on suspected drug dealers in his country, a campaign that has resulted in thousands of extrajudicial killings and sparked a global outcry. Journalists are also murdered in the Philippines. In 2017, the year of Trump's visit, the Philippines ranked as the fifth-most-dangerous country in the world for journalists. After her work uncovering the brutality of Duterte's regime, a fellow journalist and former CNN reporter in the Philippines, Maria Ressa, was accused of tax evasion, a charge regarded around the world as an act of retaliation by the government in Manila.

If the Trump folks had done their homework before arriving in Manila, they would have learned that, in 2016, Duterte even endorsed the idea of assassinating journalists.

"Just because you're a journalist you are not exempted from assassination, if you're a son of a bitch," Duterte said, in an appalling admission.

Despite this thuggish record, Trump declined to press his counterpart on human rights issues.

"Human rights briefly came up in the context of the Philippines' fight against illegal drugs," Sarah Sanders told reporters after Trump's visit with Duterte. A spokesman for Duterte contradicted her, incredibly or maybe not so incredibly, saying the subject of human rights never came up in discussions between the two leaders. Was Sanders lying? Or was it Duterte's folks? How were we to know?

Later that night, while having drinks with top White House officials, I remarked to retired army general H. R. McMaster, Trump's national security advisor, that Trump and Duterte seemed to be getting along like old friends. McMaster stared at me coldly and gave no response. I thought it was odd that he couldn't tell me one way or the other before he silently walked away.

Now, this may be where a critic chimes in that "we don't care about a bunch of whiny reporters" and their questions. Or perhaps you may ask, "Who are we to tell the people of the Philippines or China what to do?"

But that's exactly the job of an American president on the world stage. No, the president is not supposed to harass foreign leaders, insisting that they live their lives and lead their countries exactly how we do. But there are some democratic values we can defend on the world stage, such as free and fair elections and a free press. We know these institutions are worth defending because of the quality of life we enjoy in the United States. An American president could tell a world leader that these principles are worth respecting because they helped create the kind of enviable living conditions that made the United States the most prosperous society mankind has ever known.

As Trump traveled the world, it was dawning on me and, I'm sure, on many of my colleagues in the press that other Western leaders and their top officials were beginning to worry about what was happening to America. European leaders were certainly saying so publicly after their dealings with Trump. The U.S. president's sudden love affair with autocratic leaders, which he demonstrated time and again, and his erratic behavior, as demonstrated by his statements and tweets, became a national security concern during the first two years of his presidency.

Even without the worries over his launching a unilateral nuclear strike, Trump had given our allies more than enough cause for concern. More than anything else specific, there was the growing realization that the United States could no longer be counted on to play the geopolitical role that it had occupied for decades, whether that meant honoring commitments to NATO allies or pressing China's leaders on human rights violations.

All this set the stage for Trump's most unexpected overture yet: an invitation to meet with the world's most oppressive dictator, Kim Jong-un of North Korea.

THROUGHOUT 2017, TRUMP HAD BEEN INVOLVED IN A RHETORICAL arms race with Kim, which featured threats, name calling, and all manner of grade school behavior, all the while, behind the scenes, having other aims in mind. Trump clearly wanted to have the summit to end all summits with the North Korean dictator. To give credit where credit is due, Trump officials in the White House and over at the State Department, aided by some intense diplomatic efforts on the part of the South Koreans, achieved the unthinkable when they finalized the Trump-Kim summit.

Not surprisingly, there were some hiccups along the way, and for a time, the entire summit was canceled after the North Koreans missed a planning session and insulted Mike Pence. But Trump left the door open for the summit to move forward in his letter to Kim calling it off. The scuttled summit quickly became something of an embarrassment for the White House. A staffer in the White House Communication Agency, a nonpolitical military office that provides audio and video coverage of the president's movements, produced a coin to commemorate the Trump-Kim summit. One of our producers, Noah Gray, a well-known collector of challenge coins—these are frequently traded back and forth between law enforcement and military officials as a sign of friendship—had obtained one of the newly minted items. After Noah got wind of the coin, we were buzzing around the press areas of the White House. What in the world is this? we all thought. This is going to go viral. And it did.

Photos of the coin triggered an avalanche of amazement and some ridicule on social media. The coin featured Trump and Kim, face-to-face, with the words "Supreme Leader" next to the image of the dictator of North Korea. "Supreme Leader"? Secretary of State Mike Pompeo, in a sign that the administration was seeking to elevate Kim's stature, was already calling him "Chairman Kim," a sanitizing of the dictator's true role in North Korea, which is that of an oppressor of his own people. The nonpolitical staffers at the White House Communications Agency received an unfair amount of abuse over this coin, which had obviously been produced with the best of intentions. But the coin illustrated some of the concerns shared by world leaders about the prospect of a Trump-Kim summit. What was needed in confronting the dangerous regime in Pyongyang was real progress, not reality TV–style theatrics.

Within a week, to the relief of the global coin-collecting community, the summit was back on. On June 1, Trump and Pompeo walked out to the microphones on the South Lawn of the White House and announced that it was full steam ahead. There was a lot of relief behind the scenes inside the West Wing. We had heard that numerous West Wing officials, including advance staffers, had put in long hours arranging Trump's summit with Kim. Those staffers were well aware of the pride Trump took in showing off the letter he had received from the North Korean dictator, as part of their correspondence in setting up their face-to-face meeting. In short, Trump seemed more invested in this summit with Kim than other parts of his foreign policy agenda. From Seoul to Washington, there were even questions about whether he could be nominated for a Nobel Peace Prize. A Nobel Peace Prize for Trump? Whenever Trump was asked about that prospect, you could see his eyes widen. This was something he wanted badly.

About ten days later, we were all on a plane to Singapore to cover one of the most remarkable summits ever held by a U.S. president. I was in the TV pool on the day of the two leaders' meetings, which took place at a beautiful resort on Sentosa, a lush private island located just south of downtown Singapore. Simply put, my CNN team and others in the pool that day had a ringside seat to history.

Kim Jong-un, as interpreted through his translator, had a better way of describing that day:

"Many people in the world will think of this as a form of fantasy, from a science fiction movie," he said after his initial meeting with Trump. More like *Close Encounters of the Third Kim*, as the dictator was the third man in his family to rule the North Korean regime.

Trump and Kim had a series of mind-bending interactions that ended with the dictator receiving a tour of the presidential limousine, known as "the Beast," which had been flown to Singapore to shuttle Trump around the island. Trump was no longer threatening to vaporize North Korea with talk of "fire and fury" and "Little Rocket Man." This was a courtship. After the Saudis, Putin, Xi, and Duterte, a "bromance" with yet another dictator was born.

Surprisingly, we were able to shout questions to the two leaders after their first one-on-one meeting. Trump proudly declared that he and Kim were already off to an "excellent relationship," despite having only just met in person. He described the North Korean strongman as "very talented."

As you may recall from some of the coverage at the time, we tried to question Kim as well, as it was a rare but irresistible opportunity to press him on his plans.

"Chairman Kim, will you denuclearize?" a reporter with the *Los Angeles Times*, Noah Bierman, asked.

"Will you give up your nuclear weapons?" I tried, to no avail.

This was one of the rare moments when I actually received some praise from a few folks in conservative media, where it was noted that perhaps it *is* a good thing for a reporter to shout questions at a dictator.

Kim did not respond, but the show wasn't over. After a working lunch away from the cameras, the two leaders took a carefully choreo-graphed stroll through the lush gardens at the summit site. The stroll was rehearsed for days, with White House staffers playing the roles of the two leaders before Trump and Kim did it for real in front of the cameras, a White House official later told me. The press pool, in-cluding this reporter, was set up at the point where Trump and Kim would finish their walk, stop for a few moments, and then turn to the left to exit the scene. As the two leaders made their way down the path leading up to us, Trump pointed down to the ground as Kim nodded, right on cue. Trump and Kim then stopped just a few feet away from us, as the president declared the day a big success.

"How's it going, sir?" the Reuters correspondent Steve Holland asked.

"A lot of progress," Trump said. "Really better than anybody could have expected," he added.

"Has he agreed to give up any nuclear weapons, sir?" I asked.

"What are you signing?" other reporters followed up.

I had my iPhone up the whole time, recording the entire surreal scene. The video is still on my phone, actually. It's too crazy ever to be deleted. Kim, the most notorious dictator in the world, was stand-ing directly in front of me. He was a bit shorter than I expected and rather boyish, with his chubby cheeks, and seemed rather jovial. He was hardly menacing, in stark contrast with his brutal reputation. He seemed more like a politician.

A few minutes later, we were hustled into a room where Trump and Kim would sign their agreement. As we all waited for the two lead-ers to emerge and put pen to paper, there was an incredibly chaotic scene. U.S. journalists and representatives from North Korean state TV elbowed and shouted at one another for nearly twenty minutes as we jostled for position to capture the moment when Trump and Kim entered the room. Several North Korean officials and photographers tried to muscle Associated Press photojournalist Evan Vucci out of the way, but Evan refused to budge. They then tried to move over to where I was standing, next to Steve Holland. The North Koreans attempted to push Steve around, too. Holland, who is a wonderful, fatherly figure and an incredibly friendly guy, started waving his hands, telling them, "No way!" I've been around Steve for years, and I had never seen him get that mad.

Trump and Kim then entered the room and sat down at a table in front of us. Then, finally, we heard Kim's voice. Speaking through an interpreter, he told the various officials and reporters gathered in the room that he was prepared to make some major concessions to the United States and the rest of the world.

"The world will see major change," Kim said.

After they signed their agreement, I tried for a third time to ask my question.

"Mr. President, did he agree to denuclearize?" I asked Trump.

"We're starting that process very quickly. Very, very quickly," he responded.

I also tried to ask whether Trump and Kim had discussed American college student Otto Warmbier, who had died after being held in a labor camp by the North Koreans. But Trump didn't respond. My question clearly irked the U.S. team. National Security Advisor John Bolton turned around to give me the evil eye. Trump had repeatedly talked about Warmbier's case in the past. I thought, at the very least, he would bring it up and perhaps warn Kim to stop taking Americans hostage.

There was another indication that my questions had pissed off the Trump team. Brad Parscale, Trump's 2020 campaign manager, took to Twitter to call on the White House to pull my press pass, again.

Jim @Acosta should immediately have his press credentials suspended, Parscale tweeted. **He is an absolute disgrace!**

It wasn't long after the signing ceremony that we hustled over to a ballroom so he could take some questions—though we had had no idea that Trump was planning to hold a news conference at the conclusion of the summit.

"Be nice," Trump told me as he called on me for a question. "Be very respectful," he added.

"I'll be very respectful, sir," I responded. And then I asked a fairly benign question, as we were all just trying to figure out what the hell had just happened.

What had Kim Jong-un said to the president, I wanted to know, that would reassure him that the North Koreans were finished playing games?

"Very fair question," Trump responded. "He was very firm in the fact that he wants to do this," he continued, without offering any specifics. But even Trump sounded unsure.

"You never know, right," he added with something of a shrug. It was one of those rare moments of candor from Trump. He knew it was possible he was being played. "But I believe he's going to live up to that document," he continued, referring to the agreement they had just signed.

I had given my microphone back to a White House official who had come over to retrieve it from me. But off-mic, I asked Trump if he trusted Kim.

"I do. I do," he answered.

All in all, it was a pretty even-keeled exchange. Other reporters at the press conference were far more aggressive, pressing Trump on what he and Kim had just signed, what appeared to be a toothless document. Where were the guarantees that Kim would give up his nuclear weapons in a complete, irreversible, and verifiable manner? others wanted to know. It was all a leap of faith. There were no guarantees. Yet Trump had given Kim, a tyrant who had murdered untold numbers of North Koreans, the platform he was seeking:

sharing the stage with the American president. The Trump team would later learn just how wedded Kim was to his nuclear arsenal. The two leaders met again for a second summit in Vietnam. Their meetings ended abruptly with no agreement.

After the news conference in Singapore, it was off to the airport and the marathon flight back to Washington, with a refueling stop in Honolulu. Despite having extracted little more than a written agreement from Kim, Trump and his team left Singapore feeling pretty victorious. Trump was definitely in a good mood. He came back to the press cabin on Air Force One to chat with reporters. We shook hands, and he shared some of his thoughts about what it was like being face-to-face with the North Korean dictator. At the time, Trump was optimistic that he had achieved something . . . well, presidential. He had just taken questions from reporters for an hour, and he was well aware he had just rolled the dice with Kim.

Trump had come back to the press cabin of his plane to chat with reporters on countless occasions, but nearly all those chats had been off the record. On this day, as we were taking off for Washington, he didn't seem to mind being quoted. There was no animosity. There were no cries of "fake news." It was all strangely pleasant. For once, it seemed that Trump had pulled off something historic. Sure, the North Koreans were probably pulling a fast one on him, but there was a strong chance this initial summit could someday lead to a larger breakthrough. Trump sensed that. Within a few minutes, he returned to his section of Air Force One.

Looking back, I find it hard to sort out exactly what was going on inside Trump's head that day. As we later realized, he had become, once again, somewhat enamored of a dictator. As he told voters a few months later, in the weeks leading up to the midterms, at a rally in West Virginia, he and Kim "fell in love." Trump recounted the letters the two leaders had exchanged as they prepared to meet in Singapore.

"I was really being tough and so was he. And we would go back and forth. And then we fell in love, ok? No, really. He wrote me beautiful letters. And they're great letters. And then we fell in love," he told the crowd.

I'm just going to let that one speak for itself.

But speaking of strange and surreal, as we were flying back from Singapore, another member of the Trump team visited the press cabin. It was Stephen Miller. Stephen and I chatted for a bit about the summit and then turned to talking about, of all things, favorite places to eat in DC. He even asked me what my dream job was. (They were all on a high after Singapore, that's for sure.) Ours was a very pleasant exchange, in stark contrast with our confrontation in the Briefing Room over the Statue of Liberty. Another reporter in the press cabin, Catherine Lucey with the Associated Press, commented that it seemed Stephen had come back to the press cabin just to see me. I thought it odd, too, but at the end of the day, my attitude was that I had a job to do, and that meant I was perfectly capable of brushing aside their insults and personal attacks. You have to take the high road. Don't let them see you sweat. If Stephen wanted to put aside our very different views on immigration and talk about the DC restaurant scene for a few minutes, I could do that.

Not everybody on the Trump team was capable of being civil. As we stood on the tarmac in Honolulu during a refueling stop, soaking up the Hawaiian sunshine for about forty-five minutes, Steve Holland asked if I wanted to take a picture with him and Sarah Sanders. Sarah did it begrudgingly, after complaining that she didn't want to pose in a photo with me. This was all unprovoked; I was trying to be nice. She wasn't in the mood for that.

"What's the point? You're just gonna go back [to DC] and say bad things about us," she said to me. I just smiled and returned to my seat on Air Force One.

But there was a far more acidic reaction to my reporting waiting for me when I arrived back in Washington. After hours of sleeping and no Wi-Fi service (an annoying feature of flying in the press cabin on Air Force One), I scrolled through the notifications I had received on my Instagram account. There were dozens of messages from Trump supporters who had seen Parscale's tweet about the questions I had asked at the signing ceremony in Singapore. The comments left below my Instagram photos of the summit were far more sinister than Brad's threat of yanking my press pass. I was beginning to see more evidence that the maniacal ripple effect of the Trump echo chamber was expanding and getting darker.

"I can't wait for the day millions of me come knocking on your door and make you run the gauntlet o' pain all the way to the guillotine you piece of chit," an Instagram user said in a garbled and misspelled comment left on my account. "If I was president trump I think I would order the Marines to walk over to you and plant a bullet in your skull for what you did," the commenter added.

That happens only in dictatorships like North Korea, not democracies.

Arguably, this meeting with a reclusive and oppressive dictator was probably Trump's best-executed initiative since taking office. This summit had been his doing, his stagecraft, but more than that, the various petty bureaucracies in Trumpworld had finally laid down their arms long enough to get something almost right. At least it seemed that way at the moment. The agreement signed by the two leaders didn't amount to much. It had no teeth, no requirements that Kim abandon his nuclear weapons program; but it was a first step. Still, the spectacle in Singapore almost showed the kind of production that could have been possible if the White House hadn't been such a dysfunctional and operational nightmare from day one. It demonstrated Trump was capable of being more than a one-trick POTUS.

Still, I was under no illusions that this was a sign of a change within the administration. If there's one thing we've had to learn over and over since Trump took office, it's that there is no new leaf to turn over. The same would be true in the aftermath of Singapore, when Trump would embark on one of the most ill-conceived and troubling moments of his presidency: a meeting with Vladimir Putin in Helsinki.

10

Humbled in Helsinki

As the facts now demonstrate, Hillary Clinton was certainly on to something in her final debate with Donald Trump in Las Vegas in October 2016. During that debate, Clinton cited what had become a major national security concern to the U.S. intelligence community: that hackers working on behalf of Russian operatives had joined forces with WikiLeaks to release damaging information obtained through cyberattacks on Democratic officials, all in an effort to weaken the party's nominee. This was way before Special Counsel Robert Mueller's investigation was launched into possible collusion between the Trump campaign and Russia, a probe that did not prove a conspiracy. Clinton had already made the connection that, as Democratic accounts had been infiltrated, Trump had adopted much of the Kremlin's foreign policy agenda as his own: weaken NATO, abandon Ukraine, and so on.

The exchange between Clinton and Trump over Russia's apparent interference in the American democratic process must have gone over a lot of heads at the time. It was not as sensational as the revelations from the *Access Hollywood* video. "Grab 'em by the pussy" was something people could understand; hacks and WikiLeaks, at least at the time, seemed more complicated and unsubstantiated. Clinton's words at that debate did little more than trigger a nasty exchange with the

Republican contender. In the end, her warning in Vegas, that Trump could very well be Putin's "puppet," stayed in Vegas. Still, it makes for fascinating reading:

> CLINTON: So I actually think the most important question of this evening, Chris, is, finally, will Donald Trump admit and condemn that the Russians are doing this and make it clear that he will not have the help of Putin in this election?

Trump never really responded to the substance of the WikiLeaks charge and instead started a food fight with Clinton. The tactic worked for Trump, who continued to advocate for better relations with Russia, something the Kremlin obviously also wanted. He dodged the issue altogether.

> TRUMP: Now we can talk about Putin. I don't know Putin. He said nice things about me. If we got along well, that would be good. If Russia and the United States got along well and went after ISIS, that would be good. He has no respect for her [Hillary Clinton]. He has no respect for our president.

Then, a few moments later, came what was, in hindsight, a seminal moment from the campaign.

> CLINTON: Well, that's because he'd rather have a puppet as president of the United States.
> TRUMP: No puppet. No puppet.
> CLINTON: And it's pretty clear—
> TRUMP: You're the puppet!
> CLINTON: It's pretty clear you won't admit—
> TRUMP: No, you're the puppet.

CLINTON: —that the Russians have engaged in cyber-attacks against the United States of America, that you encouraged espionage against our people, that you are willing to spout the Putin line, sign up for his wish list, break up NATO, do whatever he wants to do, and that you continue to get help from him, because he has a very clear favorite in this race.

It was an eerily prescient exchange.

In a text to me, a former senior Clinton campaign adviser looking back on the Vegas debate, wrote, "Seemed too fantastic to be true. BUT IT IS." The adviser put that second part in all caps, not me.

By the summer of 2018, almost two years after Clinton called Trump Putin's puppet, Trump seemed to have gone out of his way to prove her right through his incessant attacks on the Russia investigation, his campaign against the media for reporting on it, and his erosion of long-standing U.S. policies that Putin was unhappy with. When his side meetings with Putin on the international stage weren't raising eyebrows, it was his rhetoric around NATO and his refusal to accept the intelligence community's assessment that Russia had interfered in our election. Factor in the incessant drumbeat of decidedly *real* indictments from the Russia investigation, and there seemed to be more and more evidence that the Trump-Putin relationship was questionable at best.

Prior to the summer of 2018, though, that unnerving feeling about Trump's seeming ease with Russia's autocratic ruler could be measured largely by a series of occasional interactions, court filings, and press reports. One-off encounters and statements had shown Trump's general reluctance to challenge Putin, but had left the overall portrait of their interactions to the public's imagination. What exactly was going on between these two guys? Even Trump's own national security team couldn't be sure, a former senior NSC official who served under Trump told me.

The shroud concealing much of their unusual relationship seemed to fall in July 2018, when Trump met with Putin for a summit in Helsinki. Given the enormous focus on the Russia investigation, it was a crucial time for a meeting that would put the Trump-Putin relationship on display for the world to see. Indeed, by the summer of 2018, the Mueller investigation had been in motion for more than a year, and in that relatively short time it had already shown itself to be one of the most successful and efficient special counsel operations in the history of the Justice Department. Evidence had already been presented that showed a number of attempts by Russia to penetrate Trump's orbit, with several indictments handed down and more coming continually.

While there was much about the Russia investigation that remained unclear, there were many things the public did know about what had transpired between the Trump campaign and Russia. For one thing, the Michael Flynn investigation had resulted in Flynn cooperating with the special counsel's office, but there had been also been indictments against several other fixtures in the Trump campaign's orbit. George Papadopoulos, a Trump campaign foreign policy adviser, was indicted for lying to the FBI. Paul Manafort, Trump's former campaign manager, was indicted on a variety of charges related to financial crimes and work he'd done for Ukraine. He was later convicted and sentenced to more than seven years in prison in two separate federal cases. Rick Gates, Manafort's deputy, was indicted on similar charges and was cooperating. A handful of other individuals had been indicted for lying to the FBI. And, of course, there was Roger Stone, the lifelong GOP dirty trickster who'd worked for Nixon and had managed to resurface in the Russia investigation, accused by Special Counsel Robert Mueller of being a key conduit, prosecutors allege, between the WikiLeaks effort to dump damaging emails about Clinton and officials with the Trump campaign. Federal prosecutors had also indicted thirteen Russian nationals and three Russian companies on charges of conspiracy related to the Russian propaganda effort to influence the 2016 election.

There was, of course, the meeting at Trump Tower in 2016 in which Don Jr., Jared Kushner, and Paul Manafort had all met with Russian attorney Natalia Veselnitskaya, who had ties to the Kremlin. The White House had initially lied to the public about the meeting's true purpose, saying in its earliest statement on the issue that it was about Russian adoptions, only to have Don Jr.'s emails reveal the meeting was aimed at obtaining dirt on Hillary Clinton. A more ethical, experienced campaign would have gone straight to the FBI to report the Russian overtures. Not only was that statement regarding the purpose of the meeting false, but so was Sarah Sanders's claim that Trump had not dictated the statement.

This became all too clear in June 2018, when Sanders was confronted with her own false narrative. The *New York Times* reported that the president's outside legal team had delivered a letter to the special counsel's office earlier in the year, laying out some explanations to questions from Mueller's team. One of the responses from Trump's lawyers was that, yes, in fact the president had dictated the letter on the Don Jr. meeting. Suddenly there was proof that Sanders's previous statement was wrong. On June 5, 2018, Jordan Fabian of the website the Hill and Josh Dawsey of the *Washington Post* both asked Sarah to explain herself. At this point, Sanders was beginning to use a new strategy in the briefings, referring questions to the president's lawyers.

FABIAN: What's the reason for that discrepancy?

SANDERS: Like you said, this is from a letter from the outside counsel, and I direct you to them to answer that question.

DAWSEY: Sarah, the words are literally—you said he did not dictate. The lawyer said he did. What is it? It's either one or the other.

SANDERS: I'm not going to respond to a letter from the President's

outside counsel. We've purposefully walled off, and I would refer
you to them for comment.

Like so much with the Trump White House, this whole episode—
both the Trump Tower meeting during the campaign and then the
White House's factually inaccurate response to the news of this meeting breaking—raised a fundamental question of why. Simply put,
why was there so much lying going on? Lying about Trump authoring
the statement. Lying about the actual purpose of the meeting. The
misstatements and stonewalling, it seemed to many reporters covering the Trump presidency, fit into a larger pattern of behavior. If
they didn't have anything to hide, why were there so many lies? Once
again, serious questions were being raised. Inside the Trump team,
multiple aides told me, they were just fine with misleading the press.
That was not the same as lying to federal investigators, they figured.
Not everybody got that memo, so to speak. People involved in the Russia investigation had been indicted for lying to the FBI. The longer the
investigation had gone on, the more examples there were of people in
Trump's orbit lying about Russia. And as the lies mounted, it seemed
too hard to write them off as coincidence. A key question, of course,
was how high did the lies go?

These lies looked all the more concerning when Trump's lawyers,
led by former New York City mayor Rudy Giuliani, began making the
case that a sitting U.S. president could not be indicted. Giuliani's arrival came after a rather stunning shakeup of Trump's legal team. The
president's lead outside attorney, John Dowd, had abandoned ship, as
had White House attorney Ty Cobb, who, I reported at the time, had
tired of Trump's tweets about the Russia investigation. Cobb, a former
federal prosecutor, simply couldn't go along with Trump's strategy to
demonize Special Counsel Robert Mueller, a source close to Ty told me.

A source inside Trump's legal team all but confirmed that the president's attacks on Mueller's investigation, along with Giuliani's wild

interviews with the press, were very much part of a strategy to undermine the public's confidence in the probe. The strategy was born out by a variety of polls that periodically found opposition to the Russia investigation climbing.

"Assume nothing was done without a strategy," the source said.

Dowd and Cobb believed in a strategy of cooperation with Mueller's office in order to wrap up the probe as quickly as possible. Cobb fought with Trump over his tweets about Mueller and the probe, thinking they were damaging to the president's case. Ty was one of the good guys at the White House, someone who actually enjoyed working with the press. He was often seen around DC at various White House watering holes, downing drinks with reporters, sometimes late into the night. (One night, a group of us met Ty at the Exchange, a bar near the White House that's popular with college students from George Washington University. As they often do on Thursdays after a night of kickball, the students were playing "flip cup." One group of these Millennials invited Ty and me over to play. "No no," we said. Thanks for the invite, we said. They wouldn't take no for an answer. Flip cup is basically a game where you race others to pound a cup of beer before flipping it over. There are videos on YouTube if you need further explanation. Ty nailed it on the first try. I regret to say it took me a few more attempts.)

For his part, Rudy Giuliani was less collegial. Giuliani came on the scene with a new strategy. Cooperation was out; combat was in, both in the media and with Mueller, as the ex–New York City mayor was suddenly offering himself for countless TV interviews that only seemed to add more fog to the Russia conversation. A former prosecutor who had sent mobsters to jail during his heyday, Giuliani was making some remarkable legal arguments, such as a sitting president of the United States can't be indicted and sent to jail, no matter the crime. It was an incredible thing to say. Was Giuliani telegraphing that Trump was in legal jeopardy? More likely he was just injecting some nonsense into the news cycle to change the narrative, a hall-mark of Trump's masterful manipulation of the media.

"In no case can he be subpoenaed or indicted. I don't know how you can indict while he's in office. No matter what it is. If he shot James Comey, he'd be impeached the next day," Giuliani had told the *Huffington Post*.

At the same briefing in which Fabian and Dawsey called her out, Sarah was asked about Trump having dictated the letter. I asked her if she could defend a comment from Giuliani that Trump could not be indicted even if he shot James Comey.

ACOSTA: Is that appropriate language coming from the President's outside lawyer to be talking about the President shooting Jim Comey in that fashion?

SANDERS: You would have to ask Rudy Giuliani about his specific comments. But thankfully, the President hasn't done anything wrong, and so we feel very comfortable in that.

As if that weren't enough of a hypothetical, one day earlier, Trump had tweeted that he could pardon himself.

@realDonaldTrump

As has been stated by numerous legal scholars, I have the absolute right to PARDON myself, but why would I do that when I have done nothing wrong? In the meantime, the never ending Witch Hunt, led by 13 very Angry and Conflicted Democrats (& others) continues into the mid-terms!

7:35 AM—Jun 4, 2018

All of this was hanging in the balance as the press corps prepared for Trump's trip to Helsinki. This extraordinary meeting between the two leaders was shrouded in questions and doubt: what was really going on between them? I couldn't forget that even some members of Trump's own national security team weren't totally comfortable with the president's bizarre behavior around Putin. It raised questions for them, too.

———————

AS COMPELLING AS ALL THE DIFFERENT THREADS OF THE RUSSIA investigation were, they hadn't yet been publicly woven together into a durable case of conspiracy with Moscow. Stepping back and following the massive web of lies spun over years by the most powerful man in the world, one could see it start to make sense, but there were plenty of question marks as well. As I often told people at events where I had been invited to speak, proving that Trump had actually colluded with the Russians in some kind of criminal conspiracy would be enormously difficult. Considering Mueller's reputation as the ultimate straight shooter in Washington, it's impossible to imagine the special counsel bringing anything less than an airtight criminal case against the president. Anything short of that would be devastating to Bob Mueller's legacy.

Despite some of the indictments that resulted from the Mueller investigation and the headlines it produced, arguably the most glaring and damning element of the Trump-Russia story came not from a court filing or a cooperating witness, but from the president's complete capitulation to Putin during their summit in Helsinki. Traveling with Trump in the days leading up to Helsinki, I began to get the sense that the United States was about to have a profoundly humbling moment on the world stage.

Before the fiasco in Finland, Trump stopped in Brussels, where he once again bashed members of NATO for falling short in their defense spending obligations to the alliance. He added insult to injury by conflating trade and defense issues, complaining about tariffs on U.S. products by countries in the European Union. In an interview with CBS, Trump called the "E.U." a "foe" because of its trade practices.

One German official responded by saying, "We can no longer completely rely on the White House."

Predictably, there was a clash behind the scenes at the summit
between Trump and his foreign counterparts over all these issues.
As I reported at the time, a Western diplomatic source at the NATO
summit described a "heated" exchange aimed at addressing some
of Trump's grievances. Trump left the meetings in Brussels with
America's most important military alliance once again bruised and
battered, another gift to Putin.

At a hastily called news conference that was announced as members of the White House press corps, including me, were headed to
London for Trump's next stop, the president unloaded again on NATO,
saying that he believed he had the authority to pull the United States
out of the alliance without congressional approval. It was a pretty irresponsible statement for a president to make. Sure, Congress would
almost certainly block Trump from pulling us out of NATO, but the
mere mention of that possibility sent a clear signal to Moscow that the
alliance was on thin ice—a curious message to send as Trump was
about to meet Putin face-to-face. A Western diplomat later told me
that much of the discussion behind the scenes during Trump's time
in Europe before Helsinki had centered on convincing the president
of the importance of NATO. No wonder U.S. allies were beginning to
doubt his commitment to the alliance that had kept Russia in check
for generations. That kind of conversation with an American president shouldn't ever be necessary, the diplomat argued.

Trump's destabilizing behavior didn't stop there. As the president
and the press moved on to Britain, Trump and I had another confrontation, this time at a joint news conference with Theresa May, at
Chequers, the British prime minister's official retreat outside London.
Now, I didn't think Trump would call on me at the news conference;
he preferred to call on Fox News in these settings. Plus, he had made

it pretty clear on numerous occasions what he thought of CNN and yours truly. But as a reporter, you have to be ready, nevertheless. With Helsinki fast approaching, my goal was to ask Trump if he planned to tell Putin at their upcoming summit to stay out of America's elections. I felt as though he had wavered and waffled enough on the question of Russian interference. I thought it would advance the Trump-Putin story line to find out if he was planning to tell the Russian leader to stop interfering in our democracy.

It was kind of a crazy ride out to Chequers. Our press buses barely made it through the narrow roads leading to the site of the news conference. With wooded land on both sides, we could feel the tree branches scrape across the top of the bus and break as the bus meandered its way to a beautiful apple orchard where press tents had been set up for our arrival. A few of my colleagues were teasing me, as I was reading a book about Winston Churchill and Franklin Roosevelt, penned by the American historian Jon Meacham. (I had developed a brief obsession with Churchill earlier in the year, after the movie *Darkest Hour* hit theaters.)

Prime Minister May opened the press conference with the usual pleasantries. She thanked Trump for expelling dozens of Russians from the United States after the Kremlin's alleged poison attack on an ex-KGB agent on British soil. (The Trump administration points to such actions as proof that there is nothing untoward between Trump and Putin, conveniently overlooking years of baffling comments from the president about the Russian leader.) She then announced that she and Trump would take four questions from both the American and British press. May called on a reporter from the BBC, and Trump later called on Kristen Welker, from NBC News. Welker asked the right question, which was whether Trump's criticisms of NATO and May were playing into Putin's hands. Trump didn't like the question and went on the attack.

"See, that's such dishonest reporting because—of course, it happens to be NBC, which is possibly worse than CNN," he said.

There he goes again. Unprovoked, Trump was once again attacking CNN at a news conference that was being aired around the world. If he was going to attack us by name, I thought, we should be able to ask a question, just as had happened at Trump Tower all the way back in January 2017. For me, it was simple: you attack us, we get a question. A few minutes later, Trump called on John Roberts, with Fox News.

That's when I jumped in. Trump was ready to rumble.

ACOSTA: Mr. President, since you attacked CNN, can I ask you a question—
TRUMP: John Roberts, go ahead. Go ahead, John.
ACOSTA: Can I ask you a question? (Inaudible.)
TRUMP: No. No. John Roberts, go ahead. CNN is fake news. I don't take questions—I don't take questions from CNN. CNN is fake news. I don't take questions from CNN. John Roberts of Fox. Let's go to a real network. John, let's go.
ACOSTA: Well, we're a real network, too, sir.

Trump had the gall to call Fox News a "real network." There are some good people at Fox—Shepard Smith, in particular, has been willing to hold Trump's feet to the fire—but other Fox anchors, such as Sean Hannity and Tucker Carlson, have essentially served as propagandists for Trump. In early 2019, *The New Yorker* published an extensive profile detailing the cozy relationship between the Trump White House and Fox News. I had seen all of this firsthand. The White House had carried out a sustained campaign of intimidation against CNN while giving Fox exclusive access to Trump on a regular basis. With the exception of a few stars at Fox, the network had become Trump state TV. I liked to describe it as "state-supported" TV, as Trump provided plenty of support to Fox. As a loyal viewer of the conservative outlet's morning program *Fox and Friends*, Trump frequently tweeted about the show's GOP-friendly segments, the kind of advertising money can't buy. He steered clear of Fox's straight shooters, Shepard Smith and Bret Baier. But he was happy to sit down with the TV outlet's sycophants, like Hannity, who was close with White House communications director Bill Shine, a former Fox News executive who left the network to work for Trump. As part of his severance deal with the network, Shine was still being paid by Fox while working at the White House, an astounding conflict of interest. On the campaign trail, Shine could be seen orchestrating live interviews with Trump for Fox personalities. The White House and Fox were working together hand in glove.

As for my interrupting at the press conference at Chequers, I had made my point; I had registered my complaint. And Roberts proceeded with his question.

As Trump answered John's question after calling me "fake news," my eyes turned to Theresa May, who was staring back at me as if to say, "I can't believe that just happened." A British diplomat later told me that they, too, were disgusted by Trump's attacks on the press. But what exactly are they supposed to do about it? I thought. This is our battle to fight, not theirs. As Trump and May left the news conference, I tried one last time and shouted a question.

"Will you ask Putin to stay out of U.S. elections?" I asked.

"Yes," Trump answered.

Even after our confrontation, he had answered my question.

As a quick aside, I must say I don't believe the Russia question was the most newsworthy moment from the press conference. That moment came when Trump offered perhaps his most candid comments to date on the subject of immigration. (As I've said before, as dishonest as Trump can be at times, he can also be remarkably candid.)

"I just think it's changing the culture. I think it's a very negative thing for Europe. I think it's very negative," he said about the impact of immigration on European culture. "And I know it's politically not necessarily correct to say that. But I'll say it and I'll say it loud. And I think they better watch themselves because you are changing culture. You are changing a lot of things. You're changing security."

There it is—Trump was speaking in code about what he sees in the United States, echoing the far-right extremists in Europe who have bemoaned the arrival of migrants there from war-torn countries such as Syria. To her credit, May responded to Trump's remarks by sounding more committed to the American tradition of welcoming immigrants than the American president himself. She rejected the notion that immigration had been a "negative thing" for Europe. It was quite a remark coming from the prime minister of the United Kingdom, whose leaders have historically spent a good deal of diplomatic energy maintaining Britain's "special relationship" with the United States. It's also worth noting, May was the leader of Britain's Conservative Party and had been attempting to finalize Brexit, the United Kingdom's messy withdrawal from the European Union. A fire-breathing liberal she was not.

"The UK has a proud history of welcoming people who are fleeing persecution to our country," May said, in what immediately sounded like a rebuke of Trump's immigration views. "We have a proud history of welcoming people who want to come to our country to contribute to our economy and contribute to our society. And over the years, overall immigration has been good for the UK," she added. A British diplomatic source said May's comments were a point of pride for the officials who had gathered for the news conference at Chequers. May's team was cheering her on behind the scenes, I'm told. She had repudiated Trump's xenophobia. It was another clear signal from an important U.S. ally that Trump's deeply unsettling rhetoric had to be challenged.

Trump wasn't finished with me. The next day, he posted a tweet declaring that he had gotten the upper hand at Chequers.

@realDonaldTrump
So funny! I just checked out Fake News CNN, for the first time in
a long time (they are dying in the ratings), to see if they covered
my takedown yesterday of Jim Acosta (actually a nice guy). They
didn't! But they did say I already lost in my meeting with Putin.
Fake News. . . . .

He forgot to mention the fact that I had asked him a question as he
was leaving the press conference. But that's fine. Still, he got one thing
right, which I mentioned in my tweet in response to his.

@Acosta
Takedown? I don't think so. Perhaps we should even the playing
field next time and you can take my question. (You're right about
one thing. I am a nice guy)

I remember the moment I saw Trump's tweet. My producer on that
trip, Allie Malloy, and I were walking across St. James's Park, in London, touring the city for a bit before our flights to Finland. Allie and
I both looked at the lock screens on our iPhones as the notification of
the Trump tweet about me flashed. We both started laughing. What
a time to be alive! It's a surreal experience being on the receiving end
of one of Trump's Twitter attacks. First of all, your phone immediately
blows up. "RIP your notifications," as the kids say. But this is nothing
to celebrate. There is a darker side, as this is also when the Trump troll
army joins the fray, posting a barrage of tweets supporting the president and attacking me. This is often when the death threats roll in.

Not to spend too much ink dissecting this, but I should also call
attention to the fact that Trump was, in his own way, praising me
in this tweet, which is how it was described in a number of news
reports about our confrontation. "[A]ctually a nice guy," he'd tweeted
about me. Fact check: True. This raises something I've heard from a

number of Trump aides, advisers, and friends: the president actually enjoys sparring with me. Some of this goes back to what Hope Hicks once told me, that Trump thinks, "Jim gets it." In a world where he's surrounded by sycophants, I suppose, he likes the challenge.

Trump may have thought I was a nice guy, but the folks at the White House weren't pleased. They decided to retaliate by pulling National Security Advisor John Bolton from a scheduled appearance on CNN's Sunday show *State of the Union with Jake Tapper.* This was an attempt by the White House to punish CNN for my clash with Trump at the news conference. But perhaps the White House had another motivation for pulling Bolton. The national security advisor would have been forced to explain on air all of Trump's destabilizing rhetoric from his previous two stops at NATO headquarters and in Britain. Removing Bolton from one of the Sunday talk shows provided some damage control.

There was more fallout for me after the Chequers press conference: I lost a friend. After John Roberts had asked his question, he came under attack for not having defended NBC and CNN. Tapper and others pointed out on Twitter that other networks had stood up for Fox in the past, when it had been treated poorly during the Obama administration. This was a fair point. Roberts released a statement to try to deal with the criticism.

"I know Kristen Welker of NBC. She is honest as the day is long. For the President to call her dishonest is unfair," Roberts said in a statement obtained by the *Washington Post*'s Erik Wemple. "I also used to work at CNN. There are some fine journalists who work there and risk their lives to report on stories around the world. To issue a blanket condemnation of the network as 'fake news' is also unfair."

John then repeated the same statement on the air on Fox News. It was hard to miss the underlying message in his remarks: he was willing to defend Kristen by name, but he did not do the same for me.

He said that CNN was not "fake news"—we all know that—but he allowed the "dishonest" remark to hang there.

Roberts had been a colleague of mine and, I thought, a friend for many years. We had both worked on the same CNN program, *American Morning*, for a couple of years. He was the anchor of the show, and I was one of its correspondents based in Washington. I would, on occasion, fill in for John on the anchor desk. And before our time together at CNN, we both worked at CBS News. John was the weekend anchor, and I was working out of the New York bureau. I had always looked up to John, who was in the running to replace Dan Rather on the CBS anchor desk. He was certainly one of the best broadcasters I had ever seen. I remember covering Hurricane Katrina from Biloxi, Mississippi, for CBS while he was braving the storm from New Orleans. We both led the *CBS Evening News* the night Katrina hit. Sadly, John didn't get the CBS anchor gig, and he left for CNN. I soon followed.

When I left CBS News for CNN, John had vouched for me to the network's management. It was helpful to have him on my side. Others, such as Scott Pelley from CBS, had spoken on my behalf as well. In addition to that, John knew my father from when he shopped at my dad's employer, a Safeway grocery store in Virginia. My dad would ask me all the time, "How's John? How's his family?"

By the time we all got to Helsinki, the damage to our friendship had been done. Shortly after our arrival, my producer Allie and I were walking up the street outside our hotel in Helsinki as Roberts and his producer, Fin Gomez, approached, heading in our direction. Then, all of a sudden, they both walked over to the other side of the street to avoid crossing our path. I haven't really talked to John since.

When folks wonder if I have any regrets, I have to say I really do wish I had not lost any friends during these three crazy years covering Trump. But it's happened. Unfortunately, I think it's happened to a lot of us.

BEFORE LONG, WE BOARDED THE PRESS BUSES FOR THE MAIN EVENT, the Trump-Putin joint news conference. As I set foot on the bus, I immediately spotted two of my biggest critics: Tucker Carlson and Sean Hannity, Trump's chief propagandists at Fox, were seated on the bus, too. And you know what? After all their attacks on me during their prime-time "state TV" programs, they didn't say a word to me. You'd think they would have had something to say to my face, but their faux-macho man bullshit, as it turns out, seems to stop at the doors to the Fox News headquarters.

When I arrived at the presidential palace in Finland's capital, a grand setting for the news conference, I came upon a chaotic scene. A massive crowd of journalists from around the world had gathered in the cramped holding area, all of us eager to take our seats. There was pushing and shoving. Print reporters yelled at TV photographers as they bumped into one another with their heavy equipment.

The scene would become only more crazed once we made our way inside. Within minutes, as we were waiting for Trump and Putin to finish their closed-door meeting, all hell broke loose. Finnish and American security officers had approached a man sitting a few rows behind me and asked him to leave. He refused and had to be forcibly removed from the venue. The man, who described himself as a writer for *The Nation*, was wrestled out of the press area of the ballroom, but not before he held up a sign that read, "Nuclear Weapon Ban Treaty." He insisted he hadn't done anything wrong. I can only tell you what I saw from my vantage point. Perhaps he had good intentions, but if you're a journalist, you don't bring a protest sign to a news conference.

The brief scuffle only added to the tension in the room. The press corps had been divided in half. Russians were on one side of the room; the Americans and other foreign press were assembled on the other side. I remember thinking, Am I with the bride or the groom?

(But let's not take that analogy any further.) Then the moment finally arrived, as Trump and Putin entered the room. Both men made brief statements about their meeting, and then we were off to the races.

The real news of the day came during the question-and-answer session. The Russian reporters, not surprisingly, asked what sounded like scripted questions from the Kremlin, a reminder of the truly awful state of affairs for the press in that country. Then Jeff Mason, a colleague of mine over at Reuters news service and former president of the White House Correspondents' Association, began to drill down. He did so, as any good reporter would, by asking about the news of the day. Even now, Trump's answers in Helsinki are still astounding.

> MASON: Mr. President, you tweeted this morning that it's U.S. foolishness, stupidity, and the Mueller probe that is responsible for the decline in U.S. relations with Russia. Do you hold Russia at all accountable for anything in particular? And if so, what would you consider them—that they are responsible for?
> TRUMP: Yes, I do. I hold both countries responsible. I think that the United States has been foolish. I think we've all been foolish. We should have had this dialogue a long time ago—a long time, frankly, before I got to office. And I think we're all to blame. . . . But I do feel that we have both made some mistakes. I think that the probe is a disaster for our country. I think it's kept us apart. It's kept us separated. There was no collusion at all. Everybody knows it. People are being brought out to the fore.

We were off to a bad start. The American president was calling the United States "foolish" in front of Putin. Trump's words were already dripping with submission. He said the Mueller investigation was a "disaster" for the United States. Again, if he had nothing to worry about, why was it such a disaster?

Putin made some news of his own, offering to cooperate with Mueller's investigation, but he never really denied interfering in the election. Later on in the news conference, after the Russians reporters had had another turn, Jonathan Lemire with the Associated Press got to the heart of the matter with Trump.

LEMIRE: My first question for you, sir, is, who do you believe? My second question is, would you now, with the whole world watching, tell President Putin—would you denounce what happened in 2016? And would you warn him to never do it again?

Trump would then go on to make perhaps the biggest gaffe of his political life, but to folks back in Washington, Democrats and Republicans alike, the moment felt worse than a gaffe.

TRUMP: My people came to me—Dan Coats came to me and some others—they said they think it's Russia. I have President Putin; he just said it's not Russia. I will say this: I don't see any reason why it would be . . . So I have great confidence in my intelligence people, but I will tell you that President Putin was extremely strong and powerful in his denial today.

Trump didn't realize how much controversy his comments had created until he returned to Washington, Kellyanne Conway told me. The president told Kellyanne that he had misspoken.

"He said, 'Why would I not believe him? And I meant why would I not not believe him,'" Conway remembers Trump saying.

So Conway and the rest of the president's team worked with Trump to come up with a new statement to the press, explaining what they claimed was a mistake.

"The sentence should have been . . . 'I don't see any reason why it wouldn't be Russia,'" Trump later told reporters.

Conway told me in an interview that she saw it as part of her job to tell Trump he had gotten things wrong in Helsinki.

"I am not afraid to tell him the truth. He accepts that *and expects* that. What would be the point of working here if my voice isn't heard and my view is not considered," she said.

The president all but bowed to Putin, the puppet master whom Clinton had warned about during her debate with Trump in Vegas. No Mueller indictment was necessary. Trump was guilty of showing weakness. The president told the world he would take Putin's word over that of his own handpicked intelligence officials, including Dan Coats, the director of national intelligence.

Putin was "extremely strong and powerful" in his denial? Reporters in the room were aghast. The white flag had been raised. Putin, at least on this day, had achieved a long-sought goal. After the fall of the Soviet Union and the economic collapse that followed, he had elevated the Russians back to an equal footing with the United States. And he didn't have to lift a finger. Trump had done all the work for him.

Jonathan then asked Putin what you could call the "money question":

LEMIRE: Does the Russian government have any compromising material on President Trump or his family?

Putin laughed, and there was laughter across the rest of the room. But the Russian leader had not intended to let any tension out of the room. When he laughed, he had sounded more like a Bond villain than an ally of the United States.

PUTIN: Now, distinguished colleague let me tell you this: When President Trump was at Moscow back then, I didn't even know that he was in Moscow. I treat President Trump with utmost respect. But back then, when he was a private individual, a businessman, nobody informed me that he was in Moscow.

Then came the nondenial denial from Putin.

PUTIN: Well, let's take St. Petersburg Economic Forum, for instance.
There were over 500 American businessmen—high-ranking, high-
level ones. I don't even remember the last names of each and every
one of them. Well, do you remember—do you think that we try
to collect compromising material on each and every single one of
them? Well, it's difficult to imagine an utter nonsense of a bigger
scale than this. Well, please, just disregard these issues and don't
think about this anymore again.

Yeah, that's right. Putin did not deny that he had compromising
information on Trump. And let's just address the elephant in the room:
we all knew what Putin was talking about. He was not denying that
his government was in possession of the infamous "pee tape" video of
prostitutes at the Ritz-Carlton Hotel in Moscow. In fact, based on Putin's
response, it sounded as though his spies had been in the business of
obtaining compromising information on American businessmen in
Russia but simply didn't have the capability to collect "compromising
material" on *all of them*.

Then, in one last shocking moment from what had been an insane
news conference, Trump addressed the "pee tape" issue as well.

If it were real, he seemed to be saying, "It would have been out long
ago."

And with that, it was over. As reporters shouted more questions,
Putin and Trump exited the room. CNN cut to anchor Anderson Cooper, who immediately spoke to the sentiment of commentators for the
rest of the day.

"You have been watching perhaps one of the most disgraceful performances by an American president at a summit in front of a Russian
leader certainly that I've ever seen."

I will never forget what happened next. During their news conference, Putin presented Trump with a soccer ball, a bit of a plug from the Russian president for the FIFA World Cup hosted by his country that summer. It was another attempt by Putin to lighten the mood. As the Secret Service must have known, never trust an ex-KGB agent bearing gifts.

As I walked out of the news conference, I ran into one of those Secret Service agents carrying the soccer ball out on the street. It appeared to me that he had just had Putin's gift scanned for bugs. Probably a good idea.

Walking away from Helsinki, it was hard to shake the feeling that I had just witnessed a shameful spectacle. As nasty as our domestic politics had become, as disturbing as Charlottesville had been, at least they were our politics and shared history. For Trump to act as he had in Helsinki, while the world watched, was a truly unique humiliation for our country, one that showed just how far we had fallen. It used to be the job of American presidents, both Republican and Democratic, going back decades, to stand up to Russian aggression; instead, in the face of Russia's most brazen attack on American interests in decades, Trump was actually siding with Russia. He could have looked to Reagan for guidance. Reagan once told Gorbachev to "tear down this wall." Trump had been handed a similar moment. He could have told Putin to "go to hell," and Americans back home would have cheered. Instead, he chose to prostrate himself. It was an awful sight, and it felt downright un-American.

Even for those inclined to give Trump the benefit of the doubt, it was next to impossible to justify what we had all just witnessed. Trump's most ardent supporters in Congress struggled to defend him. For anyone who doubted the Trump-Russia connection prior to Helsinki, the news conference was perplexing at best, demonstrating just how far Trump was willing to go to take Putin's word over that of the hardworking men and women of the U.S. intelligence community.

As we all later learned in March 2019, Special Counsel Robert Mueller finally wrapped up his investigation, informing Attorney General William Barr that he had concluded that the Trump campaign did not engage in collusion with the Russian government during the 2016 election. Further, Mueller said he could not prove that the president had obstructed justice. Despite Trump's comment to NBC that he had fired FBI director James Comey over the Russia investigation, not to mention his pleas to Comey to drop the Flynn case as well as the false statements to the public about Don Jr.'s Trump Tower meeting, Mueller left the question of obstruction to Barr and Deputy Attorney General Rod Rosenstein, who elected not to take the matter any further. Then, in what seemed like a signal to the public that he had uncovered some wrongdoing on the part of the Trump team, Mueller made it clear in his report to the attorney general that his findings did not "exonerate" the president. That was mind-blowing. The president had not been accused of a crime. Yet he wasn't "exonerated" either. A source on the Trump legal team told me the Mueller report was "better than we could have expected." Their legal strategy, the source told me, of cooperation by providing reams of documents to the special counsel, while blocking Mueller from actually interviewing the president (he only offered written answers to questions), was a big, fat success. Rudy was suddenly a genius?

The White House celebrated by going on the attack, accusing Democrats and some members of the media of attempting to overthrow the government. For good measure, Trump once again called the press "the enemy of the people."

"You guys are dead now," a Trump surrogate told me, referring to the mainstream media.

Still, the end of the Mueller investigation hardly put the Russia story to rest. As there had been from the beginning of that saga, legitimate questions were still on the table. Most confounding of all is this:

If there was no collusion and no conspiracy, why the hell was Trump doing all this? Why did Trump capitulate to Putin if the Russians never had the goods on him in the first place? Will we ever know?

But let's be real, shall we? We don't need a Mueller report to tell us what was staring us in the face in Helsinki. Looking back on that day, I will always see a humbling moment for America.

Don't you?

11

The Rallies

The disastrous performance in Helsinki set an ominous tone as the country turned toward the coming midterms.

Ever since Trump's election, we all knew these midterms were going to be an angry, messy affair. There was too much at stake for both Trump and the Democrats to have it any other way. Even so, I was taken aback by just how nasty it got. As a veteran of 2016, I thought I'd seen it all; in reality, 2016 was downright civil in comparison to what I would encounter on the campaign trail in 2018. Much as Trump's attacks on the media had become more heated and vitriolic since the 2016 campaign, that anger and language had also filtered down to his supporters. As we were all about to find out, Trump's irresponsible threats and insults directed at the media would have disturbing real-world consequences.

My assessment of the president during the summer of 2018 was that he was like a compulsive gambler at one of his own casinos, a man who just couldn't pull himself away from the poker table, despite one losing hand after another. But the events that unfolded on Trump's watch during the second half of 2018 had other plans. These events had a way of both magnifying the damage he was doing to the country and, at the same time, making life more difficult for him as his party tried to maintain control of Congress.

Nothing quite encapsulated the state of Trumpworld in mid-2018 like the campaign rallies for the midterms. These began in earnest during the summer and kicked into high gear in the fall. In the year and half since Trump's election, the one constant to his presidency had been his rallies. Most presidents leave their campaign rallies in the rearview mirror after they win an election. At times during his presidency, it seemed that Trump had never left the arena. While he could be grumpy and downright angry around the White House, he came alive at his rallies, which seemed to give him the love he couldn't find back in Washington. He drew his energy from the base of supporters who attended these campaign carnivals. Aides will tell you that the rallies are Trump's happy place, with thousands of screaming supporters chanting "Build the wall" and songs of the Rolling Stones blaring in the background—despite a cease-and-desist order from the legendary band.

Of the thousands of people who attend Trump's rallies, I've always found the vast majority to be good, law-abiding, though definitely very conservative Americans. These are the same working-class and middle-class Americans I have come across countless times as a journalist over two decades of covering everything from natural disasters to elections. As a product of a blue-collar upbringing myself, I've long felt I have a good handle on the people who show up at a Trump rally. My parents divorced when I was five years old, and my mom, who worked in the restaurant business starting at the age of twenty-two, raised my sister and me mostly by herself. (My dad stayed in the picture and helped raise us on the weekends, when he wasn't working at the supermarket.) Watching my mom taught me a lesson in self-reliance that I carry with me to this day. I talk about my father all the time, but in truth, much of my strength comes from my mother.

All this is to say I get blue-collar folks more than they know. Indeed, I am more like them than the man they come to the rallies to see, a self-described though not entirely self-made businessman.

Looking back at what occurred during the 2016 campaign, I find it incredible that nobody got seriously hurt. Part of the allure for some folks who attended Trump's 2016 speeches was the real prospect of actual violence. I witnessed fights break out at these events. Trump supporters sucker punched a protester. And the candidate saw no harm in fanning the flames. He was having too much fun making the protesters a part of the act, calling out to his private security to remove them from his events.

"Get 'em out!" Trump would growl into the microphone. And the crowd would go wild.

At one 2016 rally in Las Vegas, I watched in horror as Trump all but incited a melee in the crowd. When a protester appeared, Trump yelled out to security to "get 'em out," and then remarked that he wished he could take matters into his own hands.

"I'd like to punch him in the face," he said. "In the old days [protesters would be] carried out on stretchers," he continued, as the audience cheered. "We're not allowed to push back anymore," he added, in a nod to his supporters' grievances.

Punch him in the face? Protesters carried out on stretchers?

The next day, I checked with the hotel security office. Nobody there had witnessed the protester in question acting violently. Trump had made this up, a security officer told me over the phone, to play to the crowd. Reporters covering the campaign would ask one another, "Who talks like this?" We didn't know what was happening. Surely these antics would end his campaign, we would tell ourselves. But Trump and his team had discovered that these were the moments that dominated the headlines and drove the news coverage. Shortly after the Las Vegas incident, Trump won the Nevada caucuses, and he lit up the Twitterverse by telling those assembled at his victory party in Las Vegas something I will never forget.

"I love the poorly educated," he said. Yes, he said that.

A week later, there was more violence, at a rally on the campus of

Radford University, in Virginia. It all started when protesters in the crowd began interrupting Trump.

"Are you from Mexico?" Trump asked one of them.

Off to his right, roughly two dozen Black Lives Matter activists were making their voices heard. Trump called for security to escort them out of the building.

"All lives matter," Trump responded, baiting the activists.

As the protesters were being led out of the arena, a few Trump supporters gave them a hard time, which led to another altercation near our press pen, or, as we called it, "the press cage." Journalists being journalists, we all wanted to get a better look. At that moment, *Time* magazine photographer Chris Morris tried to leave the press pen to snap a few pictures and was immediately confronted by a U.S. Secret Service agent who told him to stay put. Morris, a veteran news photographer, was not going to take no for an answer and attempted to push past the agent, who then snapped. After the rally, I ran after Morris to ask what had happened.

"I stepped eighteen inches out of the pen, and he grabbed me by the neck and started choking me, and then he slammed me to the ground," Morris told me.

The Secret Service investigated the incident, but Morris, ever the professional, said he was not interested in pressing charges. Still, within minutes, video of the violent scene was playing on social media all over the world. I saw firsthand episode after episode of violence at Trump rallies. Emotions were running so high that even a professionally trained Secret Service agent could succumb to the violent energy coursing through these events. I was beginning to worry that, before long, the unthinkable would happen at a modern-day political event. I feared there would be a riot at a Trump rally.

On March 11, 2016, that's what happened. Trump's advance team made plans for a rally to take place on the campus of the University of Illinois at Chicago, home to one of the most diverse student bodies in the country. Student groups and civil rights organizations made their plans as well: to peacefully protest what had become a divisive campaign. This rally was not going to go well.

Inside the venue, I remember scanning the crowd and thinking there were not very many MAGA hats on hand. Instead, there were hundreds of people who were very clearly going to protest Trump. This time, I didn't see three or four possible demonstrators; I saw whole sections of the arena filled with people who had come to make some noise. Before long there was pushing and shoving on the floor of the arena. Then one of Trump's aides came up onstage and approached the microphone.

"Tonight's rally will be postponed," he told the crowd.

The audience cheered because they had shut down the event.

I can't tell you who threw the first punch, but within seconds after the rally was scrapped, a large fistfight involving roughly twenty Trump supporters and protesters broke out in an area behind the press cage. Americans were taking swings at their fellow Americans. Up in the stands, there was more brawling. In front of the cage, another fight broke out. This is Trump's America, I thought. People are at each other's throats.

Worst of all, there were not enough police inside the arena to break it up. About a half hour later, roughly a hundred of Chicago's finest descended the steps from all sides to round up the fighters and lead them outside. This stopped the violence inside the venue. Outside the arena, there was more trouble. Trump protesters and supporters, separated by police officers in riot gear, were screaming at each other. And the cops, some riding horseback, were starting to crack down.

One of the reporters embedded with the campaign, Sopan Deb of CBS News, was arrested. Police charged Sopan, who was bloodied in the incident, with resisting arrest. Fortunately, the episode was caught on camera, and it was clear he had not resisted arrest; he was merely doing his job. The charge was later dropped. I feared what could potentially happen to the other young campaign reporters: Ali Vitali of NBC, Jeremy Diamond of CNN, and Jill Colvin of the Associated Press.

The clashes that night felt like a bad omen. Trump would go on CNN later that night to defend himself, telling CNN's Don Lemon that the tone set at his rallies was not responsible for the violence in Chicago.

"My basic tone is that of securing our borders, of having a country," he said, adding that his events were about "love." Did you get that? The candidate who wanted to punch protesters in the face and once bragged that he could shoot somebody on Fifth Avenue and get away with it was all about "love."

Trump accused the media of exaggerating what had happened in Chicago. But some of Trump's rivals issued statements blaming him. "Tonight the seeds of division that Donald Trump has been sowing this whole campaign finally bore fruit, and it was ugly," said then–Ohio governor John Kasich. "Any candidate is responsible for the culture of a campaign," added Texas senator Ted Cruz, who also blamed the protesters. In the months that followed, Trump's aides were unapologetic about the campaign Trump ran.

"I don't have any problem sleeping at night. I just look at my bank account and go right to sleep," his former campaign manager Corey Lewandowski once told me.

As the rallies continued to be volatile, the reporters covering the Trump campaign began to take precautions. As has been reported, our teams were assigned security guards to make sure we made it to our cars after the rallies were over. There were times when these body men were a bit too intrusive; sometimes they would try to follow us to the bathroom. But having that extra layer of protection was essential. Our camera crews were also targets for the hostility of Trump supporters, who would spot the CNN logos on our equipment and begin hurling insults. At a rally in Orlando held toward the end of the campaign, a dozen or so Trump supporters began to heckle me during my live shot. A couple of these rally-goers became irate, screaming obscenities at me. One lady smacked me with her Trump campaign sign. Another man said he wanted to kick my ass out in the parking lot. He was practically foaming at the mouth with rage, spittle flying from his lips. So, yes, I was grateful to have my security detail at that event.

But the most chilling moment came at a rally in West Palm Beach, Florida. At the end of Trump's remarks, I remember seeing a sign lying on one of the press tables. When I picked it up, I couldn't believe my eyes. The sign had a Nazi swastika on it next to the word *media*. I held up that sign during one of my live shots that night to show the world what had become of Trump's rallies. The hatred he had spewed at the media for months was spreading like a virus. My thought was this: if we really had become something akin to the Nazis in the eyes of Trump's most rabid supporters, what was stopping them from hurting one of us?

WHEN IT CAME TO TRUMP'S ACT AT THE 2018 RALLIES, NOT MUCH had changed in two years. The rallies felt like old times in a sense. Trump would get up, give a speech, and encourage the usual chants of "Build the wall" and "Lock her up." He still reveled in the way he could push people's buttons on issues ranging from trade to immigration. The rhetoric itself was largely unchanged. Similarly, the crowd was often its same rowdy self: yelling, aggrieved, and mad as hell. On the surface, the whole production seemed much like 2016, but appearances told only half the story.

For many of the journalists who lived them, the rallies of 2018 were far worse. After all, they followed months and months of repeated broadsides against the media from Trump and the White House, attacks in which journalists had been portrayed as some of the vilest, most dishonorable people alive. Trump's supporters had spent the better part of three years (the last two from the White House) hearing what disgusting people we were. In that time, the verbal assaults had taken their toll, making some of us objects of vitriol on the right. Yet, for all that time, the only outlet Trump's most rabid followers had had for this anger had been to post threatening or malicious messages on social media. Now they were standing mere feet away from us, and not surprisingly, they had no problem letting us know how they felt.

The sheer hostility from 2016 was still palpable at these midterm events, but there was something else troubling, a menace hanging over the arenas that made confrontation feel less like a possibility and more like a foregone conclusion. The tone had always been unfriendly and unwelcoming, but in 2018, we reporters became increasingly mindful of the fact that anything could happen at any moment.

One huge difference, for me, between Trump's rallies during the 2016 campaign and the speeches he gave to supporters as president was that I had become a major target of the hostility. Sure, Trump supporters gave me a hard time during the 2016 campaign, but from the day Trump called me "fake news" at that Trump Tower press conference before his inauguration, everything changed. Ever since then, the acts of harassment and intimidation, including death threats, from his supporters had never really let up. Even today, they are as much a constant presence in my life as Trump's tweets.

"If Trump is removed from office in any way, you are dead," read one comment posted on my Instagram account.

"I would love to be looking into your eyes as I choke the last fucking breath out of you," read another message, posted on my public Facebook account.

And now, as we hit the 2018 campaign trail, much of this attention began to exist in person as well as online. Because of my battles with Trump, Spicer, Sanders, and Miller, and the resulting coverage on Fox News, which often painted me as some sort of journalistic villain, the crowds at these rallies paid a lot more attention to me. Eagle-eyed Trump supporters would spot me within minutes of my arrival at an arena or convention center as we file in during the hours before the president takes the stage. Sometimes we would hear the taunts as we waited in line to go through security to enter the venues.

"Hey, it's fake news," MAGA hat–wearing Trump supporters would yell. "CNN sucks," some would chant as we made our way into the event, a taste of the abuse to come.

To these Trump loyalists, I was somewhere between the bad guy at a pro wrestling event and an actual enemy of the people. How I was treated varied from one Trump supporter to another. Some came up to me and asked for selfies and autographs. Others would approach and stare without saying a word. Then there were those MAGA folks, ranging from a dozen to more than a hundred at a rally, who were much more hostile, hurling insults, giving me the middle finger, and sometimes implying or flat-out saying that bad things were going to happen to me.

A lot of these folks were just venting their frustration, I suppose, for what had been burned into their brains by Trump. He hated our coverage, so they despised it, too. Others just wanted to scream at us. But in their chants and acts of rage, they spoke volumes about the man they had come to see. They were a living, breathing extension of the forty-fifth president of the United States, using his language, his talking points, to verbally assault us. For more than two years going back to the 2016 campaign, he had been demonizing the press, and now, with us within shouting distance of them, his supporters were more willing than ever to show they'd been listening.

One of the first rallies I attended during the 2018 cycle was in Nashville. It was great getting back to Tennessee. Knoxville, to the east, had been my first local TV news market, and I had often traveled to Nashville to cover the statehouse. Trump was serving up the red meat that night in late May, referring to then–House minority leader Nancy Pelosi as "the MS-13 lover," a sneak preview of his coming attractions.

He went back to calling Clinton "crooked Hillary" and slammed the press as "fake news," but what stood out that night wasn't Trump's usual ridiculous rhetoric. It was the man, dressed in black, standing just outside our filing area and yelling "scum" and "scumbag" at me.

"You're scum," the man yelled at me. "You're a scumbag," he continued. This went on for a *half hour*. One of my colleagues with the *New York Times* asked him to stop. Then he yelled at her. It seemed like a bad sign for the rest of the year.

About a month later, I traveled down to South Carolina for another rally. As soon as I arrived at the venue in Columbia, there was trouble. Before Trump's remarks, an elderly woman approached the press cage and told me to "get the fuck out." I've known a lot of grandmas over the years, but this was the first one to tell me to "get the fuck out" of anywhere. (Usually, grandmas love me.) I have to admit, it was a bit surreal. Had I been transported to a planet where elderly people were mean and nasty? The crowd got a kick out of this episode of *Grandmas Gone Wild* and started chanting, "Go home, Jim." All of this occurred during my live shot for *The Situation Room with Wolf Blitzer*. I tried to shake the woman's hand, but she swatted it away and told me to "get the fuck outta here." I later told Wolf we weren't going to be shouted out of the building and that we would stay and do our jobs.

"Ma'am, I have every right to be here," I reminded the woman.

"Out! Out! Out! Out!" she yelled, waving her arms as the crowd around her cheered.

Apparently, I didn't win her over.

Still, it was a fascinating night because of the wide variety of interactions I had with Trump's supporters. These audiences were not a true reflection of America, mind you. They were overwhelmingly white, blue-collar, and elderly, and I hardly ever saw a person of color. But while homogeneous, these Trump superfans had their differences, too. Their attitudes ranged from salt of the earth to scorched earth. Many came up to me and apologized for the unruly behavior at the rallies.

Others uttered the most horrible things that could possibly come to mind. Oddly enough, dozens more simply wanted a selfie with me. I tried to engage with as many of them as possible. Why? you ask. In part, it was strategic. I found that as I listened intently to what they had to say, a good number of them would calm down. Ignoring them didn't work. Oh God, I tried that, too; it only made things worse. They felt disrespected, and challenged to kick things up a notch. So, the hostility level went up, not down. You try it for yourself and get back to me.

I had a pretty lengthy conversation with one woman who scolded me for my reporting. She accused me of being rude to both the president and Sarah Sanders. I kept my mouth shut and just listened. What she said was deeply disturbing. She accused me of leading the country into another civil war.

"What's going to happen is we're going to end up with a civil war. You're going to have people shooting people," she warned. "You need to tone it down a little bit. The language, everything. It's gotta stop. Be decent, please be decent. Don't ask any more stupid questions," she added, sounding relieved to have gotten that off her chest before she walked away.

I just kept thinking, Another civil war? Is that where we're headed?

And yes, there were some who would, out of the blue, show incredible kindness. I always tried to be kind to them. Shortly before Trump's speech, an older gentleman, maybe in his fifties, asked if any of us in the press could lend him a chair for an elderly woman who was not feeling well. She, like so many of the president's supporters, had been standing in line for hours in ninety-degree heat, just to get a glimpse of Trump in action. Without hesitation, I offered him mine. The man later came back to the cage with his mother to thank me. A reporter for the Associated Press in Columbia, Meg Kinnard, captured the moment.

Thank goodness, I thought. Nobody is going to believe I had a civil moment with a Trump supporter.

"You're a good man," the woman's son told me. "Your mama raised you right."

"She tried," I joked to him.

He then made a strange observation, commenting that he found it remarkable that I had recited the Pledge of Allegiance and sung "The Star-Spangled Banner" before the rally began.

I thought to myself, Yes, I know the pledge and the national anthem. I'm an American.

But the moment spoke volumes. Members of the press have been so savaged by Trump and his propagandists in the media that journalists seem almost foreign or anti-American to his supporters. In hindsight, the man's stunning observation is not that unusual at all. Trump supporters routinely look over to the press risers to see if we reporters are reciting the pledge or singing the national anthem. Allow me to assure any Trump backer reading this book: not only do the reporters covering these rallies know the pledge and even the national anthem (something the president apparently hasn't memorized— have you seen the clips of him trying to sing along?), but we are also patriotic Americans.

As the president railed against the press during his speech, the same man looked back at me and smiled. He knew I was not the enemy. At the end of the rally, his mother shook my hand, holding it for a few moments, before she paused and said, "I hope you're going to be okay." Minutes later, with our security guard trying to keep up, we ran back to our cars as other Trump supporters yelled, "Fake news!"

At the end of July, it was off to Tampa, where my producer Matt Hoye and I decided to start documenting on video some of the abuse we were taking. This was critical, as the harassing messages and threats on social media were increasing. I wanted to make sure that some of this hostile feedback was caught on video, so there could be no confusion as to what was happening to us. As a number of viral videos later demonstrated, we were subjected to a bewildering mudslide of anger and abuse. Hundreds of Trump supporters shouted "CNN sucks" as I was broadcasting live on the air. After we packed up at the end of the rally, I whipped out my phone and recorded about a minute of video of Trump supporters screaming all sorts of insults, ranging from "you suck" to "traitor." Others were giving me the middle finger or wearing T-shirts that read, "Fuck the Media." In the background, behind all the shouting, you can hear Trump's rally closer, the Rolling Stones song "You Can't Always Get What You Want." The vitriol from Trump fans that day was suddenly all over social media, as several local reporters captured the moment as well. One woman, who was giving me double middle fingers, briefly became something of an internet legend.

Trump was pleased with the outpouring of hostility. His son Eric tweeted a link to a video of the outrageous scene with the remark "Truth." Trump retweeted that tweet, which catapulted its viewership into the tens of millions. As far as I was concerned, this was putting the First Family seal of approval on abuse of the press. Anybody remember the First Lady Melania Trump's pet cause of combating cyberbullying, Be Best? This is being best? Not the president.

By the next day, my video clip of all the screaming and the middle fingers had gone viral, playing not just on *Morning Joe*, but on news sites around the world. I was flooded with requests for interviews from the foreign press. Everybody, it seemed, wanted to know what it was like being in the eye of Trump's crossfire hurricane, to quote the Stones. It would be dishonest to deny that his abuse had given me some notoriety, but there was a price to be paid for it. I had become "public enemy number one," according to one of my sources, an administration official who also saw the danger in Trump's attacks.

In the days after Tampa, the death threats were back with a vengeance. Memes were being created showing images of me balled up on the floor of a rubber room of a psychiatric hospital and so on. On my Instagram account, a visitor left a disturbing message, one of many: "Hopefully he gets beaten to death at one soon."

Not all the feedback was menacing. Thankfully, my mom texted me some moral support: "Tell it like it is. Shine on, Jim," she wrote. A former Fox News anchor whose name you would recognize wrote to tell me that she was "sending me strength." And an administration official who is close to the president wrote to say he was sorry about what had happened. I have all these texts and direct messages saved, so don't bother to say I am making this up.

All the while, I couldn't stop thinking about the people who were so full of rage and hatred in that crowd in Tampa. One woman held up a baby wearing a button on his onesie. It read, "CNN Sucks." All I could think was, My God! There are babies being raised to hate us, almost right out of the womb. What's next? In utero indoctrination?

This outpouring of venom was the natural result, I thought, of years of Trump's attacks on the media. He had normalized and sanitized nastiness and cruelty. People thought nothing of directing this level of hostility at their fellow Americans. We weren't really human to them anymore. This was the climate of fear that Trump had created. In this environment, a Trump supporter could resort to violence, I reasoned. It had become a dangerous time in America.

Perhaps the most disturbing sight in Tampa was the stunning array of "QAnon" signs we saw throughout the crowd. There were references to this fringe conspiracy theory on T-shirts, signs, and hats. QAnon refers to the twisted and false claim that celebrities throughout Hollywood are involved in pedophile rings. This is the same kind of nonsense we saw alleged in the bogus Pizzagate conspiracy theory, which falsely accused Clinton campaign manager John Podesta of being involved in sex trafficking out of a pizzeria in Washington. With QAnon, the virus had spread to slander political opponents in Hollywood. This insanity, pushed by the darkest forces of the far-right echo chamber, seemed to have no end.

My colleagues wonder why I would want to cover Trump rallies. This is why. How else am I supposed to see with my own eyes what the Trump phenomenon has done to America? The QAnon theory is a perfect example. When you have a well-known conspiracy theorist in the Oval Office, it's only natural that his most ardent supporters would travel down the same fact-challenged rabbit hole. One of the failures of the Trump era has been Trump's unwillingness to smack down these dangerous theories. As in the case of his attacks on journalists, Trump's eagerness to exploit this kind of nutty behavior could have dire consequences.

EVER SINCE THE PRESIDENT REFERRED TO THE PRESS AS THE "ENEMY of the people" in 2017, a lot of us in the media worried that it was only a matter of time before a reporter was killed. Those fears only worsened after the mass shooting attack on the Annapolis newspaper the *Capital Gazette* in June 2018. The shooting did not occur as a direct result of the president's rhetoric, but the attack did appear to be in retaliation for past reporting the newspaper had done. In the aftermath of the shooting, some *Gazette* staffers voiced their concerns about the president's comments in a letter to Trump.

"We won't forget being called an enemy of the people," they wrote. "No, we won't forget that. Because exposing evil, shining light on wrongs and fighting injustice is what we do."

Now, I know the Annapolis newspaper well, having lived in the Maryland capital for several years. It's everything a local newspaper should be, covering the political scene, crime, and high school sports and offering reviews of all the amazing seafood restaurants the city has to offer. The newspaper employs a tiny but dedicated staff, for whom no story is too big or too small. I'll never forget the time a picture of my son ice-skating at a local rink appeared in the paper. A lot of people around Annapolis have pictures of their kids or grandkids up on their refrigerators thanks to the photographers at the city's paper. Enemy of the people it is not.

The day after the attack in Annapolis, Trump toned down his rhetoric on the press at an unrelated event at the White House. "Journalists, like all Americans, should be free from the fear of being violently attacked while doing their job," he told a small crowd of supporters gathered in the East Room.

Still, at that same White House event, I thought it was important to get the president on the record on a critical question: would he stop referring to the press as the "enemy"?

"Mr. President, will you stop calling the press the enemy of the people?" I shouted from the back of the room at the end of his remarks. On my mind were the *Capital Gazette* reporters who had just died that week: Gerald Fischman, Rob Hiaasen, John McNamara, Rebecca Smith, and Wendi Winters. It seemed to me the folks at the newspaper would have wanted this question asked.

I didn't get an answer.

About a month later, Ivanka Trump told Axios reporter Mike Allen that she did not agree with her father's line of attack that the press is the enemy of the people.

"No, I do not," she replied. "I've certainly received my fair share of reporting on me personally that I know not to be fully accurate, so I have some sensitivity around why people have concerns and gripe, especially when they're sort of targeted," she added. "But no, I do not feel that the media is the enemy of the people."

Later that day, at a rare press briefing at the White House, Sarah Sanders was asked about Ivanka's rejection of her father's line of attack against the press. Sarah, shocking no one, dodged the question. So, I followed up with her.

ACOSTA: I think it would be a good thing if you were to say, right here, at this briefing, that the press, the people who are gathered in this room right now, doing their jobs every day, asking questions of officials like the ones you brought forward earlier, are not the enemy of the people. I think we deserve that.

SANDERS: If the President has made his position known, I also think it's ironic—

She was starting to dodge the question again. I interrupted. We went back and forth over that. And then, finally, she started to give something resembling an answer.

SANDERS: It's ironic, Jim, that not only you and the media attack the President for his rhetoric when they frequently lower the level of conversation in this country. Repeatedly—repeatedly—the media resorts to personal attacks without any content other than to incite anger. The media has attacked me personally on a number of occasions, including your own network; said I should be harassed as a life sentence; that I should be choked . . . When I was hosted by the Correspondents' Association, of which almost all of you are members of, you brought a comedian up to attack my appearance and called me a traitor to my own gender.

She was referring to comedian Michelle Wolf's performance at the White House Correspondents' Association Dinner earlier in the year. Wolf, while delivering a scathing rebuke of the Trump administration, had poked fun at Sarah's "smoky eye." Honestly, I had no idea what that meant at the time, until some female colleagues clued me in that it was a remark about Sanders's makeup, with an extra dig about the press secretary's tendency to lie at the briefings. Some in the press sharply criticized Wolf's performance, opining that it was beneath the dignity of the event. But, to be fair, the WHCA dinner had already surrendered much of that credibility over the years, with so many celebrities attending what was supposed to be a scholarship event for young journalists. But, again, that's a debate for another time.

In my exchange with Sarah, I reminded her that the press had not mocked her eye makeup at that event; a comedian had.

ACOSTA: We didn't try to do that, Sarah.

SANDERS: In fact, as I know—as far as I know, I'm the first Press Secretary in the history of the United States that's required Secret Service protection . . . The media continues to ratchet up the verbal assault against the President and everyone in this administration, and certainly we have a role to play, but the media has a role to play for the discourse in this country, as well.

Secret Service protection, Sanders said. What about the security that's required for us? I thought. But I wasn't about to let her off the hook.

ACOSTA: Excuse me. You did not say, in the course of those remarks that you just made, that the press is not the enemy of the people. Are we to take it, from what you just said—we all get put through the wringer, we all get put in the meat grinder in this town, and you're no exception. And I'm sorry that that happened to you. I wish that that had not happened. But for the sake of this room, the people who are in this room, this democracy, this country, all the people around the world are watching what you're saying, Sarah. And the White House, for the United States of America, the President of the United States should not refer to us as the enemy of the people. His own daughter acknowledges that, and all I'm asking you to do, Sarah, is to acknowledge that right now and right here.

SANDERS: I appreciate your passion; I share it. I've addressed this question. I've addressed my personal feelings. I'm here to speak on behalf of the President, and he's made his comments clear.

The only reasonable takeaway from that exchange is that the White House press secretary, a taxpayer-funded spokeswoman for the United States, believes the press is the enemy of the people—or, at the very least, she doesn't have the guts to disagree with her boss. What's also alarming is that she was obviously nursing some grudges left over from the WHCA dinner and was letting them affect her job in the Briefing Room. Sarah, it seemed, could dish it out but she couldn't take it. After all, she'd gone after individual journalists in briefings; she'd called CNN "fake news." But have a comedian tell a few jokes, and she can't take the heat. Give me a break.

Sanders seemed to be saying at that moment that words *do* matter, words *can* wound—which is why I had a tough time understanding how she could adopt the president's belief that the press is the enemy. She knows the consequences of that kind of rhetoric. Perhaps she'd decided it was a case of "an eye for an eye," or a smoky eye perhaps.

Herein lies the struggle we all face in the debate over Trump's rhetoric and the poisonous effect it's had on political dialogue in America. If Sarah can defend the president's comments that the press is the enemy by pointing to what a comedian said about her physical appearance, then almost anything could be held up by the right wing as justification for attacks on the news media. The problem with this "whataboutism" is that it is missing some perspective. The average reporter or politician on the left or right doesn't have the same megaphone (or MAGA-phone, as I like to call it) that Trump can turn to when he wants to vilify his adversaries. This goes to the heart of the rights and responsibilities of any American president. Sure, the president has the right to free speech, but even free speech has its limits. You can't yell fire in a crowded theater. Also, the president has sworn an oath to the nation to uphold the Constitution of the United States. Trump, I would argue, has shown he doesn't respect what is perhaps the Constitution's most vital protection—our freedom of speech.

Of course, nobody is going to impeach the president for calling us the enemy of the people. And, if anything, Sanders had just earned herself another year as press secretary. But the video from that briefing will last forever; it can't be erased from the internet. And neither can Trump's demonization of journalists. This weaponization of the bully pulpit to crush dissent and independent thought in America has been captured for the ages. History has shown us that there are real stakes and real dangers to language like Trump's, and this point in history, when the American president called journalists "the enemy of the people," will be imprinted on our national consciousness for coming generations. We will be able to read about it in our history books—if we don't end up burning them one day.

12
Fear and Losing

I could never have predicted the full extent of what the midterms would bring, or that they would converge in such unsettling and dangerous ways with the Russia investigation, Trump's immigration fearmongering, and of course his escalating war on the media. As I reported from around the country every day, it was clear that the midterms were more than just an election, or a referendum on the president's term to date; they were a pivotal turning point for the nation, answering an essential question for me: would Trump pay a price for his troubling behavior? The voters were about to have a chance to assess the authoritarian impulses, lies, xenophobia, and attacks on American institutions that had all become hallmarks of his first two years in office. For Trump, the midterms would be Judgment Day. A verdict would be rendered.

All the combustible elements from the first two years of the Trump administration, from that first Spicer press conference on, could be found in the final run-up to the congressional elections. Once again, Trump would reach into his bag of media magician's tricks to dominate the daily news narrative with explosive, hate-filled rhetoric. It had worked before, delivering the White House. But the stakes were higher this time. There was a desperation inside Trumpworld. What

unfolded in the final weeks before the midterms was nothing short
of a feverish attempt to preserve Republican control of the federal
government and spare Trump from facing meaningful congressional
oversight. A Democratic-controlled Congress, Trump knew, would
leave no stone unturned, and no closet unopened. The Russia investigation, his long-concealed tax returns, and the dark secrets of his
immigration policy could all be dredged up in committee hearings
chaired by Democrats who had been sharpening their knives from the
sidelines during two long years out of power.

Trump's last line of defense was his "base," the army of supporters
hanging on his every word on conservative media, on Twitter, and, of
course, at his rallies. It was Trump's rhetoric that ensured that these
superfans remained energized. For the press, this meant the rallies
would remain visible and immediate threats to journalists reporting on his administration. But we would soon learn there were even
greater dangers out there, dangers brought on by the frenzy of the
midterm's final months.

A few weeks after Tampa, I traveled to West Virginia. Trump was
headed to the Mountaineer State to lend his support for the GOP
Senate candidate attempting to knock out the incumbent Democrat,
Joe Manchin. It was the middle of August, a little more than two
months before the midterms, and Trump was hoping to run the table in a handful of red states where Democrats faced an uphill battle
for reelection—Manchin in West Virginia, Joe Donnelly in Indiana,
Jon Tester in Montana, Claire McCaskill in Missouri, and so on. Ever
mindful of the Russia investigation, Trump was desperate to keep
both houses of Congress in Republican hands. He knew, as did his
advisers, that Democrats could potentially begin impeachment proceedings if they somehow eked out victories in both the Senate and
the House of Representatives. But the real news that day happened
away from the Charleston convention center.

Earlier in the day, Trump's former campaign chairman Paul

Manafort was convicted in federal court of an array of financial crimes that were, at that time, unrelated to the Russia investigation. The White House responded to the Manafort news the way it had countless times, distancing the president from the former campaign chairman by describing the longtime GOP operative as having a limited role with the Trump team before the election. Trump repeatedly painted Manafort's crimes as removed from the campaign's work.

"It doesn't involve me," Trump told reporters that day. This was true at the time, but the peril for Trump was that Manafort would eventually turn against the president and cooperate with federal prosecutors. Still, for now it seemed, Manafort was determined to remain loyal to Trump, in the hope of securing a presidential pardon.

But there was another, potentially more devastating bombshell to drop that day, when Trump's ex-fixer and former personal attorney, Michael Cohen, pleaded guilty to breaking campaign finance laws by funneling money to two of the president's alleged mistresses, including the porn star Stormy Daniels. Cohen admitted to federal prosecutors that he had made the payments "at the direction of" a political candidate, a clear reference to the president that placed Trump in immediate jeopardy. Because the money was aimed at influencing the 2016 election, Cohen's actions violated campaign finance laws, prosecutors said. Adding to the melodrama of the Stormy Daniels saga, the porn star's attorney, Michael Avenatti, was taunting Trump and his outside attorney Rudy Giuliani. The Daniels story was certainly sleazier than the Russia investigation, but Avenatti had a case on his hands that put Trump in real political danger. Legal scholars argued over whether a sitting president could be indicted. But if Trump had violated a campaign finance law, he was entering the realm of the "high crimes and misdemeanors," potentially meeting the standard for impeachment.

Buckle Up Buttercup, Avenatti tweeted.

As for Cohen, his guilty plea was a stunning turn of events for the

Manhattan businessman's former personal fixer, or, as one Trump
adviser described him to me, "a less cool version of Ray Donovan," the
titular character played by Liev Schreiber on the Showtime drama.
Cohen's decision to come clean was costly to the president's team, revealing a pattern of deception that the White House had been engaged
in for months as it tried to hide Trump's involvement in the payments
to Daniels. The bad news had started for Cohen back in January
2018, when the *Wall Street Journal* first reported that he had funneled
$130,000 in hush money to the porn star. As we all know in perhaps
too-vivid detail, the secret payment was made to the actress, whose
legal name is Stephanie Clifford, to keep her from discussing her past
relationship with Trump in the final days before the 2016 election.
The payment was not declared in official filings with the Federal Election Commission. As in the case with the Trump Tower meeting with
the Russians, the initial explanations from Trump's team about the
Stormy saga turned out to be lies.

Once again, Sarah Sanders was a central figure in misleading the
public about the president's legal troubles. At the White House press
briefing on March 7, 2018, Sanders was asked by my colleague Jeff
Zeleny about the payment to Daniels.

> ZELENY: Did the President approve of the payment that was made
> in October of 2016 by his longtime lawyer and advisor, Michael
> Cohen?
> SANDERS: Look, the President has addressed these directly and
> made very well clear that none of these allegations are true.

Trump was asked directly by Catherine Lucey of the Associated
Press a few weeks later if he knew where the money had come from
to pay Daniels.

"No, I don't know," Trump said, in an outright lie. "You'll have to ask Michael Cohen. Michael's my attorney," he added, a comment that would come back to haunt him.

About a month later, on May 2, 2018, Giuliani blew the whole thing wide open when he explained that the money had been funneled through Cohen and his law firm "and the President repaid him."

At the White House press briefing the following day, I asked Sarah about her past false statement on the Stormy payment.

ACOSTA: If I could just follow up on—you said, on March 7, "There was no knowledge of any payments from the President, and he's denied all of these allegations." Were you lying to us at the time, or were you in the dark?

SANDERS: The President has denied and continues to deny the underlying claim. And again, I had given the best information I had at the time. And I would refer you back to the comments that you, yourself, just mentioned a few minutes ago about the timeline for Mayor Giuliani.

Much was made of my basic question to Sanders: "Were you lying to us at the time, or were you in the dark?" The implication was that I was asking an unfair question to get attention. Even if she didn't know the truth, Trump most certainly did, and he had lied about it, both to people in his administration and to the American public. The truth needs to mean something at the White House, and this was a glaring example of the president and his top aides lying to the American people. And the porn payoff story was more than just a tawdry news item. Had Stormy Daniels's allegation of an affair with the president surfaced in the remaining days of the 2016 campaign, it's quite possible the election would have turned out differently. The payoff to Daniels was a successful attempt to cover up what Trump knew to be a damaging story. So, these questions do matter.

It was not long after Sanders's performance that day that we saw a scaling back of the White House press briefings. Sarah went on to hold, on average, about one briefing per week. By the end of 2018, these appearances by the press secretary had all but disappeared. The briefings themselves became shorter, approximately fifteen to twenty minutes each. Conservative critics blamed the media, and guys like me, for this trend, but the responsibility lies squarely with the president and his press secretary. My sense is that Sanders was coming to the realization that she could no longer come out to the briefings on a regular basis and still maintain the last shred of credibility she had left, especially when her occasional false statements could have serious legal implications.

But a senior White House official said Trump had also seen enough of the briefings. In an admission that hardly surprised me, the official explained that Trump preferred having the live TV cameras hanging on his every word.

"It's the president," the official said. "He likes to do it. He likes to talk on the South Lawn and the pool sprays."

In April 2018, just days after Trump lied about his payment to Daniels, the FBI raided Michael Cohen's office, seizing an array of documents and records related to the Southern District of New York investigation of the Stormy Daniels case. As we learned later in the year, Michael Cohen turned against his old boss and began to help those same prosecutors.

Cohen quickly learned what life was like on the wrong side of the president. One month after the raid, the *National Enquirer*, the supermarket tabloid run by Trump's friend David Pecker, ran a hit piece on Cohen entitled "Trump Fixer's Secrets and Lies." The *Enquirer* was long suspected to be a "house organ" for Trump, willing to coordinate "catch and kill" stories that involved payoffs to people such as Karen McDougal, a *Playboy* model who had also accused Trump of an affair. The *Enquirer*'s parent company, it's been alleged, paid McDougal to buy her silence. As for that *Enquirer* story accusing Cohen of "lies," I had asked him if the piece was a message being sent to him by Trump.

Cohen's response, which we reported at the time: "What do *you* think?"

Michael Cohen's cooperation with federal prosecutors brought about his excommunication from Trumpworld. Trump would later call his former fixer a "rat" on Twitter, the kind of language used by Mob bosses before putting a hit on a snitch. Cohen would later worry that all the pressure coming from the Trump team had put his family in danger. I had spoken with Michael over the phone a few times. Because his case was still pending in court, he didn't want to speak on the record, but it was clear as we were talking over the phone that his life was falling apart. The legal career he had built working for a reality TV star turned president was crashing down around him. Trump's aides and advisers were merciless, calling Cohen a "liar" who couldn't be trusted—which raised the question: if that was so, how did he get the job with Trump in the first place? Still, one Trump adviser told me he felt "sad" for Cohen, describing him as a man who "has no country." When you leave Trumpworld, it seems, you are banished forever.

At the rally in West Virginia on that late August day, it was pure coincidence that the Cohen and Manafort news came almost at once, hours before Trump would take the stage. The timing of it demonstrated just how mired in scandal the president really was. Of course, Trump didn't mention any of it at the rally. Still, he seemed deflated as he attacked his usual targets—namely, the news media, immigrants, and congressional Democrats. I never would have expected him to discuss the conviction of his former campaign manager or the guilty plea of his former personal lawyer at length, and in any case, I imagined that many people in the arena that day were tuning out those news stories. Convinced that the mainstream media were spreading lies about Trump, they simply might have chosen not to believe that people close to him had that very day proven to be guilty of federal crimes. It was the "deep state" working with the "fake news" media to frame Trump, he would have them believe. The Trump supporters who spent the rally trying to intimidate us with stares and signs were intent on casting journalists as criminals, and yet the people close to Trump were the ones going to prison. That's a hell of a juxtaposition.

As I stood there reconciling the scene in front of me with what had happened in the courts that day, I looked over and saw a huge Trump supporter glaring at me. For a good twenty minutes he just stood there and held a menacing stare. I've often tried to wave to these folks, to see if they are looking for some kind of acknowledgment. But that didn't work with this guy; he just kept staring. Honestly, he looked psychotic. Our security guard at the rally, an equally big and intimidating guy sporting a Mohawk, and whose day job was as a local prison guard, stared intently back at the man, ready to rumble. I just wanted out of there. Even with our formidable security guard, it did not feel safe.

As we tried to quickly exit the convention center, there was more trouble almost immediately. A young reporter, Millie Weaver from the fringe website Infowars, ambushed me on the street. Out of nowhere, she shoved an Infowars mic in my face as her cameraperson was rolling. My producer Matt and our Mohawk-coifed security contractor tried to block her path so we could keep moving. Worried for a moment that Infowars would trash us for blowing past their cameras, I thought, You know what? Let her ask her questions.

Millie asked me about Facebook's decision to ban Infowars over the website's history of hate speech, including its false conspiracy theory that the mass shooting at Sandy Hook Elementary School in Newtown, Connecticut, had been a government hoax. Sandy Hook parents have sued the site over the bogus story, a real-life example of actual fake news (pardon the oxymoron). Millie's ambush interview now lives forever on the internet under the banner "Millie Weaver Schools Jim

Acosta on First Amendment." You can watch it for yourself on You-Tube. Actually, she schooled herself.

"Hey, Jim Acosta, what do you think about Alex Jones being banned?" she asked.

We had a brief debate over the issue outside the Charleston Civic Center. I talked about the value of a free press, knowing this was not what she had in mind.

"Are you concerned at all?" she continued.

"I certainly support freedom of the press," I told Millie. "I support freedom of speech. I certainly don't like what I've seen over the last couple of years [with] the president attacking the press. I think that's certainly put a spotlight on the importance of a free press. And I think that anybody who responsibly exercises that right of free speech and that right of freedom of the press, that ought to be respected."

"And don't you think it's within the president's First Amendment [sic] to criticize and make comment against the media," she countered.

"Absolutely, it's well within his First Amendment rights to make comments about the media," I responded. "But it's also within my First Amendment rights to say that I don't think it's a good idea for the president of the United States to demonize the press and to call us the enemy of the people and that sort of thing. I think that kind of speech could potentially put journalists in harm's way."

Weaver went on to compare Infowars to CNN and NBC, saying we all got called "fake news."

"My personal opinion is that you can't put CNN in the same category as Infowars, with all due respect," I said. "I think if you look at what the Sandy Hook parents are going through right now—"

She tried to cut me off, but I kept going.

"I think if you look at what the Sandy Hook parents are going through right now with respect to Infowars that there is a conversation to be had about what is being said in the public sphere and what's being said on social media and what's being told to a lot of people out there who trust what you say. And for example, I don't think it's right to say to the Sandy Hook parents out there that what happened was a hoax. I don't think that's appropriate."

The look on Millie's face was priceless. In short, she couldn't handle the truth. She knew the Sandy Hook conspiracy was bullshit. I could see she was struggling to disregard what I was saying, like a kid fighting a parent administering cough syrup.

The episode was telling. Conspiracy theories have become a powerful force in our politics because they prey on a specific fear. For gun enthusiasts, it's the fear of firearms confiscation. For xenophobes, it's the fear of millions of migrants flooding the streets of American cities. Lies work best, Trump knows, when they are rooted in fear.

AS THE NATION BARRELED TOWARD THE MIDTERMS IN THE FALL, Trump juiced his base with this kind of fearmongering. He appealed to the Infowars and QAnon crowds with his attacks on the press and by showing sympathy for their cries of censorship in social media, often sounding like the conspiracy theorist in chief at several of his rallies. But it wasn't until October that we saw Trump home in on a campaign message that combined this outreach to fringe elements with an actual policy idea. After passing one of the most unpopular tax cuts in history and trying to take health care away from millions, he turned from his legislative agenda and once more to immigration and the wave of nativist fear he'd ridden to the White House two years earlier. But whereas two years earlier he'd built his argument around the image of the wall, now, with the power of the presidency at his disposal, he was able to manufacture an immigration crisis designed to sow racial discord and drive his base to the polls.

It started that October, when Trump, to pitch his long-sought border wall, seized on the existence of a caravan of four thousand migrants making their way to the U.S. border from Central America, casting the threat posed by this group of asylum seekers in the darkest light. The Trump campaign went as far as to produce a racist ad depicting the migrants as wall-climbing invaders, which was dubbed the "Willie Horton ad" of 2018. For those who don't remember it, this was a reference to a pro–George H. W. Bush campaign commercial from 1988 that seized on Democrat Michael Dukakis's decision as governor of Massachusetts to grant a prison furlough to an African American man, Willie Horton, who went on to commit rape and murder. Even at the time, the Willie Horton ad was seen as racially divisive. So, too, was Trump's invasion ad, which was nothing more than a Hail Mary aimed at shaking up an election that had turned against the GOP, particularly in the House races that would mean the difference between House Speaker Paul Ryan or Nancy Pelosi. A bunch of the networks, including CNN, Fox News, and Fox Business, refused to run Trump's ad.

As if that weren't enough, Trump was adding new twists to his appeals to the xenophobes in his base. At his rallies, he began to speculate that Democratic dark-money forces were behind the caravan, lending credence to the conspiracy theory floated by some on the right that the billionaire philanthropist George Soros was bankrolling the migrants as a way to pump left-leaning voters into the electorate.

"Now we're starting to find out—and I won't say it 100 percent, I'll put it a little [sic] tiny question mark on the end, but we're not going to get it, but we have the fake news back there, fake news—a lot of money has been passing through people to try to get to the border by Election Day, because they think that is a negative for us," Trump told a Montana rally in October.

As if his unverified claims of Soros's involvement weren't enough, Trump was casting the caravan as some kind of perfect storm of immigration chaos, expanding his conspiracy theory to include unproven statements about Muslims infiltrating the ranks of the migrants, making their trek to the border the visual embodiment of his base's economic and security anxiety. Trump was suggesting that there were people of Middle Eastern descent using the caravan as cover, presumably to enter the United States to carry out terrorist attacks. He went as far as to put this racially loaded accusation in a tweet.

@realDonaldTrump
Sadly, it looks like Mexico's Police and Military are unable to stop the Caravan heading to the Southern Border of the United States. Criminals and unknown Middle Easterners are mixed in. I have alerted Border Patrol and Military that this is a National Emergy. Must change laws!
8:37 AM—22 Oct 2018

Despite the fact that there was no evidence that there were Middle Easterners in the caravan, Trump continued pushing that fantasy, something I challenged that same week in the Oval Office. We had gathered for a bill signing on a separate issue. Then the caravan came up again as reporters began to ask questions.

"I have very good information," Trump told reporters.

I pressed him to find out if he had any proof. He didn't.

"There's no proof of anything but they could very well be," he said, adding a new expression to the ranks of "alternative facts" and Rudy Giuliani's comment to NBC that "the truth isn't truth." "There's no proof of anything" felt like a fitting slogan for Trump's fact-challenged grip on power. In Trump's mind, any false statement, if expressed passionately enough, carries the same weight as an objective truth grounded in reality. If Trump could convince enough people that there were potential terrorists crossing the border, then he could conceivably secure enough support for any kind of policy, from a medieval wall to a family-separation policy that devastates the lives of untold numbers of children.

For almost two years, we'd all been witnessing an administration firmly detached from the truth, but in the noncrisis that was the migrant caravan, the whole country could see how Trump, if left to his own devices and without the scrutiny of a free press, could politicize and manufacture a crisis to suit his political needs.

And just because Hillary Clinton wasn't on the ballot didn't mean Trump was done attacking her, either. Trump, it seemed, was still obsessed with her. He would mention her in his speeches as though 2016 had never happened. He just couldn't let it go. He would tweet about her email controversy, repeatedly complaining that the former secretary of state should be Mueller's target, not him. A source close to Trump revealed to me that as Trump was pulling the security clearance for another adversary, former CIA director John Brennan, in August 2018, he wanted to do the same for Clinton. The president and former White House chief of staff John Kelly got into such a heated argument over Trump's desire to revoke the clearances of his rivals that their shouting match was audible to others. A congressional source confirmed the White House effort to go after Clinton. Trump essentially got what he wanted. Clinton went on to give up her security clearance voluntarily. In a letter to the State Department in late August, Clinton's lawyer David Kendall, unaware of Trump's wishes, wrote the administration to voluntarily request that the former secretary of state's clearance be removed. The State Department carried out her request the following day, according to the letters I've obtained from the saga.

Neither the absence of a crisis at the border nor of Hillary Clinton's name on the ballot were facts that mattered. And, of course, the only way to convince Trump's base to believe his version of reality was for him to continue to attack the press as he stepped up his war on the truth. In one of the real low points of the midterms, at a rally in Missoula, Montana,

Trump praised that state's lone congressman, Greg Gianforte, for body-slamming my friend and colleague Ben Jacobs of the newspapers the *Guardian*, in a fit of rage over questions he didn't like.

"By the way, never wrestle him. Any guy that can do a body-slam, he's my kind of guy," Trump said about Gianforte at the rally, firing up the crowd.

It was a perfect example of why my concerns are not just about the president's behavior. They're about his effect on the rest of the country. That night in Missoula, after Trump lionized a congressman for attacking a reporter, I saw a group of young men in the crowd looking right at me and laughing uproariously at the president's shout-out to Gianforte. One of these men, who appeared to be in his early twenties, started to make body-slam gestures, right before he ran his thumb across his neck as if to indicate that he wanted to slit my throat.

These are small gestures and threats, to be sure, but they are behavior that Trump has normalized and encouraged. Of greater concern is where you draw the line. It isn't always easy to see when a threat is just someone trying to act intimidating and when a threat represents legitimate danger. Until now, the danger had been largely theoretical, but unfortunately that was all about to change.

———————

JUST A FEW DAYS AFTER TRUMP PRAISED GIANFORTE, THE FIRST IN A series of suspicious packages, containing devices that turned out to be pipe bombs, began to arrive at the homes and offices of various high-profile Democrats across the United States. The first device was sent to George Soros, one of Trump's recent targets. The next day, another package was intended for Hillary Clinton. On the following day, CNN's headquarters in New York had to be evacuated after the discovery of yet another device, mailed to former CIA director John Brennan. My CNN colleagues, including anchors Poppy Harlow and Jim Sciutto, continued to broadcast live on the air, using their cell phones, with the help of our talented producers and photographers, who made it all happen. I couldn't be prouder of their work.

But this wasn't a time to applaud one another. Other pipe bombs were sent to former president Barack Obama, Congresswoman Debbie Wasserman Schultz, and former attorney general Eric Holder. Even actor and anti-Trump activist Robert De Niro received a suspicious package. A law enforcement source forwarded to me images of alerts sent out by the Secret Service offering exclusive details about the packages and their intended targets. This was chilling stuff. The bomber, though working with crude devices, appeared to be a domestic terrorist seeking vengeance for Trump.

Journalists are supposed to be a hardened bunch, but the attempted bombing of our offices in New York, which prompted fears that other devices might be found at CNN bureaus around the country, brought the real danger of Trump's rhetoric to our workplace. This wasn't about getting beaten up at a Trump rally anymore. CNN staff members, who lead real lives outside of work, with families of their own, could have been killed, in part, because of the poisonous rhetoric that had fueled Trump's rise to power. The network's management, including CNN president Jeff Zucker, had the job of calming terrorized staff members in one of the world's largest news operations. Yes, people were scared. This was the end result of years of Trump's attacks on CNN. We had been called "fake news." We had been called "the enemy of the people." We had heard the chants of "CNN sucks" at the rallies. But this wasn't happening just to me or any other individual CNN employee. It had suddenly become a dangerous time for all of us.

Despite those pipe bombs sent to CNN and other targets across the country, Trump and White House press secretary Sarah Sanders couldn't find the decency to stop calling the press "the enemy of the people." After the bomb scare at our headquarters, Sanders failed to show any sympathy for CNN in her first tweet after the explosive device was discovered. Her initial statement condemned the "attempted violent attacks" against Obama and the Clintons, but she didn't even mention CNN. After she was denounced on Twitter for that glaring omission, she tried to clean it up with another tweet that included CNN.

Our condemnation of these dispicable [*sic*] acts certainly includes threats made to CNN as well as current or former public servants, she tweeted, misspelling the word *despicable*.

First Lady Melania Trump also neglected to mention CNN in her initial statement on what had occurred, as she condemned "attempted attacks on President Clinton, President Obama, their families, public officials, individuals and organizations."

It was yet another stunning signal from the West Wing to the East Wing that Trumpworld's hatred for CNN had become cancerous. So, it was no surprise when CNN finally responded. Jeff Zucker, who had spent months biting his tongue and resisting the urge to spend much time weighing in on Trump's almost daily attacks on the press, had simply had enough.

"The president, and especially the White House press secretary, should understand their words matter," Zucker said in a statement issued by CNN.

Six hours later, Sanders fired back at CNN in a tweet, insisting that Trump had **asked Americans "to come together and send one very clear, strong, unmistakable message that acts or threats of political violence of any kind have no place in the USA." Yet you chose to attack and divide. America should unite against all political violence.** Sanders's tweet overlooked the fact that it was the president's rhetoric and the hostility he stoked at his events that had inspired the mail bomber in the first place. It was another shameful moment for Sanders, who had once again lost sight of her role in working with the press.

By the end of the week, the toxic Trump effect on our national discourse became clear when FBI agents captured fifty-six-year-old Cesar Sayoc, charging the fanatical Trump supporter with sending thirteen pipe bombs to CNN and Democratic targets around the country. Sayoc's white van, as the country could plainly see on the day of his arrest, was covered in antimedia signage, with much of his fury directed at CNN. One sticker on the van featured one of the favorite chants of Trump rally-goers: "CNN Sucks." Pictures of CNN commentator Van Jones and filmmaker Michael Moore could also be seen on the sides of Sayoc's MAGA van. Both men had red targets or crosshairs over their faces, as did a photo of Hillary Clinton.

Sayoc, who was living out of his van after being kicked out of his parents' home, had been a regular at Trump rallies in Florida. The former pizza delivery driver and bodybuilder had also used social media to direct threatening messages to a variety of targets, including this reporter.

@CNN @Acosta You over enemy of America CNN. Your [*sic*] next, read one tweet aimed at me.

Acosta your [*sic*] next. See you at next rally, read another.

A total of nine tweets appeared to threaten me and CNN. The most disturbing tweet, aimed at my Twitter handle, @Acosta, featured images of a decapitated goat and its severed head. These images were apparently used by Sayoc to threaten other Trump critics. Several of his tweets were posted during that first week in August, after I had been heckled by that angry mob of Trump supporters in Tampa, the same night Trump and his son Eric posted their own tweets giving the thumbs-up to all those middle fingers.

I never knew about Sayoc's threatening tweets until after his arrest. CNN's Andrew Kaczynski had screen-grabbed a number of them before the alleged pipe bomber's accounts were shut down. The fact that I didn't see these messages highlights one of the problems with social media these days: the near invisibility of what should be bright red flags pointing to dangerous behavior. Popular apps such as Twitter and Instagram are so large that these companies can't possibly see or stop every threatening message posted on their sites, thus creating a safe space for maniacs such as Cesar Sayoc to violently troll journalists in plain view. Trump was Sayoc's hero. We were his enemy.

Sayoc is exactly the kind of person we had been warning the Trump people about. We didn't worry about all Trump supporters at all Trump rallies. We feared people like Sayoc. Yes, he was clearly not playing with a full deck, but *that's* what worried us. He was the living, breathing embodiment of the tiny fraction of deranged Trump supporters some of us feared, a person who wasn't fully in control of his impulses but who had been radicalized to the point of carrying out acts of violence. We knew it would take only one of these folks to push things too far.

Now, you would think the arrest of Cesar Sayoc would have slowed Trump's roll. But you'd be mistaken. Not a chance. Five days after CNN's exchange of tweets and statements with Sanders the day the pipe bombs appeared at our headquarters, she and Trump resumed their attacks on the press. In the war on CNN and the rest of the news media, there would be no cease-fire. With one week before the mid-terms, Trump had a base to energize. Pipe bombs or no pipe bombs, he returned to calling the press the enemy:

@realDonaldTrump
There is great anger in our Country caused in part by inaccurate, and even fraudulent, reporting of the news. The Fake News Media, the true Enemy of the People, must stop the open & obvious hostility & report the news accurately & fairly. That will do much to put out the flame . . .

Trump's "great anger" tweet, incredibly, was aimed at assigning responsibility for a terrible attack that had happened just days after the pipe bomb mailings. A mass shooting at the Tree of Life synagogue in Pittsburgh had left eleven people dead. Police said the gunman,

Robert Bowers, had made anti-Semitic comments both on social media and during the massacre. In one of his rants on social media,
Bowers falsely complained that Jews were somehow part of the effort
to transport migrants in the caravan to the border. Sound familiar?
It was a disgusting lie, but one that appeared to be fueled in part by
Trump's anti-immigrant rhetoric, some of which had been aimed at
George Soros, who had been falsely accused of somehow bankrolling
the caravan. Trump obviously didn't like this aspect of our reporting
on the Tree of Life shooting. So, of course, he revved up his attacks on
the media, pouring more gasoline on his burning pile of "enemy of
the people" nonsense.

@realDonaldTrump
CNN and others in the Fake News Business keep purposely and
inaccurately reporting that I said the "Media is the Enemy of the
People." Wrong! I said that the "Fake News (Media) is the Enemy
of the People," a very big difference. When you give out false
information-not good!

Getting back to Trump's "great anger" tweet, it's also important to
note that he was taking zero responsibility for the violent events that
were terrorizing Americans across the country. Trump was claiming
that better coverage of his presidency would "do much to put out the
flame." What was he saying there? That if we gave him the news he
wanted, he would halt his rhetorical attacks? Talk about fake news.
Does anybody really believe he would have stopped his threatening
rhetoric? On that same day, Sanders happened to hold a press briefing. And I knew exactly what I wanted to ask. True to form, she was
unapologetic.

ACOSTA: Shouldn't you reserve the term "enemy" for people who
are actually the enemy of the United States rather than journalists?

SANDERS: The president is not referencing all media. He is talking about the growing amount of fake news that exists in the country. The president is calling that out.

ACOSTA: May I ask a follow-up, please? Since you mentioned that, the president said this morning, "The fake news media, the true enemy of the people must stop. They have a responsibility to report the news accurately and fairly." Can you state for the record, which outlets that you and the president regard as the enemy of the people?

SANDERS: I'm not going to walk through a list, but I think those individuals probably know who they are.

Ah, so she was in full agreement with the concept that members of the press were somehow "the enemy." If that sounds both ridiculous and dangerous to you, imagine how it came across from where I was sitting. But I pressed on for more.

ACOSTA: Would that include my outlet, which received the bomb threats?

SANDERS: I don't think it's specific to a generalization of a full outlet. At times there are individuals that is the president would be referencing.

To be honest, I was pretty pissed at Sarah for calmly stating what was some of the vilest, most un-American stuff that had ever been said in the White House Briefing Room. I was appalled. I know the folks at home were appalled. So, I kept going to see where this would end up.

ACOSTA: So you are not going to state for the record? The president is going to say the fake news media are the enemy and if you are going to continue to stand there and say that some journalists and news outlets in this country that meet that characterization, shouldn't you have the guts, Sarah, to state which outlets and which journalists are the enemy of the people?

SANDERS: I think it's irresponsible of a news organization like yours to blame responsibility of a pipe bomb that was not sent by the president and not just blame the president, but members of his administration for those heinous acts. I think that is outrageous and irresponsible.

Sanders didn't need to specify who Trump's "enemy" was at that briefing. It was painfully obvious before I'd asked my question. But I wanted all of this on record. I wanted it on video. Such words should be captured and memorialized for all eternity. Folks weren't patting me on the back as I exited the Briefing Room that day, but I wasn't looking for anybody's approval. If people think I was showboating or grandstanding in my exchange with Sanders, they can shove it. This was all about preserving a dark chapter in our nation's history. We need future generations to read and understand that there was a time in this country when the president and his top spokeswoman called reporters "the enemy of the people" in, of all places, the White House. It would be wrong to overlook such comments by sticking our heads in the sand. That would only sanitize Trumpworld's behavior and rhetoric when both should be exposed, recorded, and held up to the brightest light possible. And that was what I hoped to accomplish in the Briefing Room that day. I knew Sarah would face no accountability for her actions. She wouldn't lose her job over those comments. Indeed, they were probably acts of job preservation more than anything else. But her comments that day will outlive all of us.

For nearly three years, I had endured the taunts, the name-calling, and the abuse at countless Trump rallies. Trump had whipped up millions of Americans into a full-blown frenzy of hatred for the press. I had felt it all firsthand, whether by standing on the press riser at a

Trump rally or simply looking down at my phone to read the latest death threat posted on one of my social media accounts. Now, during these last days before the midterms, I was beginning to speak by phone with FBI agents and local police detectives who were beginning to investigate the various threats aimed at this reporter and some of my colleagues. The law enforcement community was beginning to take all of it very seriously. There were worries, of course, that Cesar Sayoc was far from the only loose cannon out there and that somebody was going to get hurt. I wasn't sleeping much those days. I was looking around corners as I walked home at night. My producer Matt Hoye and I began to discuss whether we should wear bulletproof vests to the rallies, something the Secret Service probably would not allow. Should I carry a taser gun? I wondered.

As a veteran reporter, I saw it as a bit ridiculous, but the reality was none of us knew just how serious the risks really were.

———————

WITH SAYOC BEHIND BARS, CNN STILL HAD AN ELECTION TO COVER. We had to move beyond our clash with the White House over the man dubbed the "MAGA bomber." With just a week to go before Trump found out whether his assaults on immigrants and the media would pay dividends with voters, the president was ratcheting up the rhetoric during a busy rally schedule down the home stretch. I traveled down to Florida for one of his final rallies, in support of GOP Senate candidate Rick Scott and Republican gubernatorial contender Ron DeSantis. We were nervous, as Florida rallies often featured the rowdiest crowds we would encounter. But we had a plan.

Given what had just happened with Sayoc, CNN was not taking any chances with my security. At the Fort Myers rally, I was surrounded by a group of four off-duty police officers from the Miami area. They were big and intimidating, and frankly, I was a bit embarrassed. CNN was doing right by me in offering all that protection, but as anybody who knows me will tell you, I really don't like being fussed over. And this was a lot of fussing.

When we made our way inside the venue, it was like moths to a flame. Trump supporters made their way up to the press cage to ask me all sorts of questions. One woman asked me if I had been paid by George Soros to ask questions of Trump. No, I politely told her, "George Soros is not paying me." Another man asked me if I was "on the CIA's payroll." These were some of the more bizarre examples, but they illustrate a critical point: too many Trump supporters have been so misled by conspiracy theorists, fringe websites, and conservative news outlets that it seemed normal to them that a reporter for the mainstream press could be paid by George Soros or the CIA.

It wasn't all bad that night. After the rally, an elderly gentleman named Merlin approached me with an incredibly kind gesture. He told me he had been at that rally in Tampa back in August and had given me a hard time. If you look at the video of all those folks yelling and giving me the middle finger, you can spot Merlin flipping me off in the crowd. Ever since then, Merlin told me, he had felt bad about what he'd done. He wanted to apologize. I couldn't believe my ears. Honestly, I thought I was starting to tear up. So, I asked him if it would be okay to record his apology on my iPhone. He said he didn't mind at all.

"I just wanted to apologize for flipping you off in Tampa. I got carried away," Merlin said, with his wife at his side, all smiles. "You know, it's like I was asking for facts and not opinions. That's all we want. I do get carried away so I just wanted to apologize." And with that he was gone.

I was touched by what he had done. After all those rallies and all those shouting Trump supporters and, yes, all those middle fingers, it felt good to talk to somebody who had had a change of heart. I understand that Trump supporters don't want to watch me or CNN. I get that. They can find much of what they want to hear on Fox News or

conservative websites. What mattered to me was that Merlin had realized something bigger than all that: we are still in this thing together.
He understood that we are not enemies. We are on the same team. We
are all Americans. He knew exactly how we are supposed to treat one
another, with dignity and respect.

I thought about this a lot that night and over the next few days, and
when Trump got his clock cleaned on Election Night, I was still thinking about Merlin. Yes, there was a blue wave that night: House Republicans were swept out of power, and Trump and the GOP held on to
the Senate only by the skin of their teeth. Judgment Day had come
for Trump. He was in for a whole new world as soon as the new
Democratic House was sworn in. The hearings and investigations were
all coming soon. The news cycle was dominated by that discussion.
A former senior Trump White House official had put his finger on
why Trump lost. The energy that had propelled Trump to power from
conservatives had been matched by a rising enthusiasm on the left. "A
hundred and thirteen million people came out to vote. Want to know
why? They were passionate about getting the fuck rid of Donald Fucking Trump," the official said.

But reflecting on my own experience covering the midterms and
all those crazy rallies, I was more impressed by the wave of decency
that had swept over Merlin. I knew there must be others like him out
there, feeling the same way. Fear and hatred had lost that day. So,
I was feeling hopeful about America, not because Trump had been
defeated, but because racism and xenophobia, in the form of Trump's
attacks on immigrants, had been defeated; paranoia and scapegoating,
in the form of Trump's attacks on the media, had been defeated.

At least for today.

13

A White House Smear

By the time the post-midterms press conference rolled around in November 2018, I suppose I should have seen it coming. After all, Trump had suffered a stinging defeat in the House, which was about to be controlled by the Democrats once again. The Republicans did make some gains in the Senate, but to look at it clinically, those gains were modest; they'd also lost a key Senate seat in Arizona, where former senator Jeff Flake had decided not to run for reelection, making Kyrsten Sinema the first Democrat to be elected to the Senate in Arizona since the 1990s. Needless to say, for a man who hated to lose as much as Trump did, this press conference was almost guaranteed to be messy.

As it turned out, I didn't know the half of it.

Truth be told, I had prepared myself mentally for the day the White House would seize my press pass. It had long been a possibility in the back of my mind, even before Trump campaign manager Brad Parscale suggested on Twitter that I have my credentials yanked. I knew there was precedent for Trump doing something like it. At one event early on in the 2016 campaign, he had tossed out Jorge Ramos of Univision for pressing him on his blatantly racist comment that many Mexican immigrants were rapists and drug dealers. Ejecting a reporter from a presidential campaign function was just about un-thinkable prior to Trump's run for office. But candidate Trump was crossing lines that no one imagined capable of being crossed before.

While my credentials were never threatened during the campaign, there were moments throughout the 2016 cycle when reporters from other outlets were denied access to Trump events. Jenna Johnson from the *Washington Post* and journalists from BuzzFeed were occasionally blocked from sitting in the press cage at Trump's rallies. It was the campaign's way of sending a message about stories they didn't like. CNN was in a different category in 2016. During the primaries, the Trump people counted on us. Those were the days when we offered live, usually uninterrupted coverage of Trump's rallies, something the other campaigns could only watch on their laptops, phones, and TVs with envy. The Trump campaign was not going to jeopardize that kind of free advertising by retaliating against our journalists. In fact, many of the advance people for the campaign bent over backward to make sure my crews and I made it into the rallies on time for our live shots, often escorting us to the head of the security line for the press when we were running late.

Obviously though, things changed dramatically once CNN and I were dubbed "fake news" at that infamous press conference in Janu-ary 2017. And then there were, of course, the many confrontations I had had with Trump and Spicer and Sanders. Looking back, I suppose that things had been approaching critical mass for some time.

During the fight in the fall over Trump's second Supreme Court pick, Brett Kavanaugh, I challenged Sanders to defend the president's shameful mockery of Christine Blasey Ford (a woman who had ac-cused Kavanaugh of sexually assaulting her while they were both in high school) at a campaign rally in Mississippi. By the time Sanders called on me, she had repeatedly delivered the same talking point: that Trump was not mocking Dr. Ford, but was instead just stating facts. Yeah, right. The video speaks for itself. He was mocking a woman alleging sexual assault. And per usual at Trump rallies, his supporters were laughing and egging him on.

I asked Sarah if she had any problem defending Trump. Her response was predictable and awful.

"I don't have any problem stating facts, no . . . I know that's probably something you do have a problem with but we don't," she said acidly.

Usually, a reporter would take a jab like that and absorb it. Instead, I responded, politely but pointedly.

"Actually, Sarah, we do state the facts," I fired back, "and I think there have been many occasions when you don't state the facts, if I may respond."

And then there were the many moments with the White House that fell somewhere between petty and harassing. In June 2018, White House counselor Kellyanne Conway attempted to demonstrate that I was being unpatriotic because I was typing on my iPhone while a crowd of people were singing "God Bless America" during a "Celebration of America" convened by Trump on the South Lawn. You may remember that event, as it was hastily organized to replace a celebration for the Super Bowl champions the Philadelphia Eagles. Trump was so furious that so many Eagles had declined the invitation to come to the White House that he canceled the whole thing and threw a faux-patriotic spectacle instead. This was part of Trump's culture war against the small number of NFL players taking a knee during the national anthem at league games in protest of police brutality in communities across the United States.

As I was typing up a note about the event on my phone and posting a tweet, Conway turned to me and accused me of failing Trumpworld's patriotism test. She held up her phone and started to record me, or at least pretend to.

"Oh look, it's Jim Acosta on his phone instead of singing 'God Bless America,'" she said snarkily.

So, I held up my phone to start recording Kellyanne, as she, too, was not singing along. Yes, this is but a peek through the window into the silly sideshows that play out on a daily basis at the Trump White House.

Moments like these, combined with my later confrontations with Sarah Sanders over the White House reaction to Cesar Sayoc and his pipe bombs, only cemented in my mind that my relationship with the White House was on increasingly shaky ground. My relationship with many of the Trump people, if you want to call it that, had turned toxic well before the midterms. Still, I had a plan in place in case they came for my pass. The moment they tried to grab it, I was going to record the whole thing on my phone to make sure it was documented. I had no idea if or when I'd actually have to use that recording.

On the morning after the midterms, there was no shortage of questions for Trump. At that point, he had not fired Sessions, but many of us figured that would happen in short order. There was also the issue of the Democrats seizing control of Congress. Could Trump work with the incoming House Speaker, Nancy Pelosi? What did he make of the calls for investigations into his tax returns, and so on, coming from so many Democrats on the verging of taking power? These were all key questions.

It seemed that the best way to take Trump's temperature at that moment was to confront him on the migrant caravan. During the run-up to the midterms he had used some of the most racially loaded rhetoric I had ever heard from an American president. He had claimed, without evidence, that "unknown Middle Easterners" had infiltrated the caravan. His campaign had also run a TV ad on the caravan that was rejected by the networks, including CNN (Fox News had been running the ad before taking it down). CNN labeled the ad as "racist." Sure, it was just a continuation of his incendiary rhetoric aimed at immigrants that began the day he announced his run for the presidency. But just because race-baiting was his original sin as a politician didn't mean the caravan remarks should go unchallenged. For years, I'd been listening as he took his hateful language to new lows, finding a variety of ways to paint immigrants in the worst possible light. He'd made fear of the caravan the cornerstone of his midterm strategy, but the American people hadn't bought his manufactured crisis, and now his party had lost the House. Yes, on the day after the election, the caravan wasn't just a fair question; it was the right question.

Trump began the press conference, predictably, by calling on Fox News. Their reporter asked about a possible shakeup in Trump's Cabinet and the potential for investigations. All fine questions. Next came a question on the border wall, one of Trump's obsessions. Then came one on his tax returns. Trump was getting testy already. He scolded the next reporter, Brian Karem, for his questions about Trump's tax returns and whether the president could separate his upcoming fights with the Democrats from his professed desired to work on a bipartisan basis. Trump repeatedly interrupted Karem, calling him a "comedian." Then Trump, minutes later and in a bit of a surprise to me, called on me for the fifth question of the news conference.

Almost from the start of our exchange, it was clear I was heading into territory he wasn't happy about—not because of his actual words but because he also repeatedly interrupted my line of questioning. Interruption is a ploy Trump uses regularly to sidestep giving clear answers to questions. "Excuse me. Excuse me," he will say when he doesn't like a line of inquiry. Here's a rule of thumb: if he's interrupting you, you're on to something, so keep going—which is what I did.

ACOSTA: Okay. Thank you, Mr. President. I wanted to challenge you on one of the statements that you made in the tail end of the campaign in the midterms, that this—
TRUMP: Here we go.
ACOSTA: Well, if you don't mind, Mr. President—
TRUMP: Let's go. Let's go. Come on.

ACOSTA: That this caravan was an "invasion." As you know, Mr. President—

TRUMP: I consider it to be an invasion.

ACOSTA: As you know, Mr. President, the caravan was not an invasion. It's a group of migrants moving up from Central America towards the border with the U.S.

TRUMP: Thank you for telling me that. I appreciate it.

ACOSTA: Why did you characterize it as such? And—

TRUMP: Because I consider it an invasion. You and I have a difference of opinion.

ACOSTA: But do you think that you demonized immigrants in this election—

TRUMP: Not at all. No, not at all.

ACOSTA: —to try to keep—

TRUMP: I want them—I want them to come into the country, but they have to come in legally. You know, they have to come in, Jim, through a process. I want it to be a process. And I want people to come in. And we need the people.

ACOSTA: Right. But your campaign had—your campaign—

TRUMP: Wait. Wait. Wait. You know why we need the people, don't you? Because we have hundreds of companies moving in. We need the people.

ACOSTA: Right. But your campaign had an ad showing migrants climbing over walls and so on.

TRUMP: Well, that's true. They weren't actors. They weren't actors.

As he and I continued to spar, I tried to make the point that the caravan was hundreds of miles away, which meant it was far from the imminent invasion he had been portraying it as. I mean, if it's an invasion, shouldn't the migrants be carrying weapons instead of diapers? Trump wasn't having it, and he tried to put a stop to it, but not before getting a jab at my network's expense.

TRUMP: I think you should—honestly, I think you should let me run the country, you run CNN—

ACOSTA: All right.

TRUMP: —and if you did it well, your ratings would be much better.

ACOSTA: But let me ask, if I—if I may ask one other question—

TRUMP: Okay, that's enough.

ACOSTA: Mr. President, if I may—if I may ask one other question.

TRUMP: Okay, Peter [Alexander], go ahead.

ACOSTA: Are you worried—

TRUMP: That's enough. That's enough. That's enough.

ACOSTA: Mr. President, I didn't—well, I was going to ask one other. The other folks that had—

TRUMP: That's enough. That's enough.

ACOSTA: Pardon me, ma'am, I'm—Mr. President—

This was the moment when a White House intern attempted to grab the microphone from me. I have been in this business for more than twenty years. Nobody has ever tried to rip a microphone out of my hands. As you can see in the video, I recoiled from the intern to hang on to that microphone. That's why I said, "Pardon me, ma'am." At that moment, her arm brushed past mine, making contact with me for a brief moment. After I held on to the mic, she backed away. I pressed on as Trump unloaded on me.

Trump again tried to call on NBC's Peter Alexander, but I wanted to make my point. First, I wanted to make it clear that a president should not be able to shut down a reporter at a news conference in this fashion. The Trump people had just tried to take away my microphone. Trump was trying to shout me down with insults. I felt it was critical, at this moment, to stand my ground.

TRUMP: Excuse me, that's enough.

ACOSTA: Mr. President, I had one other question if—

TRUMP: Peter. Let's go.

ACOSTA: If I may ask on the Russia investigation. Are you concerned that you may have indictments—

TRUMP: I'm not concerned about anything with the Russia investigation because it's a hoax.

ACOSTA: —that you may indictments coming down? Are you—

TRUMP: That's enough. Put down the mic.

ACOSTA: Mr. President, are you worried about indictments coming down in this investigation?

TRUMP: I'll tell you what: CNN should be ashamed of itself having you working for them. You are a rude, terrible person. You shouldn't be working for CNN. Go ahead [to Peter Alexander].

ACOSTA: I think that's unfair.

TRUMP: You're a very rude person. The way you treat Sarah Huckabee is horrible. And the way you treat other people are horrible. You shouldn't treat people that way. Go ahead. Go ahead, Peter. Go ahead.

At this point, Peter jumped in. I had turned over my microphone, and Peter had the floor. But suffice it to say, I was not ready to sit down as Trump kept attacking. The transcript is not really helpful anymore at this point, as I'm no longer holding the microphone, but you can still hear me in the video, off mic, reminding the president that we at CNN had just been sent pipe bombs in the mail. Trump was furious. This is when he called me, and my colleagues at CNN, "the enemy of the people"—but not before Peter Alexander weighed in.

Peter was the real hero of that news conference, in my view, because he did something at that point that we should see a lot more of in Washington. He stood up for a fellow member of the press, me. Folks, a lot of other reporters would have sat silently as the president berated another journalist. In fact, that had happened many times before. What makes this moment so important is that Peter did not do that. He did not let the bully win the day.

> ALEXANDER: In Jim's defense, I've traveled with him and watched him. He's a diligent reporter who busts his butt like the rest of us.
> TRUMP: Well, I'm not a big fan of yours either. So, you know.
> (Laughter.)
> ALEXANDER: I understand.
> TRUMP: To be honest with you.
> ALEXANDER: So let me—so let me ask you a question if I can—
> TRUMP: You aren't—you aren't the best.

This is when I tried to jump back in. The transcript is incomplete. Again, I no longer had the microphone. I was making it clear that he had crossed a line. Trump might be the president, but he has no right to attack us, particularly just days after one of his supporters tried to blow up my news network. It was time to stand up to the bully.

> TRUMP: Well, when you report fake news—
> ACOSTA: (inaudible)
> TRUMP: No. When you report fake news, which CNN does a lot, you are the enemy of the people. Go ahead.

There it was. Even after the pipe bombs, the president of the United States was still calling us "the enemy of the people."

By this point, the press conference had gone off the rails. Thinking back on that day, I can't help but recall the time Hope Hicks told me that Trump said, "Jim gets it," as in I get that his behavior is all an act—only, this was no act, for any of us, including Trump. In pressing my case, I had been determined to cut through the lies and the fantasy that immigrants were invading our country. And Trump hated me for it. He was red in the face, pacing behind the lectern as this was going down. After it was all over, a few colleagues said to me, "I thought he was going to come down and take a swing at you."

Trump was visibly angry throughout the rest of the news conference. I had never really seen him this testy before in front of reporters. Later on, Yamiche Alcindor, a reporter for PBS, attempted to ask him about his decision to label himself a nationalist in the final days of the campaign. This label was widely viewed by many of his critics as a dog whistle to his base, and that what he really meant was that he was a *white* nationalist. Yamiche asked whether Trump was emboldening white nationalists with that language.

"That's such a racist question," Trump replied. He called her question racist three times. It was an appalling moment in a conflict that would only get worse.

Over the course of the next couple of days, Trump would attack two other black female journalists, April Ryan of American Urban Radio Network and my CNN colleague Abby Phillip. Trump told Phillip that her question was "stupid" when she asked about Matt Whitaker, the man whom Trump had just tapped to replace Sessions as acting attorney general. He called Ryan, who had covered the White House since the days of Bill Clinton, "a loser." Add it up and you have three attacks on three black female journalists. This was not a coincidence. And all their questions were perfectly legitimate.

In the moments following that post-midterms news conference, it was obvious that my confrontation with Trump was making waves. As soon as the president left the East Room, my mission was to get on the air, so I raced outside to the North Lawn for a live shot. On my way out, I spotted Peter Alexander. We had a brief exchange and a rather awkward "bro hug." But I wanted to thank him for expressing his support in such a charged setting. There had been so many attacks on the White House press corps for having turned the other cheek when a reporter was abused by Trump. This was the first time, that I could recall, in which one network reporter had stood up for another.

During my live shot a few minutes later, Wolf Blitzer and Jake Tapper asked me what it was like being in the middle of that situation with Trump. I don't remember much of what I said, but I closed with my own version of Michelle Obama's line from the 2016 campaign, "When they go low, we go high."

"When they go low, we keep doing our jobs," I told Wolf and Jake.

CNN released a statement following the president's attack on the press at the news conference: "This President's ongoing attacks on the press have gone too far. They are not only dangerous, they are disturbingly un-American. While President Trump has made it clear he does not respect a free press, he has a sworn obligation to protect it. A free press is vital to democracy, and we stand behind Jim Acosta and his fellow journalists everywhere," it read.

It was another full-throated show of support for the press from CNN. I was very grateful. The company had issued statements on behalf of several of us before, so I thought the day would proceed rather normally. We would get back to business, put together our stories, and then do our live shots on the day's events in the evening. I did my hits on *The Situation Room with Wolf Blitzer*, per usual, and then left the White House grounds for dinner.

That was when everything in my life began to spiral out of control.

BEHIND THE SCENES, TRUMP AND HIS AIDES WERE FUMING. THE president obviously hated the way I had confronted him at the press conference. You don't get dubbed "the enemy of the people" every day in this city. But Trump's attacks on the media, which we typically brush off as bluster, were about to be taken to a new level. One of my sources told me that White House communications director Bill Shine, the former Fox News executive, was the driving force behind what was about to happen next. But officials at the White House have thus far refused to specify exactly who was behind it. Perhaps it was all of them.

As I was returning from dinner that evening for my next live shot with Anderson Cooper, a notification flashed on my phone. Sarah Sanders had announced that my "hard pass" had been suspended. An essential press credential, the hard pass allows a reporter to move through the Secret Service checkpoint for journalists without a huge hassle every day. As a White House reporter, you can technically function without a hard pass, but it's extremely difficult. A reporter could still obtain a "day pass," but that would grant me access to the White House grounds only one day at a time. The hard pass is a rather coveted credential for any reporter in Washington, as it means you can enter 1600 Pennsylvania Avenue at just about any time during normal business hours. There is no hassle in going through the White House press office and the Secret Service. With a hard pass, you simply go through the security booth, and you're in. Losing that kind of access to the White House is a pretty big blow if you're covering that beat. Without that hard pass, you could miss—no, you *will* miss—actual news inside the White House, as events can happen at any moment. If you have to rely on obtaining a day pass, you could be waiting out at the Secret Service booth to be granted access to the grounds while your competitors are inside attending a briefing or news conference.

As for the revocation of my press pass, Sanders hadn't even given me a heads-up that it was coming. For a moment, I was stunned. And then I read the press secretary's statement.

The statement was a disgusting smear, carried out by the U.S. government and paid for with American tax dollars. Sanders had accused me of putting my hands on the intern, when, in fact, the opposite had occurred. The intern had approached me, had come into my personal space, and attempted to pull the microphone away from me. As any layman can clearly see in the video of the encounter, the intern put her hands on me as she went for the mic. And to be clear, I don't blame the intern for what happened. She thought she was doing her job.

Sanders justified the action taken against me with a despicable tweet, posted from an official government account announcing the White House decision. It remains on Twitter for all the world to see:

@PressSec
President Trump believes in a free press and expects and welcomes tough questions of him and his Administration. We will, however, never tolerate a reporter placing his hands on a young woman just trying to do her job as a White House intern . . .

"[A] reporter placing his hands on a young woman just trying to do her job" is how Sanders described it. I had been attacked before for my work. I had been called a grandstander and a showboater and so on. I had never, ever been accused of assault. That's what Sanders did here.

I WAS ABSORBING THESE WORDS WHILE STANDING ABOUT TWENTY yards from the White House compound. My eyes glazed over, as it was all a bit surreal. Within a few minutes, I reached the Secret Service booth. Immediately, an officer looked out the window and saw me. Seconds later, another officer exited the booth from a side door and moved in my direction.

At that moment, the officers informed me I had been denied access to the White House, a place I had gone to work just about every day for more than five years. Remembering my plan for just this moment, I pulled out my phone to record the exchange.

"You can take it up with the press office," one of the officers told me.

"But I'm not allowed to come in right now," I said.

"You'll just have to take it up with the press office," that officer said again.

As we had this exchange, the other officer blocked the door into the complex. I experienced such a bizarre feeling. Is this guy guarding the door so I can't come in? Like I'm some kind of criminal?

At that point, I began to head back to Pennsylvania Avenue with the realization that I was going to miss my 8:00 p.m. live shot. As I was about to call the desk at CNN and give them the news, the officer who had blocked the door approached me again. Once again, I pulled out my phone. At this point, I did not know what was going to happen. Am I going to be arrested? Am I going to jail? I wanted everything on camera.

He asked me to turn over my hard pass, so I started narrating the moment, as if it were a live shot, thinking, Don't stop. Keep rolling. It occurred to me that this was possibly unprecedented and probably worthy of documentation for any future legal action on my part.

"This is Jim Acosta. I am in front of the White House. This Secret Service officer is asking for my hard pass. Obviously no hard feelings to the officer. But I am now giving my hard pass to the Secret Service," I said into my phone.

I handed my lanyard to the officer, who set about removing the hard pass from its clear plastic case.

"It's been here for a while now," the officer said, struggling to remove the pass.

"Thank you for your service," I told the officer. And with that, my pass was gone.

My head was spinning. It dawned on me that this, theoretically, could be the end of my career covering the White House. Then I thought, Wait a minute. They can't do this. This is bullshit. They don't get to pick and choose who covers the president.

Then other thoughts occurred to me: What will CNN want to do about this? Will they want to fight? What will my colleagues in the press think? Will they join me? These were not easy questions. Some of this, I thought, went back to that day at Trump Tower when Trump called me "fake news." As I learned during that experience, some journalists (Peter Alexander, for example) will speak up and support a fellow reporter; others will support a fellow reporter but be too afraid to stand behind him; and still others won't care or will even see a potential benefit to siding with the president. As crass as it sounds, standing on the sidelines in a battle between another journalist or news outlet and the White House has its upside: The White House will see you as somebody with whom they can do business. They can give you scoops, interviews, and access—things I couldn't give them.

For now, though, I had to push all of that to the side. First, the revocation of my hard pass needed to be made public immediately. Sarah had put out her statement; now I needed to respond.

I did so with a tweet of my own, retweeting Sarah's tweet falsely accusing me of having assaulted an intern with a simple message. It's still up on Twitter.

@Acosta
This is a lie.
https://twitter.com/PressSec/status/1060333176252448768

But I needed to do more than just tweet. After missing my live shot at the top of the hour for Anderson Cooper, I raced over to CNN's Washington bureau to speak with Anderson in person on set. As I told him, I hadn't placed my hands on anybody. During a brief segment at the end of his show, I defended myself.

Before I went on the air, I spoke by phone with CNN president Jeff Zucker, who counseled me to remain calm, stick to the facts, and simply tell the viewers what had happened. Anderson quoted reporters from other outlets who were at the news conference that day and who stated that I had not done anything to the intern in question.

"This is a test for all of us," I told Anderson. "I do think they're trying to shut us down."

As I made my way home, I tried to make sense of the day's events. It seemed to me that the people inside the White House had all lost their minds. They were so upset about the midterms, it appeared, that they had become unmoored from rationale thought. They were flailing, like a drowning swimmer—and frantically reaching around for somebody else to drag down to the bottom.

All over social media, folks were speculating that the microphone grab by the intern had been a setup. The thinking behind this theory was that Trump had been so damaged by the midterm results that he needed to change the narrative by going after his favorite foil, the news media. I think that's probably giving the people in Trumpworld too much credit. My sense then, and it's still my belief, is that this was just Trump and the White House coming unglued. Remember, these are the same folks who said they were too dumb to collude with the Russians. Sure, attacking CNN would help Trump change the narrative. But why, then, had he then gone on to describe questions from Yamiche Alcindor as "racist." No, this was Trump being Trump. He had been backed into a corner, and he was fighting back. But he was losing. And at this White House, they don't lose graciously.

Sanders would go on to prove that point with her next course of action. As anybody who watched the video could plainly see, I did not place my hands on anybody. But being a bad liar, Sanders doubled down and posted another tweet. Sarah, it seemed, was well aware she was being hammered on Twitter for her ridiculous first attempt at smearing me. This time, she stepped back from the "placing his hands" language and responded by taking White House gaslighting to new Orwellian heights.

@PressSec
We stand by our decision to revoke this individual's hard pass. We will not tolerate the inappropriate behavior clearly documented in this video.

Bizarrely attached to the tweet was a doctored clip of my encounter with the intern—a brief, sped-up version of the video that magnified and exaggerated the momentary, incidental contact the intern made with me as she came into my space and grabbed the microphone. One other unmistakable change to the video tweeted by Sanders was it was now silent—you could no longer hear me saying, "Pardon me, ma'am," an omission immediately detected by others as well. The White House had presented the public with more than alternative facts—this was an alternative reality, tweeted out to the entire world.

According to news reports at the time, the "karate chop" motion I was accused of making was apparently the creation of an individual associated with the fringe website Infowars. This marked another mind-boggling action taken by the White House. As many observers noted at the time, it was astounding and surreal that the White House, or the U.S. government, would stoop to using a doctored video from a discredited website to smear a journalist. It was something an authoritarian government would do. It was something China or Russia would do.

It was also, it occurred to me, the height of hypocrisy. This was, after all, the same president who had once bragged that it was okay to grab a woman by her genitals. It was the same president who had been accused of sexual assault by multiple women. It was the same president who had supported other alleged abusers, Roy Moore in Alabama and Rob Porter on his own White House staff. Who were these people to accuse me of anything? Also, it's difficult to understand how I can be accused of assault when I was just trying to hold on to a microphone.

One thing, at least, was clear: the White House was finally playing for keeps. The endgame was obvious. This wasn't about changing the narrative. The Trump people wanted me out and were willing to smear me to make that happen. I knew I had not done anything wrong. I looked at the video a few more times just to be sure. Had I "karate chopped" the intern's arm, as the doctored video showed? No, I had not. That was obvious.

Then something else strange happened.

An outpouring of support came in to me privately. Former coworkers whom I had not seen in twenty years were emailing me to express their outrage over what was clearly a smear aimed at silencing me. Some of these old colleagues were posting their sentiments on Facebook. It was a solid show of support that gave me the determination to keep fighting.

Behind the scenes at CNN, we were weighing our options. Obviously, the White House had overreacted. But something more profound had occurred: they had violated my rights as a journalist. For starters, Sanders and her boss, Bill Shine, had not even notified me of their decision. Second, they had offered a ridiculous rationale for swiping my hard pass. If they had had a good case, they wouldn't have needed an altered video to prove their point. Also, Trump, as his people know all too well, encourages a rough-and-tumble environment at his press conferences. He lives for it. When I look back at the video of the press conference or read the transcript, I see the White House as the clear aggressor. Trump began to interrupt me as I asked my question. He is the one who launched into the insults, calling CNN the "enemy of the people" and so on.

For me, the stakes felt greater than just my job or the prospect of never covering the White House again. This was only a couple of short weeks after a Trump supporter sent pipe bombs to CNN and others, after personally threatening me on social media. I would be lying if I didn't admit to feeling fearful at the time. To some Americans, I had become the enemy of the people. The death threats were once again polluting my social media accounts. In addition to that, there were Trump supporters who were parroting the White House attacks online, accusing me of assault and worse. Worried about the mental state of the many people posting such comments, I thought for the first time that it was possible somebody would actually try to kill me for doing my job. During the next two weeks, I was constantly looking over my shoulder. I had gotten death threats before and shaken them off, but this was too many.

———

IN THE MEANTIME, THERE WERE MORE IMMEDIATE CONCERNS, practical ones. I needed to get my hard pass back. CNN did ask the White House to reconsider, but it didn't want to back down. (Shocker.)

Fortunately, the schedule for the rest of that week gave us a little time to consider our options. I was off to Paris to cover Trump's trip to France to mark Armistice Day, the one-hundredth anniversary of the end of World War I. No hard pass was necessary for the beginning of the trip, as I was able to go live from the CNN bureau in Paris, with its amazing views of the Eiffel Tower. But the weekend was about to get trickier, as Trump was scheduled to hold some events that would require a White House hard pass. The first event came on Sunday morning, when Trump joined the leaders from France, Germany, the United Kingdom, and Russia (yes, Putin) to mark the end of World War I. Fortunately, the French were organizing the event. My producer Matt Hoye and I had discussed the situation the night before. The White House, we reasoned, would not relent and cough up my hard pass, so we decided to use a back door. I called a contact with the French government, who produced a credential. *Vive la France!* The official, who shall remain anonymous, said the French government would be happy to have me on hand.

So, that Sunday morning, Matt and I made our way down to the Arc

de Triomphe, where Trump was attending his first Armistice event.
The scene in Paris that Sunday was quite a memorable one, as French
president Emmanuel Macron ripped Trump for his nationalist, unilateral view of the world.

"Patriotism is the exact opposite of nationalism," Macron said in
the pouring rain at the Arc de Triomphe. Nationalism, he added was a
"betrayal of patriotism." It was clearly a rebuke from Macron. Trump
had just described himself as a "nationalist," right before the midterms.

Warning of "old demons reawakening," Macron implicitly linked
Trump's brand of politics and the wave of nationalism spreading
across much of Europe to the rise of fascism, the same scourge that
had threatened to wipe out mankind in the twentieth century.

"History sometimes threatens to repeat its tragic patterns, and
undermines the legacy of peace we thought we had sealed with the
blood of our ancestors," Macron continued. It was a brutal, pointed
takedown of Trump.

The French official who had helped me with my press pass told me
Macron's speech was aimed not just at Trump, but at the whole world.
Was the world listening? I wondered. Macron, who had behaved like
something of a "bro" with Trump in their previous encounters, complete with macho handshakes, had rebuked the U.S. president by taking a Kennedyesque stand for freedom. In what must have been a
surreal moment for a French leader, standing on the same streets of
Paris that had been liberated from the Nazis, Macron made the case
for the kind of multilateral, global leadership that had kept much of
the world at peace for more than half a century. I had personally never
witnessed an American president taken to the woodshed by a fellow
foreign leader in that fashion. There was Macron, defending what
used to be U.S. principles. An insult to some Americans, I'm sure, but
Macron, it seemed to me, was doing it out of a love for America and all
her sacrifices to save the French people.

I was there to witness it all and report it out live for CNN. In a bit of logistical wizardry, my producer Matt was able to get me on the air simply using his iPhone. We Skyped into the control room and were on the air to report this historic moment, all without a White House press pass.

Later that day, we faced a bigger challenge. Trump, who had been hammered with criticism for skipping a trip to a cemetery one day earlier because of the rain, was heading out to another cemetery site. We raced out of the city to cover the event, about ten miles outside Paris. It was pouring again. As we arrived on the scene, a Secret Service official questioned whether we had the proper credentials to attend the event. We flashed our French pass, and he didn't turn us away. (Maybe he hadn't gotten the memo.) We continued to show off our gift from the French government and made our way to the cemetery for Trump's only speech of the trip. As any reporter who's covered presidential events will tell you, making your way to the site where the U.S. president will be is no easy task. And this case was no different: the security perimeter was a meandering trek, one mile around the cemetery.

Alas, as we reached the Secret Service checkpoint to enter the cemetery, it was made clear to us that we weren't getting inside. A supervisor calmly but coldly informed us that we were not credentialed to enter the event.

"Take it up with the press office," he said. And that was it.

For the first time in my five years covering the White House, I had been denied access to enter a presidential event. It's odd. At that moment, I wasn't really disappointed or frustrated. It was more a feeling of bewilderment, and then clarity. They were serious about this ban, which meant it was time for me to be just as serious. I was determined to make sure this unconstitutional nonsense did not stand.

In a sense, the White House had just done us a favor. As it turned out, discussions were already under way inside CNN to challenge the revocation of my hard pass in court. The White House Press Office

had just demonstrated the real-world impact of its ban on my reporting. Without any advance notification of the revocation and without
any kind of due process for taking that sort of extreme action, the
White House had done something no president had dared attempt in
decades. President Trump had likely just violated the civil rights of an
American journalist. And we were all about to find out exactly what
the United States of America, with its enduring system of checks and
balances, was going to do about it.

14

Revocation and Redemption

After I had been turned away by the Secret Service at that cemetery in France, I wondered how long we could conceivably fight this out. The odds for a clean victory, I thought, were probably remote.

My flight home was delayed four hours, so I sat at Paris–Charles de Gaulle airport checking my phone for updates on what was about to take place next in the dustup over my press pass. At that point, CNN had made the decision to file a lawsuit against the White House, seeking the return of my credentials. Our attorneys at CNN, along with a formidable outside legal team, had been discussing options for how to proceed. The instructions to everybody were simple: no talking about what was about to happen (and certainly no tweeting—that was for me).

So much for best-laid plans. Word got out anyway.

Former White House correspondent Sam Donaldson, who had been a thorn in the side of the Reagan administration, had offered his support in our case. Donaldson and I had met earlier in 2018, at the CNN management retreat. Sharp and funny as ever, Sam had come to offer all of us a morale boost, letting us know that our coverage of the White House was fully in keeping with the tradition of aggressive reporting on the presidency.

"People who stick their head above the crowd get hit by rotten fruit," Donaldson told us.

As I was wrapping up my trip to Paris, Donaldson was being interviewed on the CNN program *Reliable Sources*, which covers the media, and he inadvertently disclosed to anchor Brian Stelter that he was offering his assistance in our case. This was a huge boost for our cause, as Donaldson, who had made a name for himself for his reporting on Ronald Reagan, could very simply point to his own record as evidence that tough questions, assertively posed to world leaders, are not only part of an accepted practice at the White House, but an essential component of how news outlets cover any presidency.

"I hope I'm not mistaken, but it's my understanding that CNN and Acosta have sued, that there will be a court hearing on Tuesday on this very matter we've been discussing," Donaldson told Stelter.

That, of course, surprised Stelter, who had not seen this reported anywhere, at least not yet.

"I've been told that because I've been asked to give an affidavit, which I've prepared, to be submitted to the court," Donaldson added.

Sam had the scoop. We hadn't sued just yet, but we were about to take the plunge. Donaldson had accidentally let the cat out of the bag. I didn't mind one bit. Indeed, I thought it fitting that Sam Donaldson had broken the news. It was gratifying to have a legend like Sam on our side. He, too, had been called a "grandstander" and a "showboat" in his time, during his days covering Reagan. You can still find clips of Sam's greatest hits on YouTube. He would shout questions at Reagan, who would cup his hand around an ear, pretending he couldn't hear what was being asked. Sam knew that folks were going to attack us if we were tough on Trump; it was expected. But it shouldn't stop us. Sam and I had kept in contact since that CNN management retreat. He had emailed me after the revocation of my hard pass and urged me to "keep charging."

When I landed back in Washington, I found an email that required my immediate attention. A conference call was scheduled to take place within the hour about the lawsuit. As I was waiting in line at customs, I listened as our attorneys—CNN's lead lawyer, David Vigilante, and our lead outside counsel, Ted Boutrous—explained our case. Putting aside our unanimous feeling that our First Amendment rights had been violated, the attorneys were particularly interested in a previous court decision that pointed to a more obscure but very important aspect of the case that hadn't really occurred to most folks. Simply put, by yanking my hard pass without any prior explanation, the White House had violated my right to due process. In other words, we also had a Fifth Amendment argument on our hands.

Our attorneys were referring to the 1977 case of *Sherrill v. Knight*. In that case, reporter Robert Sherrill applied for credentials but was denied by LBJ's White House. You want to talk decorum? Sherrill had gotten himself into hot water by punching an aide to a Florida guber- natorial candidate. That incident, it seemed, was enough for the Secret Service to reject his application for a press pass when he became a White House correspondent for *The Nation*. Where the Johnson White House, along with the Secret Service, made a mistake was in refusing to notify Sherrill of the rationale behind the decision, prompting the lawsuit against the government. A federal judge in the case ruled that the Secret Service and the White House had violated Sherrill's due process rights. The First Amendment, the court decided, protected Sherrill's rights as a journalist to enter the grounds of the White House to do his job. A DC appeals court ruling found that "the pro- tection afforded newsgathering under the First Amendment guaran- tee of freedom of the press requires that this access not be denied arbitrarily or for less than compelling reasons." The same thing, our lawyers were prepared to argue, had happened in my case.

As you might expect, I didn't sleep much that night. Before I went to bed, the head of CNN public relations, Allison Gollust, informed me that media reporters were going to break the news on the filing of our lawsuit in the morning. CNN was taking Donald J. Trump, president of the United States, to court. It was the case of *CNN v. Donald J. Trump*. Also named in the lawsuit were Sarah Sanders and Bill Shine, Trump's recently hired communications director. As a matter of procedure, we also sued an unnamed Secret Service agent and the director of the Secret Service, as that agency had technically pulled my hard pass on behalf of the White House. I hated that part, as I had always had very good relations with the Secret Service. I knew full well that the officer who confiscated my press pass was just doing his job.

In addition, the lawsuit included a declaration from me. Admittedly, it's a bit odd to read this sort of thing in a court document, but this is how the process works. In the declaration, I talk about how the revocation of my press pass would decimate my career, making it impossible for me to work as a White House correspondent for any other news outlet. Would this engender much sympathy? Probably not. But I had to put into writing exactly how the government's decision to pull my pass would basically shut me down as a journalist covering the White House. It was fair to say at the time that if I were banned from entering the White House grounds, then other news outlets would be unable to hire me as a White House correspondent.

The next morning came, and the notifications were flashing on my iPhone: "CNN, Acosta Sue White House over Press Pass" and so on. The *Washington Post*, the *New York Times*, CNN, NBC, Politico, Axios, and others were all reporting the news, which was also spreading to foreign outlets around the world. On social media, critics were quick to pounce, accusing me once again of making myself the story, as though I had a choice in the matter. In this case, I could either become the story or lose my job.

CNN's executives and attorneys recommended that I stay off social media during the court proceedings. This was wise counsel. We didn't need a tweet to send the wrong message to the judge hearing our case, and we certainly didn't want to inadvertently give the White House any ammunition.

The Trump administration appeared ready to do battle. Sanders announced that the White House would "vigorously defend" itself in court. But something stood out in the press secretary's most recent statement; she had rather conspicuously changed the White House rationale for yanking my hard pass:

> We have been advised that CNN has filed a complaint challenging the suspension of Jim Acosta's hard pass. This is just more grandstanding from CNN, and we will vigorously defend against this lawsuit. CNN, who has nearly 50 additional hard pass holders, and Mr. Acosta is no more or less special than any other media outlet or reporter with respect to the First Amendment. After Mr. Acosta asked the President two questions—each of which the President answered—he physically refused to surrender a White House microphone to an intern, so that other reporters might ask their questions. This was not the first time this reporter has inappropriately refused to yield to other reporters. The White House cannot run an orderly and fair press conference when a reporter acts this way, which is neither appropriate nor professional. The First Amendment is not served when a single reporter, of more than 150 present, attempts to monopolize the floor. If there is no check on this type of behavior it impedes the ability of the President, the White House staff, and members of the media to conduct business.

Sanders was obviously backpedaling from her initial statement, which had (ridiculously) accused me of placing my hands on an intern. This time the language was toned way, way down: "he physically refused to surrender a White House microphone to an intern, so that other reporters might ask their questions. This was not the first time this reporter has inappropriately refused to yield to other reporters."

"Physically refused to surrender" is a hell of a reversal, I thought. So did our lawyers. I had "refused to yield to other reporters," Sanders's statement added. Excuse me, but have you watched a White House press briefing? I am certainly not the first reporter to ask a follow-up question. Give me a break. This was all but an acknowledgment from the White House—and sometimes I have to remind myself this was *the White House*—that they had botched that original "karate chop" statement.

Other reports agreed with this assessment. "The White House Is Changing Its Tune on Why It Yanked Jim Acosta's Press Pass" was the headline in the *Washington Post*. It all added up to a good development for our case.

Positive developments aside, I was getting nervous. Our day in court was coming, and there was a lot riding on the case. Yes, it was a good and necessary thing that we were challenging the White House in court, but I'd be lying if I told you I wasn't worried that the whole thing could backfire, because it could. One potential obstacle was standing in our way, as a Trump-appointed judge, Timothy J. Kelly, would be hearing the case. This was an up-close-and-personal reminder of a president's impact on the judiciary system. Trump and Senate Majority Leader Mitch McConnell had made it a priority to pack the courts with conservative jurists. And with a GOP Senate, they were more wildly successful at this than a lot of people in Washington had ever dreamed.

My fear, at the time, was that Judge Kelly would quickly rule against CNN, which would have meant a protracted legal battle, perhaps all the way to the U.S. Supreme Court, a process that could take months or years. Under such a scenario, the debate over who did what during the news conference would have raged on. And more important, I would have faced a long period without my press pass. My career as a White House correspondent would have been effectively ended by Trump. The man who had dubbed me "fake news" and "the enemy of the people" would have won.

Looking back, I wish I had never entertained the thought that Judge Kelly could rule against us simply because he had been appointed by Trump. Our legal team had cautioned that we should have more confidence in the independence of the judiciary. But alas, this was the Trump era. Faith in our institutions had eroded, even for me. Despite thinking of myself as a true believer in our system of government, I was feeling pretty depressed about our prospects and succumbing to a fair amount of cynicism. The Trump era had gotten to me. Everybody else was looking at things through a partisan lens. That's certainly how Trump views the world, questioning the motivations behind the actions of people in every corner of government, from career civil servants to Senate-confirmed judges. For two years I'd been watching this process play out, but I'd never fallen victim to it myself until now.

One of our lead attorneys, the legendary Ted Olson of *Bush v. Gore* fame, attempted to cut through the tension. As we shook hands in the lobby of the offices of Gibson, Dunn and Crutcher, Olson smiled and made light of the accusations of "grandstanding" directed at me by the White House.

"Grandstanding," Olson growled with a grin. "I can't believe there is grandstanding going on at the White House."

I laughed. We all did. Olson, with one hilarious line, had put his finger on the absurdity of the attacks coming from the White House and, I suppose, from some of my other critics. Like the line from *Casablanca* in which the Vichy prefect of police declares himself "shocked" to find there is gambling going on at Rick's café even as he pockets his winnings, Olson was rightly mocking the notion that "grandstanding" at the White House would ever be a punishable offense.

Still, Olson could be just as serious-minded as he was hilarious. In an earlier interview with CNN's Brooke Baldwin, he explained the stakes in our case and told her, "The White House cannot get away with this."

———————

THE HEARING ITSELF WAS BOTH FASCINATING AND FRIGHTENING AT the same time. Judge Kelly displayed an impressive poker face through it all. He respectfully pressed both sides pretty strenuously about their cases. I never testified. Instead, as the courtroom sketch artist captured, I sat stone-faced throughout the arguments. Make no mistake, though. I was nervous.

The lead Department of Justice attorney arguing on behalf of the Trump administration, James Burnham, caught our attention by making a broad and sweeping case that the president could bar anybody from the grounds of the White House that he saw fit.

"There's no First Amendment right" for reporters to have access to the White House complex, Burnham argued. "I don't think anyone would dispute, if [the president] wants to exclude all reporters from the White House grounds, he clearly has the authority to do that." He went on to say that I could cover the White House and Trump simply by watching TV.

I couldn't believe my ears.

Burnham went on to assert that the president could even remove news outlets he didn't like, essentially arguing that Trump or any future occupant of the Oval Office could pick and choose who covered the executive branch of the government. This was a mind-blowing and dangerous claim of presidential authority, I thought. Were Judge Kelly to rule in Trump's favor in our case, it stood to reason, the First Amendment could be hit with a damaging blow.

Judge Kelly appeared skeptical of Burnham's overreach, asking the government's lawyer whether the White House could say to a reporter, "We don't like your reporting, so we're pulling your hard pass."

Burnham's response was jaw dropping. "As a matter of law . . . yes," he replied.

Judge Kelly had some probing questions to ask as well. Interestingly, he wanted to know who had been behind the decision to remove my pass. "Do you have any information to suggest that it was anyone other than Ms. Sanders that made the decision?" he inquired.

Burnham didn't have a good answer. "No, not that I'm offering today. I'm not denying it, but I don't know anything beyond what's been filed," he answered.

Kelly, who appeared to be paying attention to the news coverage, had taken note of the shifting explanation from Sanders as to why my press pass had been revoked. What had happened to the allegation from the White House, accompanied by the altered video, that purported to show that I had placed my hands on the intern attempting to take back the microphone? he wondered.

"Why don't you set me straight," Kelly said. "Let me know what was the reason and address this issue of whether the government's reason has changed over time."

"We're not relying on that here, and I don't think the White House is relying on that here," Burnham later said of the doctored video.

Let me repeat that. The government's own lawyer said they weren't going to rely on the video.

Still, Kelly gave me some reason to worry. He pressed our lead attorney in court, the great First Amendment lawyer Ted Boutrous, on my conduct at the news conference.

"We've all seen the clip," Kelly said, noting that I had "continued speaking after [my] time expired" and "wouldn't give up [the] microphone."

Ouch, I thought.

Unflappable, Boutrous calmly but pointedly took issue with the government's claims about my behavior, noting the obvious flaw in the White House argument that it could retaliate against journalists it didn't like.

"What are the standards?" Boutrous wondered. "Rudeness is not a standard. If it were, no one could have gone to the press conference." Besides, he added, Trump was pretty rude himself.

"[The president] is the most aggressive, dare I say rudest, person in the room," Boutrous said. "He encourages that kind of rough-and-tumble discussion. . . . Knowing Trump, he'll probably call on Mr. Acosta the day he gets his press pass," he continued.

Boutrous did not know how right he was, but some of this back-and-forth bothered me, I confess. This should not be a debate about rudeness, I thought. I believed I had been standing my ground while under attack by the president. How many times do we let the bully beat us up on the playground? Still, if yielding this point to the judge served the greater good, so be it.

Then Boutrous got to the larger point: that the president was essentially trying to select the reporters who covered the White House. That's something news organizations get to decide, not the president. "The president doesn't have the right to choose who CNN sends to the White House," Boutrous said.

Amen, Ted!

He went on to argue that part of the reasoning for the White House decision was its dissatisfaction with what it perceived to be CNN's "liberal bias." Just before our hearing, the Trump campaign released a fund-raising email to its supporters that seized on the CNN case against Trump and the White House. The email attacked CNN for having a "liberal bias." Boutrous pointed to the email as evidence that the decision against me had been driven in part by discrimination that was "content based."

I was looking closely to see if I could make out the Justice Department attorneys' reaction to Ted's use of the fund-raising email. Sitting at their table, they appeared to bristle at it as damaging to their case.

"Told ya," I saw Burnham mouth to one of the other government attorneys at their table, as if to acknowledge that yes, the email was not helpful to the administration's case.

Boutrous then lambasted the White House over the false claim that I had placed my hands on the intern, along with the shameful use of the doctored "karate chop" video.

"It's absolutely false," Boutrous said. "They've abandoned that," he added about the assault accusation.

As for the more dangerous argument from the administration, that officials could conceivably bar reporters from the White House without any effect on what we did as journalists, Boutrous took a hammer to that claim as well, accusing the Justice Department of disregarding the news-gathering process for reporters on the beat. Reporters meet with sources on White House grounds. Journalists attend briefings held by administration officials. All that would be out the door if we were forced to merely watch the Trump bunch on TV.

"That's not how reporters break stories. It's simply a fundamental misconception of journalism," Boutrous said.

But it was Burnham who was able to have the last word at the hearing. He argued that CNN had more than fifty employees credentialed to cover the White House. The network's rights were not threatened if I got the boot, he added.

"The president never has to speak to Mr. Acosta again," Burnham said. "The president never has to give an interview to Mr. Acosta. And the president never has to call on Mr. Acosta at a press conference."

If Trump decided to ice me out from here on in, Burnham posited, what difference would it make if I had a hard pass to enter the White House grounds?

"This seems to me like an odd First Amendment injury that we're talking about," Burnham said.

I thought to myself, Has Mr. Burnham *met* Trump? Of course he'll call on me again.

But there was a big problem with the government's case. It had failed to address the Fifth Amendment rights, outlined in *Sherrill v. Knight*, which were critical to my complaint against the White House. In short, I hadn't been given due process. Burnham didn't really deal with that question.

Yet Judge Kelly, in a preview of his decision, told the government's lawyers that he was bound by the *Sherrill* case. This was of some comfort to me as he wrapped up the hearing, which lasted nearly two excruciating hours. The judge said he would have a decision for us on our request for a temporary restraining order, essentially a two-week hold on the White House revocation of my hard pass, the following day.

I remember turning to our CNN public relations supervisor from the DC bureau, Lauren Pratapas, who was sitting next to me in the courtroom. After the hearing was finished, we both breathed a sigh of relief. It was exhausting. It was stressful. Some of it sounded good. Some of it sounded not so good.

Still, there was a big factor working in our favor, as we had received a heartwarming outpouring of support from our colleagues in the press. Thirteen news outlets, including Fox News (!), NBC, and Politico had all joined in an amicus brief in support of our lawsuit against the administration. Other outlets later jumped on board. It was, for all intents and purposes, a united front.

"It is imperative that independent journalists have access to the President and his activities, and that journalists are not barred for arbitrary reasons. Our news organizations support the fundamental constitutional right to question this President, or any President," the brief from the news organizations stated.

Judge Kelly could not just ignore that kind of solidarity coming from the entire Washington press corps. Sure, it might not tip the scales in our favor, but it was a critical show of support. Even Fox was on our side, we all kept saying. After all those prime-time segments on Fox News ripping me and my colleagues to shreds, this bastion of conservative media was standing with us.

Following the hearing, we huddled in a small holding room outside the courtroom to discuss what had happened. The lawyers and I all agreed that I would continue to remain silent while the judge was considering the case.

Olson, who had sat at the CNN team's table during the hearing, adding the weight of his presence to our legal arguments, explained why he thought Kelly would rule in our favor.

Judge Kelly, Olson reasoned, would seize on the *Sherrill* ruling, he thought, as a quick and clean way out of what could become a complicated First Amendment case. Both CNN and the White House could battle it out over whether my First Amendment rights had been violated, Olson said. But when it came to the due process question, the White House didn't have much of a leg to stand on. I hadn't been given any due process. Judge Kelly, Olson thought, would hand us a victory based on *Sherrill v. Knight*.

The following day, there was more drama. Judge Kelly decided to postpone his decision for another twenty-four hours. The lawyers advised me not to read too much into that. The weather, as I recall, was pretty awful that day. I was holding out hope that another factor, albeit late in coming, was also weighing on the judge's mind. The White House Correspondents' Association, of which I am a member, filed an amicus brief on that Thursday. Odd timing, we thought. We could have used that show of support prior to the hearing. And to be honest, I was disappointed the WHCA had not been on our side as we walked into the courtroom. But it was better late than never.

The president of the WHCA, Olivier Knox, told me part of the reason for the delay was the very nature of the volunteer nine-member board.

"It's like herding cats," Knox said.

Another factor was that the organization was considering being a part of a larger amicus brief, filed along with other press freedom groups, then reconsidered.

"I thought it was good to stand apart from the crowd," Knox said.

My WHCA sources told me Knox and other members of the group argued on my behalf with Sanders behind closed doors. Sanders, I'm told, was warned that her office's decision to revoke my press pass "would be a sizable self-inflicted wound."

"The entire press corps would be united," Sanders was told by the WHCA.

Sanders was unmoved, I'm told. "They were really running hot for the first couple of days" after the press conference.

As for Shine, he could hardly be counted on as an advocate for the White House press corps. During meetings with the WHCA, Sanders was sometimes open to the concerns expressed by the board's members about various logistical issues and coverage questions. Shine would only complain about what was being reported by the mainstream media, barely containing the fact that he had come to the White House from Fox News.

But the administration's overreach during the hearing, in arguing that the president could bar any journalist he chose, gave the WHCA more than enough reason to act. The organization's statement got right to the point: "The President of the United States maintains that he has absolute, unbridled discretion to decide who can report from inside the White House. Under the President's view of the law, if he does not like the content of an article that a journalist writes about him, he can deny that journalist access to the White House. If he does not like the viewpoint that a journalist expresses about him, he can deny that journalist access to the White House," the statement read.

I was truly happy with the last part of the statement, which really got to our point about the real danger of the administration's argument before the court, that Trump could take his false criticisms against the press to the next level. He could begin to crush critical coverage of his administration. If successful, Trump could potentially bully all of us into submission.

"If he does not like a question that a journalist asks him, he can deny that journalist access to the White House. If he decides that a journalist's story is 'fake news,' he can deny that journalist access to the White House. In fact, according to the President, if he alone considers a journalist a 'bad' or a 'rude' person, he can deny that journalist access to the White House. And he can do so without providing that journalist with any due process whatsoever. The President's view of the law is wrong. While he may have absolute discretion to exclude a member of the press from his Trump Tower residence, he does not have absolute discretion to exclude a member of the press from the White House."

The authority the president was claiming, the WHCA warned the judge, went way too far. My case, which had begun with a ridiculous act of retaliation on the part of the White House, had mushroomed into a full-blown challenge to the abilities of a free press in America to cover the highest office in the land.

Now, if you think I was patting myself on the back over this, you're wrong. Truth be told, I was actually beginning to worry, deeply, that my exchange with Trump could do serious damage to my profession and to a lot of my colleagues. If this Trump-appointed judge were to decide against CNN in any way, it was not an overstatement to argue that there could be an immediate chilling effect on the press in America. I worried about April Ryan. They had tried to punish my colleague, Kaitlan Collins, for her questions. They could go after her, too. The White House could start ousting journalists it didn't like. Governors and mayors across the country could start blocking reporters from official events. All those government officials would have to do, I worried, was point to *CNN v. Trump*, and that would be that.

This whole thing could come crashing down, I thought, and I

would be blamed. I would be radioactive. Other news outlets would probably not touch me. This very well could be the end of my career.

Needless to say, I didn't sleep much that night. Adding to my stress level was the steady stream of threatening messages I was receiving on social media. One deranged man sent a series of violent emails too disturbing to publish.

The next day came, and we made our way to the courthouse. My bureau chief, Sam Feist, along with our PR executive Lauren Pratapas, CNN attorney David Vigilante, and the Gibson, Dunn and Crutcher legal team quickly entered the building. We made some small talk and tried to tell a few jokes, but there was no cutting through the tension. We were on pins and needles, nervously anticipating the judge's decision. There were a few predictions. I'm not sure any of us thought the judge would grant a temporary restraining order that would immediately restore my hard pass. The cynicism bug had gotten all of us.

And then . . . we could not have been happier with the result.

Judge Kelly, as Olson had predicted, leaned on the *Sherrill* decision in his ruling. The White House "must provide due process if they are to revoke Mr. Acosta's hard pass," he said.

Interestingly, the judge seemed to suggest that there was some credence to the government's claim that there was no First Amendment right to enter the White House grounds. But even that was a hollow victory for Trump and Sanders. Once journalists are admitted onto the White House grounds, the judge continued, reporters have a First Amendment right to be there.

As the judge was speaking, one of the Gibson Dunn lawyers, Joshua Lipshutz, gave me a look that's hard to put into words. He kept nodding at me in astonishment as the judge read through his ruling, as if to say, "Wow . . . this just keeps getting better and better." And it did. It got better and better.

Judge Kelly admonished the White House at several times during his ruling, noting that the government could not pinpoint who had made the decision that had led to the revocation of my hard pass. My sources told me Shine, Sanders, and Trump had all agreed to do it, but that Shine was the driving force behind the push to boot me out of the White House. And perhaps the government's lawyers just didn't want to admit that in court. In a small victory for me, the judge chastised the White House over its use of the doctored video, describing it as being of "questionable accuracy." That's as close to a sick burn as a federal judge can get. It was a rebuke to Sanders from a judge her boss had placed on the bench.

Kelly went on to grant the temporary restraining order and instructed the White House to return my hard pass. We were, needless to say, ecstatic. We had won.

"Our sincere thanks to all who have supported not just CNN, but a free, strong and independent American press," CNN said in a statement.

I finally broke my company- and self-imposed silence, telling reporters outside the courthouse, "I just want to thank all my colleagues in the press who supported me this week. I want to thank the judge for the decision that he made. And let's go back to work."

THEN I COULDN'T HELP MYSELF. AFTER WE GOT IN THE CAR, I LET off a little steam.

"We beat Trump!" I yelled.

Perhaps they could hear me all the way across town at the White House, as Sanders and Trump both tried to save face, surprising no one. During a brief availability with reporters, Trump insisted that he was a proud supporter of a free press.

"We want total freedom of the press," he said. "But you have to act with respect when you're at the White House. And when I see the way some of my people get treated at news conferences, it's terrible. So we're setting up a certain standard, which is what the court is requesting," he added.

Insert laugh track here. Trump was telling me "you have to act with respect when you're at the White House." His words struck me as the height of hypocrisy. Had he treated the White House with respect? Once again, he was at war with the truth. Trump has not elevated the presidency.

Sanders cherry-picked what she wanted to read in the judge's decision.

"The court made clear that there is no absolute First Amendment right to access the White House," she said in a statement. But she ignored the fact that Judge Kelly had said that reporters covering the presidency do have First Amendment rights once they are admitted into the White House. I found it bizarre that she would continue to parrot the Justice Department's absurd and overreaching claim about access to the White House complex. Trump had just said, "We want total freedom of the press." And Sanders was arguing for something well short of that.

They couldn't even get their gaslighting straight.

But there was no time to focus on all that. As I said outside the courthouse, "Let's get back to work."

CNN president Jeff Zucker emailed to congratulate me and basically said the same thing. Get back to work! The plan was for me to go back to the White House, retrieve my hard pass, and file a piece that evening for *The Situation Room with Wolf Blitzer*. The only thing I asked in return was that I be able to leave early to make my daughter's dance recital. In light of the ordeal I had just been through, permission was granted.

As excited as we were about the judge's decision, Trump supporters were still lashing out on social media. Some of the comments once again raised red flags.

Kill Jim Acosta, one tweet read. At that moment, CNN security officials mandated that I receive around-the-clock protection for the next few days. It was another jarring moment, but I had to put it aside. I had to get back to work.

As I returned to the White House, warnings were coming in from our producer there that day, Allie Malloy, that dozens of news crews were awaiting my return. Oh crap, I thought. Folks were going to say it again: "You're making yourself the story!"

Feist accompanied me back to the White House. And Allie was right. Approximately fifty producers, photographers, and reporters were standing in the driveway of the White House to capture the moment. It was a little odd being on the other side of the stake-out. Unsure what to do at that moment as I faced the cameras, I remember nervously asking everybody if they had a question for me. They did not. So, I basically repeated what I had said outside the courthouse. One reporter asked me what advice I would give young journalists.

"Do your job and tell the truth," I replied. Honestly, I wish I had said more at the time. I'm a TV reporter; I always want to say more. But CNN was eager to limit my comments that day. So I kept it brief. Theoretically, we were still in the middle of a court battle. Yes, we had been granted a temporary restraining order, but at the time, there was still a chance we would have to continue to fight our case in front of Judge Kelly. Brevity was wise counsel.

One of the photographers at the White House, a "still" (as we call them) named William Moon, snapped a shot of my hard pass as it caught a ray of sunshine. I couldn't believe my eyes when he sent it to me. Technically, we are not supposed to take a picture of our hard passes. The Secret Service frowns upon that, I suppose, because it could encourage criminals to use them to produce counterfeit credentials. But this photo was perfectly fine to share because you couldn't really see the hard pass in it. It was just a burst of bright light hanging at the bottom of my lanyard. I stared at the photo and thought to myself, What a crazy week.

Who would have thought, after all those rallies and press conferences and after all that abuse I had absorbed over the last three years, that I would end up in court fighting for my rights as a journalist? Who would have thought I would win that battle?

Not me.

So, I went back to work, turned in my piece, and actually made it to my daughter's dance recital. But I wasn't out of the woods yet.

———————

AS I WAS DRIVING HOME LATE FRIDAY NIGHT, AN EMAIL FLASHED ON my phone. It was from Sarah Sanders (Shine was copied on it), informing me that the White House had decided to seek the revocation of my hard pass. Despite their defeat in court, decided by a Trump-appointed judge, they weren't giving up the fight. Ah right, I thought. This was Trumpworld. You never admit a mistake; you double down. Sanders's reasoning was that they were giving me ample notification and due process, this time around.

I immediately called Sam Feist, who had been copied on the email. My first thought was to just leave it alone. This sounded like desperation to me. The Trump people were not accustomed to losing. So, this may have been just more flailing to save face. I suggested to Sam that we not speak a word of this outside a small circle inside CNN. That way, Sarah's letter wouldn't leak from us. It has to leak from the White House. The ball, we reasoned, would then be in their court.

Unlike the first time around, when I tweeted Sarah's statement and the video of my hard pass being yanked, mum was the word. Let's enjoy the victorious news cycle as long as we can, we thought. And let's see just how eager Sarah is to start World War III all over again.

I had reached out to my lawyer, respected Washington attorney Robert Barnett, to get his advice on the Sanders letter. He predicted that Sarah's gambit would be unsuccessful. You can't retroactively start a process for something that had already happened, Barnett said.

"It's never a good idea to poke a federal judge in the eye," he added.

For the weekend, our strategy seemed to work. The White House may have expected we would immediately protest, but we were silent. All day Saturday and much of Sunday over that weekend, the headlines were all positive for CNN. The stories were about how we had won. We had won!

Then Sunday night came. The White House must have leaked the story. Mike Allen with Axios reported on the existence of the letter. Other reporters were beginning to confirm the story. The only silver lining was that we had kept Sarah's ridiculous letter out of the headlines for a good forty-eight hours.

CNN immediately requested an emergency hearing with Judge Kelly, who had just adjudicated the matter on the previous Friday. We wanted the White House to understand that we could play hardball, too. After all, there was no reason to take the escalation from Sanders lightly. Her new letter stated that Trump "is aware of this preliminary decision and concurs."

Our motion for an emergency hearing described the latest White House salvo as an "attempt to provide retroactive due process." But maybe the White House would get away with this one, I thought. Judge Kelly had insisted that the White House needed a process for revoking hard passes. This was a rather lame attempt at due process, but it might meet the judge's standard. I was again filled with dread. Sanders had said in her letter that my suspension would go into effect after the temporary restraining order had ended. But the White House was trying to pull a fast one, attempting to defy the judge's order while, at the same time, trying to comply with it. This struck me as too cute by half. Maybe we would be all right.

In a message to the Justice Department, Ted Boutrous was blunt with the government's lawyers, describing the Sanders letter as "further evidence of your clients' animus towards Mr. Acosta based on his work as CNN's chief White House correspondent." Boutrous had put his finger on it. The White House was acting out of spite. They couldn't help themselves. And we needed Judge Kelly to put a stop to it.

Then a funny thing happened Monday afternoon, less than a day after Axios had reported the news of Sanders's letter. A tweet from John Roberts of Fox News appeared on my screen. John had broken the news that the White House was restoring my press pass. Sarah or John's old boss Bill Shine must have tipped him off. I emailed Sarah. Is this true? She confirmed that it was. Within a couple of minutes, she had released a statement.

"This afternoon we have notified Jim Acosta and CNN that his hard pass has been restored," Sanders said. Then, once again, she tried to save face: "We have also notified him of certain rules that will govern White House press conferences going forward." Then, with the graciousness we all came to expect, she took one last slap.

"We have created these rules with a degree of regret," she added.

Yes, I'm sure you have a lot of regrets, Sarah. I'm sure you do.

The new rules were painfully unserious, like something cooked up by a kindergarten teacher in a MAGA hat. Here they are:

1. A journalist called upon to ask a question will ask a single question and then will yield the floor to other journalists;
2. At the discretion of the President or other White House official taking questions, a follow-up question or questions may be permitted; and where a follow up has been allowed and asked, the questioner will then yield the floor;
3. "Yielding the floor" includes, when applicable, physically surrendering the microphone to White House staff for use by the next questioner;
4. Failure to abide by any of rules 1–3 may result in suspension or revocation of the journalist's hard pass.

As I told some of my colleagues, the Trump people don't like to lose. And during this episode, they had clearly gotten spanked. Further, they had lost to the people they hated the most, the press. One of their own judges had rejected their assault on the press. As for these new rules, nobody took them seriously, including the president. White House journalists continued to ask follow-up questions. And Trump continued taking them because he enjoys the sparring, at least when he thinks he's coming out on top.

The following day, Trump proved my point. He walked out onto the South Lawn of the White House, on his way to an event, and took questions from reporters. And by questions, I mean multiple questions from multiple reporters. Reporters asked lots of follow-up questions. David Martosko of the *Daily Mail* asked a handful. (You could say David was refusing to yield to other reporters, but he should have done that; he's a reporter.) And there was no drama. Almost immediately and with little fanfare, Sarah's rules were out the window.

When Trump came to me, I asked him about the murder of Saudi journalist and *Washington Post* columnist Jamal Khashoggi. Despite an assessment from the CIA that the Saudi crown prince Mohammed Bin Salman Al Saud had orchestrated Khashoggi's gruesome murder in a consulate in Istanbul, Trump had issued a bizarre statement that day that sided with the Saudis on Khashoggi's death, saying of the Saudi crown prince, "[M]aybe he did and maybe he didn't." I asked Trump about his dismissal of the CIA assessment. He didn't really answer the question. So, I asked a follow-up. Again, there was no drama as Trump engaged.

"Are you letting the Saudis get away with murder, murdering a journalist?" I asked.

"No. This is about America First," he responded. Standing up for a reporter is how you put America first, I thought. But Trump was on his way to the next reporter and the next question. At the conclusion of that go-round, Trump pointed at me as if to say, "You're back." And I was.

Then something happened that made me sick. As he moved down the line to other reporters, Trump refused to answer a question from my friend April Ryan. April had asked whether the White House would investigate Ivanka Trump's use of a personal email account to send and receive messages about government business. Trump just pointed at her with a scowl on his face. He then turned to others in the crowd and asked, "What else?" As tough as she is, April appeared hurt by Trump's nastiness at that moment. I know she brushed it off, but it pained me.

As much as I enjoyed being back at the White House doing my job with my hard pass back in my pocket, I knew our victory in court was never going to change Trump's behavior. We had won the battle, but the war on the press wasn't over. Far from it. Sarah and the folks at the White House never apologized for smearing me and attempting to destroy my career—though I never expected that anyway.

Now, this may not please the haters, but I don't spend much time curled up in the fetal position, crying myself to sleep every night. I welcomed Trumpworld's hatred. Besides, I would much rather focus on the mountain of positive feedback that comes rushing in from all corners. There are the anonymous White House officials who have stopped me on the street to tell me to "keep going." (Yes, that has happened.) Pilots on some of my flights crisscrossing the country have sent back notes from the cockpit telling me to "keep up the pressure." Don't let yourself think for a second that the abuse we take at the White House or at the MAGA rallies somehow tells the whole story. It doesn't.

I have heard from so many people from around the world, as have my colleagues in the press. Folks come up to us at train stations, supermarkets, and restaurants. They believe in this thing called a free press. They know we have a tough job cutting through the lies. They know we are sacrificing so much. They have seen all the abusive behavior. And the folks at home have told us, resoundingly, "Don't stop." Or, as Sam Donaldson put it, "Keep charging."

NOT LONG AFTER I RETURNED TO WORK IN THE WHITE HOUSE, I WAS able to play a small role in the coverage of the passing of President George H. W. Bush. I was outside the National Cathedral in Washington. The service had just concluded. It was a moving ceremony. The entire world, it seemed, was mourning with the Bush family as they said goodbye to Bush 41. I had a chance to report on the encounter between the Bush and Trump families, describing it as "The Greatest Generation meets Make America Great Again," a reminder that America was great long before the forty-fifth president. It felt good to report on another president besides Trump for a change. George Bush would have never called the press the enemy of the people.

After it was all over and the movers and shakers of Washington high society were heading home, I spotted a familiar face moving toward me. It was Tom Brokaw, the legendary NBC anchor who had written the book *The Greatest Generation*. We had never met before.

"Staying out of trouble?" Brokaw asked with a laugh.

"A little," I replied with a smile.

Epilogue:
America, If You're Listening . . .

In the weeks following the restoration of my hard pass at the White House, several of my colleagues at other news outlets, and even a few Secret Service officers, had some good fun needling me about the whole saga, part of the gallows humor of the White House beat.

"Are they letting you back in here?" folks would ask.

Yes, I would say, laughing.

But I had received some warm gestures of support as well. At an awards dinner in Washington, the retiring Republican senator Jeff Flake, who had also sparred with Trump, gave me a shout-out.

"Go get 'em, Acosta. Don't back down," Flake said.

At the White House Correspondents' Association's annual holiday reception at the JW Marriott in Washington, Sarah Sanders and Bill Shine approached me in what appeared to be a transparently insincere attempt to lighten the mood.

"Don't back away," Sarah said as she and Bill walked up to me. "We come in peace."

They then roped me into joining them in singing a rather half-hearted version of "The Twelve Days of Christmas," with some of my counterparts in the press gathered around, watching curiously.

"Five golden briefings," I joked, weakly. There was strained laughter. It was all very awkward, so I took a swig from my wineglass and slipped away.

Folks have asked me if things have gotten back to normal with the White House. No, of course not, I respond. How could they? Things were not normal at the White House before I lost my press pass.

After the midterms, Trump continued to test America's durable Constitution. He shut down the government to force U.S. taxpayers to build his border wall, the project that in 2016 he had vowed Mexico would finance. When he didn't get his way during the shutdown, he declared a national emergency to circumvent Congress with a scheme to divert already appropriated funds to his border barrier quest. Some fellow Republicans accused the president of actually violating the Constitution, a rare proof of life from a party held hostage by its leader. The late senator John McCain, Trump's longtime nemesis, would have been proud.

But what more could Trump attempt with another term in office? At some point, I reckon, both parties will give in and let Trump have his way on the wall. But do Democrats really believe Trump will reciprocate with truly bipartisan initiatives to address, say, the epidemic of mass shootings that has ravaged communities from Newton, Connecticut; to Parkland, Florida; to Las Vegas? He obviously won't tackle the urgent crisis of climate change, which he still sees as a hoax, despite what all the scientific evidence tells us.

When it comes to the border, facts are sometimes not on Trump's mind. At a news conference in the Rose Garden, where he announced his immigration emergency, he lashed out at my attempts to hold his feet to the fire. When I reminded him that respected studies show that immigrants, even the undocumented, commit crimes at lower levels than native-born Americans, he cried "fake news."

"You don't really believe that," Trump said.

"I believe in facts and statistics," I told him during another one of our confrontations.

One national emergency Trump appears to have ignored altogether is the potential for Russia to hack into America's democratic process once again in 2020. For all the heated debate over whether Trump's aides and associates colluded with Moscow, there are some clear conclusions contained in Special Counsel Robert Mueller's report about Putin's interference in 2016. Mueller found, as had the U.S. intelligence community long before Mueller's appointment as special counsel, that the Russians had successfully carried out an operation to alter the outcome of the U.S. presidential election. Top administration officials, including the director of national intelligence, Dan Coats, have warned that the Russians will try it again in 2020.

On April 18, 2019, Special Counsel Robert Mueller released his report on the Russia investigation. While Trump was not charged with conspiring with the Russian government in 2016, he was notably not cleared of obstructing justice. The Mueller report stated Trump ordered White House counsel Don McGahn to fire the special counsel. McGahn ignored the order. Trump was alarmed by Mueller's appointment, remarking to aides, "This is the end of my presidency." It was also revealed that Sarah Sanders admitted to investigators that she had lied about Comey's firing.

It's worth noting that after Democrats captured the House of Representatives in the 2018 midterms, Trump began to express concerns that he could be impeached, I was told. He saw it as a "real possibility." My sources said White House officials believed the accusations of campaign finance violations, tied to the payments of hush money to Trump's alleged mistresses, were most problematic.

When taking stock of the Trump effect on the world, we should think bigger than the Russian threat. Perhaps we should assess the damage we are doing to ourselves in betraying the values that have always stood America in good stead. Consider the case of *Washington Post* columnist Jamal Khashoggi, the Saudi journalist who resided in Virginia, whose children are U.S. citizens, and who was assassinated inside a Saudi consulate in Istanbul. The assessment from the U.S. intelligence community was that the Kingdom of Saudi Arabia, likely at the direction of Crown Prince Mohammad Bin Salman, orchestrated the murder of Khashoggi in retaliation for his commentary about the government in Riyadh.

In their defense, the Saudis at first said that Khashoggi had left the consulate alive; in fact, there was closed-circuit video showing as much. But as CNN's exceptional reporting of the journalist's murder demonstrated, it was a body double dressed in Khashoggi's clothing who made the videotaped exit from the consulate. Khashoggi, we later learned, never left the building. Instead, the journalist was detained inside, where, U.S. and Turkish governments assert, Saudi operatives murdered him and then dismembered him with a bone saw.

The Saudis attempted to mislead the world about what had happened to Khashoggi, at one point blaming his assassination on "rogue killers," a lie repeated by Trump to the press. It was as if O. J. Simpson were writing the kingdom's press releases. The Riyadh government's shameful and amateurish attempt at a cover-up, exposed in part by dedicated journalists but also by their geopolitical rivals in Turkey, underlined the danger of handing the world over to autocrats like the Saudi royal family.

When the American president ultimately sided with the Saudis instead of with the press, he made it clear that the kingdom would not be held accountable in any meaningful way for the murder of a journalist. The life of an "enemy of the people," it seemed, was not worth defending, the Trump team figured, if it meant sacrificing the cozy relationship the United States enjoyed with Riyadh. This all but gave the green light to other governments around the world to target the press—not that Vladimir Putin needed the go-ahead; still, other tyrants big and small were watching. Now foreign leaders call stories they want to smother "fake news." Trump's anti-truth virus is spreading.

A free press is surely a vital element of the democratic vaccine against assaults on the truth. Still, it's almost impossible to look at our situation heading into 2020 without asking how much worse things could get for journalists.

I thought about the high price journalists now pay for asking hard questions during the weekend after my press pass was returned. There I was, standing in the street tossing a football with my son (as we often do), and about fifty feet away from us stood a man with a gun on his belt: a security guard assigned to my family and me in response to the death threats that had been pouring in as part of the backlash to the judge's ruling in CNN's favor. There had been other attempts at harassment. A "swatter" sent police to my home to frighten my family, claiming there was a violent incident taking place there. The police arrived in the middle of the night, guns drawn. Fortunately, my children slept through it all.

I ask my fellow journalists and my fellow Americans: is this to be our fate?

The dangers cannot be ignored. When the so-called MAGA bomber, Cesar Sayoc, pleaded guilty in federal court in March 2019, he expressed remorse for endangering journalists and Trump critics, but he later insisted to the judge that he never intended for the devices to explode.

"The intention was to only intimidate and scare," Sayoc said in a letter to the judge.

The MAGA bomber's arrest didn't press Pause on the threat to journalists covering Trump. In February 2019, a MAGA hat–wearing Trump supporter attacked a BBC cameraman at one of the president's rallies in El Paso.

Journalists must continue to speak out against these acts of violence against the press. We should not be bullied into silence.

By 2020, we will have reached year five of Trump's war on the press and on the truth. By that point, America will have changed in profound ways, ways that even now we cannot predict. A free society, I would argue, cannot sustain the collective weight of the kind of abuse we've endured without its institutions, and its people, undergoing a profound metamorphosis. Across the country, people will have come of age exposed to a dangerous rhetoric that distorts our collective sense of reality and that will have consequences we cannot yet fully appreciate.

To better understand the gravity of this moment in our nation's history, I consulted a handful of presidential historians and scholars. If you share the view that this is a perilous time for America, take heart. You are not alone.

"We are in very dangerous waters right now," Rice University historian Douglas Brinkley told me. "A key part of authoritarianism is to smother a free press," he continued. "If [Trump] can turn the press into 'fake news' and 'the enemy of the people,' that really takes away his biggest roadblock to authoritarian government," he added.

Other historians I consulted weren't quite ready to say we are on the road to authoritarianism, but they were equally worried about the sorry state of affairs in the nation's capital and its impact on the rest of America. Princeton University presidential historian Julian Zelizer assigned the blame for much of the nation's current woes on an outbreak of hyperpartisanship being exploited by Trump. Let's hope that's all this is. But Larry Sabato, from the University of Virginia's Center for Politics, went further than that, saying that Trump "can fairly be described as a cult leader; millions of his followers believe anything he tells them, and the truth be damned." Sabato continued: "Since Nixon's final days in 1974, I've never wondered whether a president would consider leading a coup to retain power—until now."

I asked Larry if he was okay with my using these quotes. His response? "Use any of it you want, Jim. . . . Give 'em hell." (I will.)

At the conclusion of the testimony of Trump's former personal attorney Michael Cohen, arguably the most profound moment came when the committee's chairman, Rep. Elijah Cummings, a Democrat from Maryland, delivered an impassioned speech about the state of American politics.

"We have got to get back to normal," he shouted. "When we're dancing with the angels, the question we'll be asked: In 2019, what did we do to make sure we kept our democracy intact? Did we stand on the sidelines and say nothing?" Cummings added.

I think the chairman is on to something. If we stay on this path of abnormality, there almost surely will be consequences. If we continue down this road, it is not a stretch to say that, here in America, we will have witnessed a sad transformation. Tens of millions of Trump supporters may no longer believe what is written or reported by journalists working for major news outlets. Further, Trump has demonstrated time and again that he will stoke animosity toward the mainstream press inside his base to benefit his sympathizers and apologists in conservative media. The question is: how much can the system take before there is a crash? After all, you can't speak truth to power if those in power can crush the truth.

Having traveled to every corner of the country and attended those raucous rallies and absorbed all that hostility and venom, I'm less worried about what Trump is doing to America than I am about what we have done to ourselves. If a politician's supporters are so blinded by their own passions that they can walk up to a journalist at a political event and scream that she's a traitor, or anonymously threaten a reporter's life on social media, then we, as a society, are surrendering something far greater than politics. We are surrendering our decency, and perhaps our humanity. It is perfectly fair to ask how does this end without suffering.

In the final analysis, there is only so much blame that should be shouldered by the president of the United States. Citizens still have the ability to sort right from wrong, to recognize the difference between real and fake news. Don't let the truth die in a tweet. That would be a horrible way for it to go.

When I speak to groups of people who want to know what it's like covering the White House these days, the thing I'm asked perhaps most often is how we see our way out of these dark times for our country. I certainly don't have all the answers. But the first thing I tell folks is that I am less concerned about "Trump Derangement Syndrome," as some of the president's supporters describe the outrage among his critics, than I am about what I call "Trump Depression Syndrome." Too many people are feeling dejected, even defeated, based on the news of the day, or the tweets in the morning. Will this moment pass? I believe it will. But how do we get there? Here's my thought on that: We are simply going to have to have more faith, not just in the facts, but in each other. We need to have more faith that we still can count on our neighbors, even the strangers in the red MAGA hats or the pink #RESIST T-shirts, to form that more perfect union. We are divided, but not irreparably, in my view. Despite what's happened, I still have faith in all of us.

Getting to that place of a more lasting unity will be a difficult task. There must be a common understanding that words matter. They have meaning. Words have power. I believe the term "the enemy of the people" will come to help define this era, when one group of people was pitted against another in ways that I had not seen in my lifetime. Before the sun sets on this democracy—and may that day never come—it must be said that the press is not the enemy. We are defenders of the people. Some of us, not I, have sacrificed everything for this profession, from war zones to, unfortunately, newsrooms. Journalists have done this out of a deep devotion to the people. It is a devotion born out of a love for all people. That is a truth worth defending, as journalists are people too.

Acknowledgments

This book would not have been possible without the help of some truly special people in my life. I especially want to thank my entire family for their patience during the writing process. The wonderful folks at CNN have also been very supportive. So, I'd like to acknowledge Jeff Zucker, Michael Bass, Allison Gollust, Rick Davis, David Vigilante (and the rest of CNN's legal team!), Sam Feist, Virginia Moseley, Antoine Sanfuentes, Steve Brusk, and Matt Hoye. There are so many other show producers and anchors who've invited me onto their programs over the course of my twelve years at CNN. I'm immensely grateful to all of you.

Additionally, I would like to recognize my colleagues in CNN's White House unit, past and present: Laura Bernardini, Brianna Keilar, Dan Lothian, Jeff Zeleny, Pam Brown, Sara Murray, Kaitlan Collins, Joe Johns, Athena Jones, Abby Phillip, Boris Sanchez, Michelle Kosinski, Kevin Liptak, Allie Malloy, Jeremy Diamond, Dan Merica, Sarah Westwood, Meghan Vasquez, Betsy Klein, Noah Gray, Kristen Holmes, Becky Brittain Rieksts, Bonney Kapp, and Elizabeth Landers. New York–based producers Laura Dolan and Julian Cummings, as well as former colleagues Jon Klein, James Kraft (now with NBC), and Edith Chapin (now with NPR), were also very supportive during my time at CNN.

I would be remiss if I didn't give a shout-out to our talented crew of photojournalists on this demanding beat: Khalil Abdallah, Peter Morris, Jay McMichael, Bill Alberter, Geoff Parker, Burke Buckhorn, Mark Walz, John Bodnar, David Jenkins, Tony Umrani, and Tim Garraty.

AS FOR THE WRITING OF THIS BOOK, I MUST TIP MY HAT TO THE passionate Lisa Sharkey at HarperCollins, who first approached me about this project, as well as my astute and tireless editor, Matt Harper. Matt's guidance has been nothing short of brilliant throughout this endeavor. As always, I am grateful to Robert Barnett for his wise counsel and support.

There are many sources without whom I could not have covered this challenging and unorthodox administration. Of course, I cannot name them here, but they should know they are rarely far from my mind.

Finally, I wish nothing but the best to you, my fellow citizens, for taking the time to read this book, which is straight from the heart. God Bless America.

About the Author

JIM ACOSTA is CNN's chief White House correspondent, currently covering the Trump administration. He previously reported on the Obama administration from the White House and around the world. He regularly covers presidential press conferences, visits by heads of state, and issues impacting the executive branch of the federal government.